Thank you for purchasing **The Indie** ⎯⎯⎯⎯⎯⎯⎯⎯⎯⎯⎯⎯⎯⎯⎯⎯⎯⎯⎯⎯⎯⎯⎯⎯⎯⎯⎯⎯⎯⎯⎯⎯⎯⎯ I would have purchased this resource in a flash, had something like it been available when I first began to promote my own CD. The truth is that there was no resource like it, and as a result, I wasted hundreds of hours surfing the Internet wading through dead links and outdated sites trying to find the good stuff.

For ease of use, this resource is broken down into five sections. Each section contains a different way in which you can promote your music (ie: getting your music reviewed). Within each of these sections the contacts are categorized according to genre, and in most cases, the genres are catagorized geographically.

When looking for contacts that fit your style of music, there are TWO very important points to keep in mind:

1. *There is a large amount of genre "bleeding" from section to section*. This means that if you are in a punk band, you will not only find sites that cater to your needs in the "Punk" sections, but you will also find a number of sites that welcome your style of music in the "Metal" and "Mainstream" sections. You can even find some sites that accept punk music in the "Experimental" sections. The sections are based upon the <u>primary</u> musical style that each site lists as their preference.

2. **This crossover is especially true with the "Mainstream" radio stations**. The majority of the stations listed in the "Mainstream" sections are college or university stations that have a show catering to <u>every</u> style of music (Country, Hip Hop, Death Metal, Goth…etc), so make sure you check them all.

You will also notice that in most cases, I have listed the URL as the sole connection to a particular site. Listing the URL, contact name, e-mail address and physical address groups together too many variables that can change. My philosophy is that the URL will get you to the site. Once you are there, you can then find the most **updated** contact names, e-mail addresses, physical addresses, phone numbers, fax numbers etc.

I hope you enjoy exploring the many sites, and wish you the best of luck with your music and your career. If you feel that you made a worthwhile investment by purchasing the Indie Contact Bible, please tell your friends about it. Send your comments and suggestions to me. ALL suggestions will be taken into consideration.

Hope to hear from you!

David Wimble
President, Big Meteor Publishing

Table of Contents

Introduction i

Section One: *Reviews of Independent Music*

Mainstream Music 1
    North America 1
    South America 20
    Europe 20
    Australia - New Zealand 28
    Asia 30
    Africa 30

Country Music 30

Dance Music
    North America 34
    Europe 35
    Australia 36

Experimental Music
    North America 36
    South America 43
    Europe 43
    Australia 47
    Asia 48

Hip Hop 48

Jazz/Blues/Folk Music 53

Metal
    North America 56
    South America 63
    Europe 64
    Australia/New Zealand 69
    Asia 69
    Africa 69

Progressive Rock 69

Punk
    North America 70
    South America 79
    Europe 80
    Australia 83
    Asia 84

World Music 85

Regional Publications
- North America 85
- South America 88
- Europe 88
- Australia 88

Section Two: *Radio Stations that are Willing to Play Independent Music*

Mainstream
- North America 89
- South America 120
- Europe 121
- Australia – New Zealand 128
- Asia 130
- Africa 130

Country Radio 130

Dance Radio 134

Experimental Radio
- North America 137
- Europe 140

Hip Hop Radio 143

Jazz/Blues/Folk Radio 145

Metal Radio
- North America 150
- Europe 152
- Australia 152

Punk Radio 153

World Music Radio 154

Radio Shows that Spotlight Local Musicians 156

Section Three: *Services that Will Help You to Sell Your Music Over the Internet*
- All Styles 175
- Specialty 189

Section Four: *Sites that Will Allow You to Upload Music Files.*
- All Styles 193
- Specialty Sites 201

Section Five: *Sites that Will Allow You to Upload Information About Your Band For FREE*
- All Styles 207
- Specialty Sites 210

Section One
Reviewers of Independent Music

Mainstream Music

This section contains contacts that are willing to listen to the "lighter" genres of music – Pop, Twee, Rock, Rock & Roll, Indie Rock, Acoustic Rock, Light Alternative etc. As I mentioned in the Introduction, many of these reviewers are willing to listen to <u>any</u> style of music.

North America

United States

1/2 Creeper
www.geocities.com/SunsetStrip/Underground/5641

181.4 Degrees from the Norm
www.181-4.com
The Net's freshest music magazine!

33 rebellions per minute
www.geocities.com/SunsetStrip/Mezzanine/6613/
Detailed, enthusiastic album reviews. Thoughtful, tuneful, eccentric music given preference.

40below
40below.cjb.net
40below is a site that was made to promote bands that deserve the exposure. Bands can email the members that run the site to be put up on the site in various ways. The site also includes news, tablature, interviews and much more

7-Ball
www.7ball.com/front.index.htm
Christian Publication.

A Boy and His Pet Heart
escape.angband.org/abahph

Aaron Poehler's Music Journalism Archives
www.angelfire.com/in2/aaronmusicarchives
Huge archive of reviews/articles—writer for Flipside, TailSpins & EYE.

Access to the Music Zone (AMZ)
www.amzmusiczine.com

Acoustic Guitar Magazine
www.acguitar.com

AcoustiCDigest.com
AcoustiCDigest.com
Specializing in Classical Crossover and Acoustic Intrumentals.

Action Attack Helicopter
www.actionattackhelicopter.com
We're an online zine that covers independent emo, hardcore, punk, and the like.

Addicted to Noise
www.addict.com

Aiding & Abetting
www.cent.com/abetting

AIMusic
www.aimusic.org
Advancing Independent Music.

Alan Haber's Pure Pop
www.purepop.com

all-reviews.com
www.all-reviews.com/music.htm

alt.culture.guide
www.telalink.net/~samurai

The Alt-Pop MP3 Review
www.unc.edu/%7Emarmbru/mp3
Reviews "alternative pop" music by unsigned/indie bands who put out free mp3 files of their music on the Internet.

Altar Native
www.altarnative.com

Alternate Music Press (AMP)
www.alternatemusicpress.com

AM Publications
www.ampubs.com

American Feed
www.stillstationary.com/americanfeed.html

Amp3.com
www.AMP3review.com

The Ampli-Flier
www2.dtc.net/~scepter

Amplifier
www.twomp.com/amplifier

The Angry Thoreauan
www.angrythoreauan.com

Anti-Elitist Audio Zine
subrealsongs.com/antielitist
Internet radio show/review webzine for DIY artists and bands.

Atlanta Journal
www.accessatlanta.com

Atomic Chaser
www.geocities.com/~atomicchaser

Atrophy Zine
members.aol.com/atrophyman

Auburn Plainsman
www.theplainsman.com

Audities
www.audities.com/audities

Aumnibus
www.aum.edu/aumnibus

Aversion.com
www.aversion.com

Babysue
www.babysue.com

The Band Next Door
www.thebandnextdoor.com
The Band Next Door is the web marketplace for sharing and discovering the best in local, indie, and underexposed music. Check out our top-quality original content, or submit an article or review on a band you want to let the rest of the world know about. The Band Next Door- because the world is crammed with great music you might otherwise never hear.

BANDRADIO
www.bandradio.com
Demos are reviewed for Band of the Week honors.

Bangin' and Screamin'
www.iteams.com/bangin

Bangsheet
www.geocities.com/~bangsheet

Bassline Buzz
Jaymes Mckenzie
jaymesmckenzie@basslinebuzz.com
www.basslinebuzz.com
The Ultimate Indie Review Site Weekly New Music Review Site for indie & unsigned artist/bands.

Belladonna Journal
www.triplo.com/belladonna

Big Orange Crayon
www.bigorangecrayon.com/
An indie pop/rock zine run by a kid named Nick.

Big Takeover
www.bigtakeover.com

Billboard
www.billboard.com

BEST SHEET MUSIC.com your guide to the best sheet music, tab and lyric sites on the Internet!
www.bestsheetmusic.com

Boomshaka
www.boomshakamusic.com

Brat
www.brat.org

bu2z
www.bu2z.com

Buddyhead
www.buddyhead.com

Burn Yer Radio
www.burnyerradio.com/

Buzzer
Vivian/Nicole buzzerzine@hotmail.com
www.geocities.com/SunsetStrip/Gala/
1476/buzzer.html

Buzzine.com
www.buzzine.com

BVS Reviews
members.aol.com/bvonstiers

Carbon 14
www.c14.com

Carletonian - Carleton College
www.carletonian.carleton.edu

cameZine
www.m8.com/camezine
Christian Alternative Magazine.

Casco Bay Weekly
www.cascobayweekly.com

Catascopic
www.catascopic.com

Caught in Flux
www.appelstein.com/cif/cif.html
Covering old and new musical favorites.

CAZ Media
cazmedia.com/mmi/mmientry.shtml

The CD Review
home.earthlink.net/~rydogg1

CD Reviews.com
www.cdreviews.com

CD Shakedown
www.cdshakedown.com
Weekly reviews of new music releases, mostly pop, rock, alternative, and singer/songwriter.

The Celebrity Cafe
www.thecelebritycafe.com
TheCelebrityCafe.com does primarily Q&A interviews, but also has, reviews, commentaries, music trivia, music contests, the famous album of the day award and more.

Check it Out (BIG)
www.bigzines.com

Check This Out!
ctomag.com

Chicago Medley Arts
www.enteract.com/~chicagom/medley.html

Chico News and Reviews
www.newsreview.com/chico

ChinMusic Magazine
www.girlyhead.com/ChinMusic.html

Christian Music Review Headquarters
placetobe.org/cmp/cmrh

Christian Pirate Radio
www.christianpirateradio.com

City Life (Las Vegas)
www.lvcitylife.com

Clemson Tiger -Time Out Section
hubcap.clemson.edu/Tiger

Cleveland Free Times
www.freetimes.com

Clovis Records
www.clovisrecords.com

Club Exit
www.geocities.com/~clubexit/cezine.html
Christian Publication.

College Music Journal - CMJ
www.cmj.com

Columbus Alive
www.alivewired.com

Consumable Online
www.westnet.com/consumable

Contemporary Christian Magazine - CCM
www.ccmcom.com

Continental Magazine
dblcrown.com

Cool Grrrls
www.coolgrrrls.com
The worldwide grrrls' guide to all that grooves, featuring show & CD reviews, interviews, and more.

copacetic
www.geocities.com/~copacetic-

Copper Press
www.copperpress.com/2poster.html

Cosmik Debris Magazine
www.cosmik.com

Creative Loafing (Birmingham)
www.clnetwork.net/scripts/
oneweb.nl.birmsite

Creative Loafing (Savannah)
www.creativeloafing.com/savannah/
newsstand/current

The Critical Review
www.criticalreviews.com
The best in music and books. Drop by and say 'Hi!'

Crushworthy
www.geocities.com/~crushworthy

Cupid Kidnap
www.cupidkidnap.com

The Cutting Edge
www.geocities.com/SunsetStrip/Venue/1006
Christian Publication.

CUZ
members.aol.com//CUZzine
Submissions welcome; CD reviews & free band/zine/record label advertisements.

Cybercitymag
www.cybercitymag.com

CyberPress Music (getsigned.com)
www.getsigned.com

Dagger
Tim Hinely   daggerboy@prodigy.net
PO Box 7605 Santa Rosa, CA 95407-0605
DAGGER is an indie pop/rock zine that I've been doing for nearly 13 years. each issue has about 7 or 8 (sometimes more) interviews or articles on bands and literally hundreds of record reviews. plus "much more." send $3.50 for a sample copy... and thanks!

Daily Camera
www.bouldernews.com

Daily Digital Opinion/SPiNME.com
www.spinme.com/ddo

The Daily Vault
www.dailyvault.com

Deadwinter
members.aol.com/Footsteps0

Deep Water Acres
www.dwacres.com

DeepFried Bug Vision
www.bugvision.com

Demo Universe
www.demouniverse.com

DePaulia
condor.depaul.edu/~depaulia

DIGIMUSIC Magazine Music Mall
federico panero fpanero@digimusic.net
www.digimusic.net
Digimusic is a multi-faceted website that offers you webcasts, live concerts, music industry directories, reviews, and more

Dirty Linen
www.dirtynelson.com/linen

Dogprint
www.dogprint.com/
A site for both the magazine and the label. focus: candy pop, electronic, lo-fi, ambient, D'n'B. photography, links.

The Doll Column
Niki Selken nselken@cats.ucsc.edu
www2.ucsc.edu/~nselken
An indie ezine of music reviews, poetry, and art.

Downeast Record & CD Review
community.webtv.net/DowneastReviews
We review CD's in all genres and are set up to promote the indie artists primarily.

Dr. Jay's Album Reviews
www.geocities.com/Paris/Metro/9650

Drawer B
www.drawerb.com

Dreamatic Online
www.dreamatic.com

the easy way
www.inetworld.net/thrill

Eclectic Earwig Reviews
www.geocities.com/trogotagel
Your online source for jazz, jazzrock fusion, progressive rock, electronic, ambient, psych/space rock and more eclectica.

Edrenaline – MP3.com
edrenaline.mp3.com

eguide
www.eguidemag.com
The entertainment magazine for the eastern Texas region.

Electron Music
www.electronmusic.com

Entertainment Blvd.
www.entertainmentblvd.com

Epinions.com
www.epinions.com/musc

Eventide
www.yourbestguess.com/eventide
Music, film, politics, and progress.

excerpt zine
dangermedia.org/excerpt

EXIT
www.geocities.com/SunsetStrip/
Frontrow/2647/index2.html

Exit 13
members.tripod.com/ex13/main.htm

EYE Magazine
www.eyemag.com

Eyepiece Network
www.eyepiece.com

Faction Press
members.aol.com/gonzodvz/faction.htm

Fallout Magazine
www.fallout-magazine.com

Feedback Magazine
www.feedbackmag.com

The Female Musician
www.femalemusician.com
Multimedia music productions for women in music. Educational and Entertaining Radio/ TV Series /resourceful web site.

FEMMUSIC.com
www.femmusic.com

Firecracker
www.angelfire.com/ny/snappleland

Fish Rap Live (UCSC)
prtr-13.ucsc.edu/fishrap

Five/One Magazine
www.five-one.com/51mag

Flagpole
www.flagpole.com

Flick Music
www.flickmusic.com

Flipside
flipside@ix.netcom.com
Reviews lots of indie music.

Flow Online
PO Box 641518, Los Angeles CA 90064
www.flowonline.com
Monthly online entertainment 'zine.

Focus Magazine
www.eatmag.com

Frames Per Second
www.angelfire.com/az/Aram

The Free Music Archive
www.free-music.com

FRIGHT X
www.frightxmagazine.com

The Fritz
www.thefritz.com

ftm Music Inc.
ftmmusic.com

Full Moon Fever
www.fullmoonfever.com

futurehit (TALKMUSIC.com)
www.talkmusic.com

fyou.com
www.fyou.com

Gajoob (Quality Impressions)
www.gajoob.com

Gallery of Indispensable Pop Music
homepages.go.com/homepages/
p/o/p/popgallery

GatorBuzz
www.gatorbuzz.com/

Geek America
www.geekamerica.com/
Stupid people don't...

Get Fancy!
Melyssa A. Harmon GetFancy@aol.com
600 E. Maple Street Suite 7,
Bellingham, WA 98225
Rather than compete with major label-oriented trade magazines and commercial radio promotion teams, the goal of Get Fancy! is to work with those professionals in bridging the gaps between the unsigned artist, independent label, major label and commercial radio as a tool that industry pros can use in their search for new talent.

Girlmedia.com
www.girlmedia.com/girlbands
GirlMedia's GirlMusic, website for only female musicians. Girl band listings as well as appearance on the radio show.

Girl Musician Online
www.girlmusician.com
Girl Musician Online has been designed with the female singer/songwriter in mind with an emphasis on the independent recording artist.

The Global Muse
www.theglobalmuse.com
A web base promotion service that offers Mp3 reviews, CD reviews, Band Marketing Advice, Artist Listings, and Artist programs.

GoGirlsMusic.com
www.gogirlsmusic.com/gogirls
Supporting independent women artists because chicks rock!

Going Underground
come.to/going-underground

GOOD STUFF
listen.to/goodstuff

Grand Central Music
www.grandcentralmusic.com

Green Mountain Music Review
www.gmmr.net
Dedicated to music aficionados resisting the blanding of America.

Grid Magazine
www.gridmagazine.com

Grip Monthly
www.virginiamusicflash.com

GRRL ROCK Has Become **Femmusic.com**
www.GRRLROCK.com

Grrl.com
www.grrl.com/musicreviews.html
If it makes a sound I'll review it....but it doesn't mean I'll like it!

Guitar Player Magazine
www.guitarplayer.com

Gumby in Space
www.pauserecord.com

GURLmusic
www.gurl.com/music

Hear &Now Music News
Celeste hear_and_now@hotmail.com
www.angelfire.com/wv/musiceyeball/index.html
Features a variety of music; indie, punk, electronica, emo, ska, etc.

Heckler
www.heckler.com/
Skate/snowboarding mag for young-uns, music reviews accordingly.

Heldlikesound
www.heldlikesound.com

High Times
www.hightimes.com

Highball Media
www.highballmedia.com

Hip Like Junk
www.blue.icestorm.net/hiplikejnk

Hip Online
www.hiponline.com/reviews
The premier online guide for music.

hipMama
www.hipmama.com/
hipMama is for parents who didn't check their personalities at the door.

HM Mag
christianmusic.org/cmp/hmmag/
Christian Music.

Hodgepodge
hodgepodge.burnit.net

The Hollow Planet
members.primary.net/~gmarshal
A comprehensive site featuring informative, challenging politics and entertaining indie rock.

Hollow Point Highway
www.hollowpointhwy.com

Howzitsound
www.howzitsound.com

The Humbled Reporter
humbled.com/reporter
Christian Music.

Hungry Bands.com
www.hungrybands.com

Ice Magazine
www.icemagazine.com

iDGiT
www.surfonline.com/idgit

iHerald.com
www.iherald.com

---

musiceditor.com
the new on-line A&R resource
opening doors in the industry for artists who deserve to be heard...

NEW MUSIC - MP3s - A&R FEEDBACK

Illinois Entertainer
ie.onza.net

Impact Press
alt.theslant.com/impact

Improvijazzation Nation
users.tm.net/rotcod/cds.htm
Zzaj Productions creates and produces YOUR music (as well as their own) HONESTLY!

In Music We Trust
www.inmusicwetrust.com

In the Pocket
stations.mp3s.com/stations/0/
in_the_pocket_pop__rock_e-.html

In Your Town Tunes (Comcast)
www.InYourTownTunes.com

Independent A&R
www.indiear.com

Independent Music Site
www.indiemusicsite.com

Independent Reviewer - Erik Deckers
www.kconline.com/deckers

Independent Reviewer – PJ Birosik
Musikintl@aol.com
154 Berasso Road,
Boulder CO, 80302, USA
Regular music review columns in over 28 trade and consumer publications plus on-line including NAV, CDNOW, allmusicguide, Creative Loafing, Crossroads, etc. Send CD with bio and distribution info, photo optional. I will accept all styles except rap, hip-hop and country.

Independent Reviewer - Shane Matsumoto
paradigmlost@hotmail.com
Writes for Gajoob and Found Music.

Independent Reviewer - Western Holmes
www.westernhomes.org/

Independent Songwriter
www.independentsongwriter.com

Indie Detour
www.hollowpointhwy.com/indie.htm

Indie Journal
www.strangecloud.com/indiejournal
Reviews, interviews, internet radio, mp3 site guide, poetry, art and more.

Indie Pages
www.indiepages.com
We've got info about your favorite indie bands, labels, mailorders, and zines, along with sounds and reviews.

Indie Scene
www.indiescene.com

indieaudio.com
www.indieaudio.com/

Indielive.com
www.indielive.com

IndieMonkey
www.indiemonkey.com
Dedicated purely to minor label and self-released artists. Indie Monkey features interviews, reviews and opinion pieces. Oh and it is owned by a geriatric ex-filmstar monkey!

Indie-music.com
Suzanne Glass suzanne@indie-music.com
www.indie-music.com
Indie-music.com has band feature reviews. Venue, radio, label, media and resource lists. Original articles by founder Suzanne Glass and guest authors. Exclusive discounts with other music companies. Log on and get your free listing. Then explore the massive information available at your fingertips. The ultimate little black book... all FREE for musicians! It's about the MUSIC!

Indulged
www.indulged.com

Indy Rock
www.indyrock.com/music

indygirl
www.planetgirl.com/indygirl.html

indyMusic.com (VIM Inc.)
indymusic.com

Ink 19
www.ink19.com

Ink Blot
www.big-shot.com/inkblot/default.htm

Inquisitor Zine
www.inquisitor.com

Instant Mag
www.instantmag.com
Your online guide to good rock.

InterMixx
www.intermixx.com

InterZone
www.interzone.addr.com

Incredibly Small Concert Hall
www.smallhall.com/mhall.html

Iron Feather Journal
Iron Feather & Hanna ifj@mycal.net
PO Box 480-004,
Denver, CO 80248   USA
ironfeather.com
A cybertekpunk magazine in print since 1987. We welcome any and all forms of music to be reviewed in our magazine. We will do a full review and also include contact infos, logos, etc. We also like to interview bands & DJs. We really dig reggae, rock, metal, blues, electronica, dance, pop, lounge, goth & industrial, noise, etc. We also will review punk, country and mainstream.

JAM Magazine (based in Portland)
www.jamzine.com

JAM Magazine (based in Florida)
www.floridajam.com

Jam Music Magazine (based in New Hampshire)
www.jammusicmagazine.com

Jelly
www.jellyroll.com
Crisp reviews of honest music in the great American tradition.

Jersey Beat
www.jerseybeat.com
Our motto: You try to play it, we try to like it. Serving the DIY community since 1982.

Just Plain Folks
www.jpfolks.com

Juxtapoz
www.juxtapoz.com

Kibbutz Music Reviews
www.tufts.edu/~mzwirn01/kibbutz.html
Idiosyncratic biweekly Web/Usenet album & concert reviews.

Kickstand
www.kickstandzine.com

The Kinda Muzik You Like
www.KindaMuzik.net
An indie/rock/pop webzine with webradio, reviews, rare streaming/mp3 and more.

The Knowledge
www.theknowledge.com

Kristian's Songwriter Critique Circle
www.insidetheweb.com/mbs.cgi/mb950694

KUCI Radio
University of California
www.kuci.org

Kweevak's CD Review
www.kweevak.com
Independent music promotion web site with lots of mp3 downloads, music industry links, rare live & studio tracks, music promotion services and autographed CD giveaways!

lazyeye
www.timmcmahan.com/lazyeye.htm

Left Leg
www.snuggles.org/leftleg/

LEO Weekly
www.louisville.com/leo

Lexicon
www.lexiconmagazine.com
New Wave to Modern Synthpop and everything in between.

Life As a Lie
members.tripod.com/lifezine

Life In Death
lifeindeath.freeservers.com

The Life Science Site - Music Reviews
Paddy Carroll paddycarroll@hotmail.com
www.nua-tech.com/paddy/music.shtml

Light Rotation
www.users.interport.net/~apfel/
Light pop only.

The Lighthouse
tlem.netcentral.net/toc.html
Christian Music.

Link Magazine
www.linkmag.com

Little Rock Free Press
www.aristotle.net/FREEP

Local & Regional Bands of America
geocities.com/SunsetStrip/Backstage/1329

Local Music Store
www.localmusicstore.com
A Collection of Independent Reviewers.

Localize It!
www.localizeit.com

Lollipop
www.lollipop.com

Lost at Sea
ursis.com/LAS
Music, Art, Photography, Literature, Media, the Environment and more!

The Loud Bassoon
www.polyholiday.com/loudbassoon

Luminous Flux Records
www.fluxnet.com/submiss.html

Lyrical Line
www.lyricalline.com

LyricsReview.com
www.lyricsreview.com

Magnet
www.magnetmagazine.com

Maximum Ink
www.maximum-ink.com

Maximum Rock and Roll
www.maximumrockandroll.com

Memphis Commercial Appeal
www.gomemphis.com

Menagerie Cyberzine
www.midtown.net/~limey1

Metro San Jose
www.metroactive.com/metro

Metroland Online
www.metland.com
Albany's Entertainment Magazine.

The Metropolitan Spirit
www.metspirit.com

Minor 7th
www.minor7th.com
Reviewing CDs which prominently feature guitar (especially acoustic): folk, jazz, fingerstyle, blues, new age, world, ambient.

Minx Magazine
www.minxmag.com

Mish Mash
members.tripod.com/~mashmusic

The Mobile Harbinger
entropy.me.usouthal.edu/harbinger

Monkey Dog CD Reviews
www.dnai.com/~gmatting/monkeydg.html

Monsters In My Bed
Jocelynflosdiner@aol.com

Motorbooty
www.motorbooty.com

Mountain Living Magazine
www.mountainliving.com

MP3 Artist Archive
www.mp3artistarchive.com
MP3 Artist Archive lists independent musicians, links to their music and CD's for free. Bulletin board, chat room and Shoutcasts.

MP3MusicReviews.com
www.mp3musicreviews.com
Love new music? Read reviews about songs by indie and unsigned bands at "www.mp3musicReviews.com"

MP3Reviews.com
www.mp3reviews.com
We actively scour the Internet to find the newest and best musicians and artists that promote their music by using the mp3 audio technology. We also accept submissions from artists directly on our site. Visit us to find some great new bands from all over the world, or to submit your band for review.

mp3Xreview
www.mpxreview.com
Reviews MP3s only.

Muddle
www.muddle.com

Multientertainment.com
www.Multientertainment.com

Muse: the Journal of Women in Music
www.val.net/muse

Music Biz Magazine
www.musicbizmag.com

Music Box
www.geocities.com/SunsetStrip/Club/7487

Music Connection
www.musicconnection.com

Music Corner
members.aol.com/musccorn

The Music Den
www.musicden.freeservers.com

Music Dish Reviews
www.musicdish.com
Trade publication showcasing the cutting-edge players and developments in the online music industry.

Music Haven
musichaven.tsx.org

Music Manic
www.musicmanic.com

Music Monthly
www.geocities.com/~musicmonthly

Music Morsels
www.serge.org/musicmorsels.htm
Free monthly ezine targeting musicians, songwriters and industry professionals providing self-help on advancing music careers. Industry columnists, interviews with national recording artists on how they evolved from obscurity to infamy, major and independent CD reviews, Unsigned band spotlight and an Industry profile every month along with listings of music industry opportunities for independent musicians. To subscribe, send an email to MusMorsels@aol.com

Music Reviews
www.nua-tech.com/paddy/music.shtml
A wide-ranging site, containing thoughtful reviews/recommendations of: world music, techno, blues, classical, gospel, rock & more.

Music Scene
www.muscene.com

musicgeek
www.musicgeek.com/

The Musician's Homepage
www.enteract.com/~digialex

Musician's Network
www.MusiciansNetwork.com/zine

MusicEmissions.com
Dennis Scanland dscanland@hotmail.com
www.musicemissions.com
MusicEmissions reviews every sort of indie music under the sun.

musicomet
www.musicomet.com

Musicrom.com
www.musicrom.com

Musiczone Online
Katrina Alliason katrina23@mailcity.com
P O Box 857, Tempe, AZ 85280-0857
www.musiczone-online.com
An online music magazine specializing in detailed artist information and reviews.

Mutant Renegade
www.Mutant-Renegade.com/main.htm
Half music half theme publication, we review everything.

Muzik Man's Sound Script
www.muzikman.com
Music reviews, interviews, news and informative links.

Nada Mucho
www.nadamucho.com/

The New Artist Review
www.newartistreview.com

New Century Review
members.aol.com/bookermps

The New Music Showcase
www.newmusicshowcase.com
The ultimate Internet promotion medium available to Independent artists.

New Routines
www.homestead.com/newroutines

newCDnews.com
newCDnews.com

netDrives.com
www.netdrives.com/home_layers.htm
Review MP3s.

The Night Guide
www.thenightguide.com
Dedicated to promoting performing independent artists everywhere. News, reviews, resources, web design services.

The Night Owl
www.thenightowl.com

No Cover
www.nocover.com
No Cover is the largest free music magazine in California. We distribute 100,000 copies worldwide, with a large presence in San Francisco, LA, Orange County, Riverside County, San Diego, Phoenix, Las Vegas, Santa Barbara, Hawaii, and Tijuana, Mexico. One of our mottos is "We know what you like before you do". this is not meant as a pretentious statement, just that the bands we feature are relative unknowns. Currently, 25% of unsigned bands featured on our cover get signed shortly after. For example; Anyone, an act from Huntington Beach was playing locally with a small following around the OC scene. Whithin 6 months of being in our cover they were involved in a bidding war finally settling on Roadrunner and landing Munky from Korn as their producer. This is the essence of No Cover, and our mission.

No Tequila
www.calpoly.edu/~jbounds/notequila.html

Bay Island Records, Inc. an independent record label
dedicated to new original music!
www.bayislandrecords.com

No Ugly Babies
www.angelfire.com/biz/nouglybabies
A monthly zine from Indiana dedicated to all things pop and rock.

Noise Queen
www.geocities.com/WestHollywood/
Castro/7507
It's a queer/friendly music/books/video/ politics/fiction 'zine.

Noisy Fans of America
www.noisyfans.com

Not Quite Israfel
www.bluemarble.net/~darcy/
notquiteisrafel.html

Nude as the News
www.nudeasthenews.com
Focusing on the expansive current state of rock.

NY Rock
www.nyrock.com

Oni Bubba's Den of Sin
members.tripod.com/~onibubba

Open Up and Say (OUAS)
www.openupandsay.com

Opus' Album Reviews
www.opuszine.com

Out of Order
annie.newdream.net

Outer Shell
members.aol.com/outershel

Outer Sound
www.outersound.com/

Papercut
papercut.rworld.org

Pathetic Caverns
www.pathetic-caverns.com

Pause & Play
www.pauseandplay.com/
Weekly pop/rock artist interview column, with vast archives.

Perfect Sound Forever
furious.com/perfect

Performer Magazine
www.performermag.com
Want your CD reviewed? Do you have news on your band? Send your CDs and press releases to the office in your area for publication.

Performing Songwriter
www.performingsongwriter.com
I am also a freelance reviewer for CDNow, Request and Mr. Showbiz.

The Phantom Tollbooth
www.tollbooth.org
Christian music.

Pig Publications
www.pigpublications.com

Pillowfight.com
www.pillowfight.com

Pitch Weekly
www.pitch.com

Poo Punk
poopunk.cjb.net

Pop Culture Detox
www.popdetox.com

Pop Culture Press
www.popculturepress.com
Pop and the rest of the musical spectrum. Plus a free CD sampler!

Pop Shots
popshots.org

Pop Stops
members.aol.com/jjenet
Weekly pop, rock & alternative CD reviews.

The Popcorn Music Review
home.twcny.rr.com/popcorn

Pop-Culture-Corn
www.pccmag.com/toc.html

PopMatters
c/o Sarah Zupko, PopMatters Media, Inc.,
P.O. Box 11015, Chicago, IL 60611-0015
www.popmatters.com
We run approximately 200 CD reviews per month, plus concert reviews, interviews and artist profiles.

Potpourri and Roses
c/o Brian Broccoli, POB 25692,
L.A., CA 90025 USA
www.geocities.com/SunsetStrip/Arena/3984/
From punk to polka- hey, if it's from Earth, it's all World music.

Preamp
www.preamp.com

Pulse!
www.towerrecords.com
Associated with Tower Records.

Puncture
Katherine Spielman
puncture@teleport.com

Pure Pop
www.purepop.com

Purple Tights
purpletights.com

Purr Magazine
www.purrmag.com

RAD Cyberzine
www.radcyberzine.com

Raging Smolder
www.avmcyber.com/rsmr
The Home of the Independent Music Review! We review everything we receive!

Rant N Rave
www.rantnrave.org

Ranter's World
www.rantersworld.net

Rats In The Hallway Webzine
members.tripod.com/~fakey

Raygun
www.raygun.com

The Record Reviewer
www.music-reviews.com

Renaissance Online
www.renaissancemag.com
Bringing cultural diversity to the Internet community.

Renegade Newsletter
membrane.com/renegade

repliq
www.repliq.net
We deliver new reviews of music (primarily mp3-formatted) every day. We are very much open for submissions from our audience. In time, we shall handle all kinds of music, but currently, electronic / techno/ hip-hop and the likes are handled alongside pop/rock/alternative music. We also have a reviewer handling classical (!) music.

Request Magazine
www.requestmagazine.com

Resonance Magazine
www.resonancemag.com

The Review Addict
dsl.org/review

Reviews Unlimited
www.reviewunlimited.com

Rhythm and News
www.rhythmandnews.com

richochetmusic.com
www.ricochetmusic.com
Christian Music.

Rock & Read Magazine
www.rocknread.com/home.html
Supporting rock bands and musicians of all levels.

Rock n Roll Reporter
www.rocknrollreporter.com

Rock Rag
home.earthlink.net/~rockrag

Rockazine
www.rockazine.com

Rocket Fuel Online
www.rocket-fuel.com

RockLove
www.rocklove.com

Rockrgrl
www.rockrgrl.com

Rockzines.com
www.rockzines.com

rockzone.com
www.rockzone.com
From Fugazi to The Smashing Pumpkins. From Jimmy Eat World to Rage Against The Machine. If it's Rock, It's here. The music. The Scene. Everything in between.

Rooster's Reviews
members.aol.com/roostrview
Mostly Christian, but will review all types and styles.

Rooted
www.rooted.com

Running In Circles
www.geocities.com/SunsetStrip/Birdland/3555

Salt For Slugs
www.saltforslugs.com
Contemporary Literature for the Random Reader.

Salt Lake City Weekly
www.slweekly.com

Sample Magazine
www.sample.wustl.edu
Washington University's Magazine of Musiculture. All items for review should be sent to: Sample Magazine, Box 1205, 1 Brookings Drive, St. Louis, MO 63130.

Scram
surf.to/Scram
Unpopular culture, beatniks, garage rock, novelty acts and anything offbeat.

Screachen Publications
www.screachen.com

Seattle Post-Intelligencer
www.seattle-pi.com

Seattle Weekly
www.seattleweekly.com

Section 3
www.section3.com

Seven Five-0
www.sevenfiveo.com

SF Weekly
www.sfweekly.com

Shark Sandwich
www.geocities.com/SunsetStrip/Towers/7050
An online zine that has interviews, show pictures, and reviews covering garage rock, pop punk, indie rock, and more.

Shock Value
members.aol.com/SVwebzine

The Indie Link Exchange
A new free and easy way to promote your website!
www.indielinkexchange.com

Signal Drench
drench.simplenet.com/sd

Silly Little Trouser Monkeys
Brad Bugos bushwkProd@aol.com

Sisdels Groove
members.tripod.com/~SisdelsGroove

Skyscraper
ucsu.colorado.edu/~bottomle
Covers music from indie rock to hardcore to punk to emo to metal to rock.

Skyway
www.freespeech.org/poploser/skyway/

Slender
www.slendermusic.com

SLIPCUE
www.slipcue.com
A noncommercial music-based e-zine focussing on indie pop, Cuban, Brazilian and hick music, with reviews by Berkeley, California's Joe Sixpack. Joe believes that music criticism is "not brain surgery or rocket science" and offers his reviews only as one person's opinions, free of commercial bias. Slipcue includes the world's largest English-language Guide to Brazilian Music.

Slipstream Magazine
Kristina Vallejo kvallejo@austin.rr.com
www.slipstreammagazine.com
Online music magazine featuring reviews, interviews, and cd reviews of signed and unsigned bands of all music genres

Smother
www.smother.net

Sn@kebite
www.btinternet.com/~snakebite

Snack Cake
www.snackcake.com

sonicnet.com
www.sonicnet.com

Soul Purpose
SoulPrpse@aol.com

Soundwaves
www.swaves.com

Space Age Bachelor Pad Magazine
www.space-age-bachelor.com

Space City Rock
www.tenagra.com/~jhart/space_city

Sparks Magazine
James Esch jesch@keystonenet.com
eserver.org/sparks/sparks.html

The Speaking Tree
www.speakingtree.com/speakingtree

Spectator
www.spectatoronline.com/current/index.asp

SPIN
spin.com

Splendid
www.splendidezine.com

Spoiler
www.spoiler.com

Spongey Monkey
www.ametro.net/~spongey

Sponic
www.sponic.com/

Spooky Poop
850 Carsonia Ave
#a-204 Reading PA 19606
members.tripod.com/~spookypoop/
Spooky poop has been in existance since 1992, and deals with the independent side of music - no matter what kind!

spOOn
members.tripod.com/spoonzine
We do accept music submissions in any file type that can be attached to an email.

Stereo-Type Magazine
www.stereo-typemag.com

Sticks n Stones
www.geocities.com/SunsetStrip/Venue/7374

Stinkweeds Online (formerly Mechanical Milkbone)
www.stinkweeds.com

Stomp and Stammer
www.stompandstammer.com

Stomping Ground
www.stompingground.com

Stonker
www.twdzine.com/stonker

stranger things magazine
www.strangerthingsmag.com
The love child of pop culture and ultimate reality.

subReal Songs/Anti-Elitist
subrealsongs.com/antielitist

Suite 101.com
www.suite101.com/welcome.cfm/pop_music
Send CDs/press kits for reviews/artist profiles. High-traffic site.

Superette Zine
Sandi superettezine@hotmail.com
www.freespeech.org/poploser/superette/
Pop music plus a girl's life equals superette!

Superstar in Stereo
www.superstarinstereo.com

The Swarthmore Phoenix
www.sccs.swarthmore.edu/org/phoenix/print.html

The Swinging Shindig
hometown.aol.com/shaunaskye/myhomepage

Swizzlestick
members.tripod.com/swizzlestickzine

The Synthesis
www.thesynthesis.com

Taco Truffles
www.tacotruffles.com

TailSpins
tailspin@interaccess.com
Reviews more indie music than nearly any other magazine.

Talk Music - Future Hits
www.talkmusic.com

Terrell's Tuneup
members.aol.com/spudclaw/tuneup.htm

Tidal Wave
www.tidalwavemag.com
Journal of pop music with a penchant for indie rock/pop.

tinycake
www.tinycake.com/h/jshome.html

TleM (The Lighthouse)
tlem.org
Christian Music.

Toast Magazine
www.toastmag.com

Tower of Song
cool.icestorm.net/towerofsong/index2.htm

Twee Kitten
www.tweekitten.com

U Magazine
www.umagazine.com

Underground Music Monthly
UMMusic.com
Online magazine and website dedicated to helping independent musicians.

The Underground Sound
ourworld.compuserve.com/homepages/ugr/sound.html

Undevoured
www.undevoured.com

University of Colorado Advocate
www.cudenver.edu/public/advocate
Need original, indie music. Help!

Uno MAS
www.unomas.com

unsealed
beam.to/unsealed
Original content featuring reviews, interviews, opinion and other tastey morsels.

The Unsigned
www.unsigned.com

Urban Prophet
urbpro.tripod.com
On the UPO website, you will find reviews of submitted material from artists and labels all around the world.

usounds
www.usounds.com

VoiCE
www.voicemag.net

Wall of Sound
wallofsound.go.com

The War Against Silence
www.furia.com/twas

Web 'n' Zic
www.webnzic.com/enter.htm

Webthrust - Pieces
www.Webrust.com
An essay publication covering all facets of the arts.

Weekly Alibi
www.alibi.com/alibi/current

Weekly Indie MP3
www.weeklyindiemp3.freeservers.com

Well Rounded Entertainment
well-rounded.com/music

Whatever
www.whatevermagazine.com

Why Magazine
www.whyzine.com

Willamette Week
www.wweek.com

Wish I Might
www.velvetclub.com/magazine

Women of MP3.com
artists.mp3s.com/artists/57/the_women_of_mp3com.html

Womanrock.com
womanrock.com

World Wide Music Reviews
www.realtimerecords.com
Great site by freelance music reviewer/writer/singer/songwriter Bobby Torres

The Worst Fanzine
Kevin Morris psi40@hotmail.com
fanzine.at/theworstfanzine
If it rocks we want it, all rock music included.

Xemplary Music Reviews
www.xemplary.net

yahtzeen
www.yahtzeen.com

Zum
www.sirius.com/~zum
Our jocks specialise in: Punk, Stoner,Psych, Progressive, Folk, Metal, Indie.

Canada

009
Marilyn and
Michellerhiannon22@hotmail.com
Interviews with duotang and b'ehl;rants and raves; stories; poems; games; contests and all things sloan and x files.

Above Ground Testing
www.angelfire.com/on/abovegroundtesting

Agree to Disagree
members.xoom.com/a2d

Back Of A Car (BOAC)
home.istar.ca/~beeman/contents.html

Broken Pencil
www.brokenpencil.com

Building Adam
www.hwcn.org/~ad825/baindex.htm
Building Adam is the irregularly-produced hard copy zine, with the accompanying website which should leave a BA flavour in your brain.

Chart Magazine
www.chartattack.com/monthly

Drop D
www.dropd.com
BC music has priority. Then Canada, then the world.

Ductape
members.tripod.com/~ductapefanzine

Extreme Magazine
www.extreme-online.com

the GATE
www.go.to/theGATE

IndieCan
members.tripod.com/~indiecan

indiehour
www.angelfire.com/or/indiehour
A Toronto-based webpage that promotes Independent artists for free.

Melting Snow
members.tripod.com/~weatherpattern

Monday Magazine
www.monday.com/monday

Muse's Muse
www.musesmuse.com
Indie reviews, songwriting tips, tools and interactivities.

MUSon
www.vari-media.com/muson

the Nerve
www.thenerveonline.com

Ontariomusic.com
www.ontariomusic.com
Reviews, Sounds, Video, Photographs, Interviews, Biographies, Show Listings, Site Hosting, Promotions, Music Store and more for all musical genres.

Queen of the Universe
Jeannette Ordas
nettiequeen@hotmail.com
www.angelfire.com/bc/queenoftheuniverse

So It Goes
welcome.to/soitgoes
Brit Pop.

Soda Magazine
www.sodamag.com

SOUP
www.soup.on.ca

Speck
www.medatman.com/speck

Spill
www.spillmagazine.com
Toronto's Hippest Underground Music Magazine. Now has an Indy band of the month feature.

Tapegun
www.interlog.com/~tapegun

Thrust Quarterly
come.to/thrust

BEST MUSIC BOOKS offers HUNDREDS of music books that can help to shape your career including *"How To Be Your Own Booking Agent and Save Thousands of Dollars"* by Jeri Goldstein and *"Guerilla Marketing"* by Bob Baker.
www.bestmusicbooks.com

VAJ
www.etext.org/Zines/VAJ/v13p2.htm

Velocity Mag
www.velocityonline.com/
Entertainment and pop culture distributed monthly throughout Canada.

South America

Brazil

071
www.geocities.com/SunsetStrip/
Mezzanine/1470

Brazilian Rock Eletronic Magazine
brazilianrock@litoral.com.br

Conga Conga Conga
www.Geocities.com/Hollywood/
Makeup/9828/laconga.htm

organic alterNETive
www.ufsm.br/alternet

Rock Brigade
www.rockbrigade.com.br

Rock Demo Website
www.rockdemo.com

SonarIvo A P Escóssia
www.geocities.com/SunsetStrip/
Stadium/1389

TSIANTAKIS corp
www.geocities.com/SunsetStrip/Venue/8032

Whiplash!
whiplash.simplenet.com

Chile

ESPECIAL 35°
members.spree.com/sip/especial35
Includes all type of musical tendencies: alternative, indie, latin american scene, electronic, punk, hardcore, avant garde, stoner rock, heavy metal....

Europe

Belgium

Shakin Fever
surf.to/shakinfever
A Webzine bringing news and info about surf, rockabilly, psychobilly and good old rock'n roll. The zine is now partly edited in english but will be fully bi-languagal very soon.

Finland

Custom Built
surf.to/custombuilt

Eastpop
www.eastpop.com

Music Mission
www.kauhajoki.fi/musicmission

SOUNDi
www.soundi.fi

France

Abus Dangereux
www.multimania.com/vicious/abus.html

Le CARGo
www.terant.com

ces Sons Déments Ki me Hantent (S.D.K.H.)
sdkh.citeweb.net
Critiques de disques et concerts, nouvelles musicales, listes de discussion. Albums and gigs reviews in French, music news, mailing lists...

Critic Instinct
nwurd@canz.com
www.critic-instinct.com

Djouls.com
www.djouls.com

Electric Light
www.welcome.to/electriclight

Inrockuptibles
www.inrockuptibles.presse.fr

James!
home.planete.net/~jpascal/James.html

Kerosene
www.kfuel.fr.st

L@bel Vie
home.worldnet.fr/~labelvie

Nova Planet
www.novaplanet.com

Panic
www.chez.com/panic

POPnews
POPnews, 172 rue d'Alesia,
75014 Paris, France
www.popnews.com/popnews
We are one of the major French music webzines. Very keen on discovering new talents we also publish regular compilation CD of our favorite "newcomers". POPnews is read by over 5000 people per month (60% French, 20% Belgian, 10% English, 10% others). on top of this people we have a list of 2000 registered readers who receive the articles on a weekly basis.

sefronia
wwwusers.imaginet.fr/~ouaah/LeMessager
CD review free e-mail magazine (in french). Subscribtion/Samplers/Infos : Francois ouaah@imaginet.fr

SDZ
members.xoom.com/sdz
A french underground zine available on the Net as well as on paper. We cover everything that rocks!!

TamTam
tamtam.music@insat.com
www.tamtam.insat.com

Zatapathique
www.altern.org/zata

zicline.com
www.zicline.com
Chaque semaine toute l'info musical du jazz au metal, presentations de CD, concours, concerts. Each week all music infos from jazz to heavy metal , new CD presentations, games with music gifts, live shows.

Germany

Discover
www.discover.de

Giants Lore
itsnova.mach.uni-karlsruhe.de/~meiswink/giantslore

Music Mag
www.musicmag.de
Charges a fee for reviews.

PNG (Persona Non Grata)
www.popculture.de

Poltergeist
mitglied.tripod.de/dachshund
Version 1.5 feat.interviews with The Rocking Horses, Gel, Gizmo, Midget and the Kenadas!

Rock Pages
www.ip-verlag.de/szene/welcome.htm
A classical and new Rock-Mag only on the Net.

Sound De Verlagsgellschaft
www.sound.de

Greece

Babylon
www.babylon.gr/

Italy

Discorso Musica
www.omitech.it/DM/dm.htm

La Musica Inrete Pop Magazine
popmag@inrete.it
web.inrete.it/musica/musica.html

Music boom
www.musicboom.net

Mirko Spino
www.undo.net/rumori
Freelance reviewer that writes for BLOW UP and many other Italian fanzines (JAMMAI, ITSELF, EQUILIBRIO PRECARIO and others).

The Netherlands

Music Discoveries.com
musicdiscoveries.com/charts/radio/amstelveen.html

Project A
www.projecta.net/iffr

Saucy Trout
saucytrout.com/

Tracks Online
www.tracksonline.com

Norway

Luna Kafe
www.fuzzlogic.com/lunakafe/index.shtml

Popgenerator
www.stud.ntnu.no/~matsj/zine

Women and Music
home.sol.no/~kwinther

Portugal

musicNET
www.musicnet.forum.pt

Rock 'n' Cave
www.rockncave.pt

Russia

Music News Weekly
www.nestor.minsk.by/mg

Rock City, Rock Fuzz, Toad, Boonker
Yuri Burnosov advis@admin.debryansk.ru
Yuri writes for several Russian paper zines including the above mentioned.

Spain

Fanzine De Colores
ttt.eui.upv.es/~juamaro/toxicosmos/decolores.htm

Ruta 66
www.kebradisc.com/ruta66.htm

Sweden

Allt på ett kort
www.algonet.se/~popoga

bara ALLT
home4.swipnet.se/~w-44991/ba

benno
www.benno.com

Bomben
bomben.nu

The Broken Face
brokenface.exitflagger.com
Psych, noise, folk, drone, pop and rock 'zine.

Elva
www.rymd.com/elva

Ettnollett
www.nordling.com/ettnollett

Fastback
www.algonet.se/~mbg/fastback

Midwestern Skies
www.melodic.net

Passagen
www.passagen.se

Portrait Magazine
www.portraitmagazine.com
About everything that can be called "popular culture", but mostly modern rock music. Bands who are interested in getting their music spread in Sweden are encouraged to send a demo.

Promenad
hem1.passagen.se/promenad

Revolver
www.revolver.nu

Scandinavian Indie Reviews
www.lysator.liu.se/~chief/reviews.html

Truckfighter
www.truckfighter.com

United Kingdom

14 Sandwiches
members.tripod.co.uk/~sandwiches14
E-zine based in the north of England with reviews, interviews and features casting a wide view over the indie scene.

A Cheery Wave From Stranded Youngsters
Kevin Pickstock
PickstockK@luton.gov.uk
Rated indie fanzine welcomes contributions for occasional freebie compilations.

Akiko
www.akiko.ndirect.co.uk

Almost Cool
www.almostcool.org
Updated on a weekly basis, the site focuses on indie and electronic music and has an archive of well over 300 reviews.

Alphabetty
www.rockin.to/alphabetty

always echoes
www.always-echoes.co.uk
New online fanzine that shows the lighter side of the heavy sound.

Ashamed and Bored
www.csv.warwick.ac.uk/~maupn/ashamed
Guildford based indie zine in its online form, covering the best in local and national sounds, from post-rock to punk-pop.

Available in Shops
www.diskant.f9.co.uk/shops

Below the Surface
freespace.virgin.net/chinch.mu
The foremost underground music 'zine. Nuff said. With slight seriousness.

BLAG
members.aol.com/blagmail

BonaFideStudio
Deanna info@bonafidestudio.co.uk
www.bonafidestudio.co.uk
Open 24 hours recording and rehearsal studio (and much, much more!!!) in Central London. We also offer: Reviews, Artist Page, Notice Board, Sound Tutorial etc. Run by musicians for musicians, we are different - we really do care. Check us out!

borrowORob
www.borroworrob.com/mag_main.htm

The Brain Farm
members.easyspace.com/eatradio

Breaking Waves
Robin Seamer robin.seamer@virgin.net
94 Sutherland Rd,
Southsea, Portsmouth PO4 OEZ
Indie pop and alternative zine that reviews demos, gigs and interviews both established and new bands. Also features discursive and comedy articles. Varies between £1.00 to free.

breakthru
www.breakthru-magazine.com
A music magazine about people making it in music. As a publication it is designed to inform its readers about the workings of the industry, while at the same time acting as a platform to help expose the unsigned and newly signed artist.

"Find yourself a Music Deal" in the Bandit A&R NEWSLETTER

Bandit profiles Labels, Publishers, Managements, Production Co's worldwide which are CURRENTLY looking for new acts, songs & masters. There is a US edition and also a UK/World-wide edition. so you can target your material worldwide.

Bandit has been published monthly for over 12 years and has helped many people throughout the world get all kinds of deal!

GET YOURSELF A FREE SAMPLE COPY !!

visit www.banditnewsletter.com
e-mail bandit@aweber.com
(subject ICB offer)

Busker's Ball
www.busker.freeuk.com

CHA CHA CHA
browse.to/ccc

Clean Shaven
www.badmusic.net

the cocktail lounge
www.rollo17.freeserve.co.uk
An indie heart, a pop soul and rock socks.

COME ZERO
members.tripod.com/mozaque/comezero

Cultural Review
www.w-mids.freeserve.co.uk

Dancing About Architecture
www.dancingaboutarc.com

Dancing Penguin
www.dancingpenguin.com

Darcy's on the Pull
www.kenickie.com/darcy.htm

Dazed and Confused
www.confused.co.uk

Diskant
www.diskant.f9.co.uk

e.p.
www.vigilante.co.uk

earitation
www.earitation.com

Elsol's Album Reviews
homepage.tinet.ie/~rwhelan/index1.html

Excellent Online.com
www.excellentonline.com
The Home for North American fans of UK Music.

Exclusive Fanzine
www.exclusive2.freeserve.co.uk
A fanzine from the UK specialising in review/interview/articles on indie music from around the world. We review all music sent to us, in both the paper magazine format and on the web site.

Fancybiscuits
Carl Bradley fancybiscuits@hotmail.com

Flashback
www.flashback.org.uk

Fluxeuropa
www.fluxeuropa.com

The Fly
www.channelfly.com
A new and alternative music site featuring webcasts, legal MP3s, features, interviews, competitions and music news covering the best UK acts from JJ72 to Oasis.

Freaky Trigger
www.netcomuk.co.uk/~tewing/freaky.html

Freebase Magazine
www.freebase.com

geekrock
www.geekrock.com
An online gig guige & music resource covering 600 venues in theUK and Europe.

Graham Vine – Independent Reviewer
graham.vine@bt.com
56 Colchester Road, St Osyth,
Essex, CO16 8HB UK
My reviews are published by all the local magazines in my area, and I know these have led to sales.I look forward to reviewing your music and building up a partnership with your good selves.

Headcleaner
web.ukonline.co.uk/keith.dumble/
hopper/head.html

Hearsay
www.hearsaymagazine.demon.co.uk

Higher Than the Sun
members.tripod.com/arsed

Home and Away
Pete Cole   homeandaway86@hotmail.com
PO Box 16,
Aldershot, Hants GU12 5XY, UK
www.liveclub.co.uk/h&a
A short & sweet, honest bi-monthly hard & soft copy fanzine that covers studio/live reviews of guitar/punk/pop bands.

The Horse
www.uk-image.net/horse

Hot Press
www.hot-press.com

I Am the Rock
www.iamtherock.co.uk

Intoxicated 'Zine
www.intoxicated.clara.net
One of the UK's longest running rock zines!

Irish Music Box
www.dojo.ie/musicbox

ISR Online Reviews
www.isr-uk.net
One of the world's leading online music magazines.

jockrock
www.vacant.org.uk/jockrock/jockrock.html
Resource for Scottish indie-underground music with news, record and gig reviews, band and label guide, plus sound samples and streaming webradio.

Konketsu
www.nonverbal.com/konketsu

Limecat MP3 Reviews
www.geocities.com/SunsetStrip/
Concert/9968

Live Online
www.live-online.com

Luke
Rob.Forbes@btinternet.com
We specialise in independent North American music, be it power pop, insurgent country, folk roots, garage punk, lo-fi rumblings or just plain old alternative

Massmurderon
Paul massmurderon@hotmail.com
Cheap shoddy and crap. If you want to see how bad - 17 St. Thomas Road, Norwich NR2 3RP, UK.

Mild Curry
members.aol.com/polo47/mildcurry/
mild.html
A free online fanzine with issues every 2-3 weeks. Covers indie/punk and metal.

Mind the Gap
surf.to/mindthegap

The Modern Dance
www.madasafish.com/~moderndance/
An A to Z music review Internet magazine that follows no fashions - probably the most eclectic there is!

mudmag.co.uk
www.mudmag.co.uk

Muse
www.muse.ie

New Music Express (NME)
www.nme.com
The Official UK No 1 music web site.

No Pictures
www.diskant.f9.co.uk/nopics

No Ripcord
welcome.to/noripcord
A free online music fanzine specialising in reviews and features of indie/alternative bands. We are also aiming to start an independent record label.

Nothing To Declare
www.ed.ac.uk/~nine/ntd.html

Nuisance
www.angelfire.com/ak2/nuisance

Online POP
www.onlinepop.co.uk

Organ Zine
www.organart.com

papercuts
www.papercuts.co.uk

Peel The Stain
www.peelthestain.freeserve.co.uk

pennyblackmusic.com
www.pennyblackmusic.com

pH Magazine
www.phantomfm.com/ph

Pop is Love
www.popislove.co.uk
Featuring daily updated news and weekly updated reviews and interviews, Pop Is Love is all you need. Full stop. Er, except beer. Full. Stop.

Quirk
fly.to/quirk
Music meets lifestyle in and around London.

Qwirky Purple
Dammo qwirkypurple@hotmail.com
www.qwirkypurple.co.uk
Qwirky indie/alternative website containing interviews, live reviews, single & album reviews, demos, up-and-coming bands. Soon we will include live soundfiles and downloads of tracks by featured artists. We are also hoping to include a CD swap page.

Rainsound
www.geocities.com/SunsetStrip/Studio/9230

Rant UK
www.rantuk.com

The Realm of Old Mother Hubbard
www.realmofomh.co.uk
Album reviews, gig reviews, interviews and more with a UK and Ireland bias from Old Mother Hubbard.

Red Roses For Me
www.redrosesforme.co.uk

RetroActive Baggage
www.baggage.co.uk

Robots and Electric Brains
www.geocities.com/SunsetStrip/Backstage/1472/
Eclectic zine for music with that extra something special (come.to/robots)

Saccharine
www.cl.cam.ac.uk/users/kr205/saccharine/home.htm
A UK based fanzine covering all good music everywhere.

Scotland Calling
www.sc-online.co.uk/

Skippy's Cage
www.skippyscage.com

BEST SHEET MUSIC.com your guide to the best sheet music, tab and lyric sites on the Internet!
www.bestsheetmusic.com

Slampiece
freespace.virgin.net/slampiece.inc/home.html

sleazenation.com
www.sleazenation.com
A lively labyrinth that allows visitors to sample our cultural hotbed and communicate with like-minded souls.

Sliver Space Boots
www.geocities.com/SunsetStrip/Studio/9830/frames9.htm

sMaggots Zine
www.geocities.com/SunsetStrip/Studio/6093

Sorted
www.irelands-web.ie/sorted

Speeder
talk.to/Speeder

Spitting Glass Stars
spitting_glass_stars@lineone.net
www.geocities.com/spittingglassstars
Stars features interviews and reviews of both small and established bands. Music ranges from punk to pop to rock to indie...whatever we feel like reviewing! As well as music there's lots of other nonsense to read and some silly pictures to look at. The website will eventually have all the articles from the back issues on it, and is growing all the time. Latest issue is £1 + A5 sae, or a trade. Contact by e-mail or check out the website for more details.

State 51 - Motion Reviews
www.state51.co.uk
Showcasing the best new music, across all genres. updated daily.

The Storm Lounge
Talek Glover reviews@stormlounge.co.uk
www.stormlounge.co.uk
We will review indie, punk, lo-fi, rock, metal and other forms of independant music. We are a UK based site.

Supanova Radio
www.supanovaradio.co.uk/
We review Punk, Stoner, Psych, Progressive, Folk, Metal and Indie music.

surface vs depth
www.angelfire.com/wy/neonlights/main.html

Tangents Online
www.tangents.co.uk

T-Funk
www.t-funk.co.uk

This is Not TV
www.zen.co.uk/home/page/alec.cook/tintv

Tom's MP3 Reviews
home.clara.net/tcsb
Independent reviews of MP3 tracks from a range of sites covering different genres including Indie/Alternative, Electronica, & more!

TWANG
dimension.spodnet.uk.com/~twang

unbarred
www.unbarred.co.uk
unbarred deals with bands that aren't usually covered by larger publications. It deals with all sorts of styles, from indie, rock, pop and dance; also gigs, concerts, records and CDs. It is updated regularly and provides profiles, mp3 samples, interviews, previews, reviews and competitions making it a music magazine that the real music fan cannot do without.

underpop
www.catmobile.co.uk/underpop

The Universal
www.geocities.com/SunsetStrip/Arena/8538

Unnatural and Wrong
www.thumped.com/unnatural

Unpeeled
www.counsel-house.demon.co.uk

Urbane Terrorists
www.envy.nu/urbaneterrorists
Indie music zine that concentrates on British music.

Weeyaa music mag
www.snapper0.demon.co.uk

The Wiseacre
www.wiseacre.clara.net
Weekly music reviews in all manner of styles.

Zeitgeist
www.zeitgeist-scot.com/
Reflecting The Underground through music and lifestyle and art.

Australia - New Zealand

Australia

2RDJ FM Contact!
crash.tig.com.au/~andrew/contact.html
Reviews international Indie/alternative/new wave pop demos.

Renegade Review
renegadereviews.homepage.com

Beat Magazine
www.beat.com.au

ChaosMusic
www.chaosmusic.com
Indie artists WANTED!!! Sell your CDs/sound files, no up-front costs.

Chester
www.darkshadow.com.au/chester

Chunky Yet Funky
www.zyworld.com/chunkfunk/smeg.htm
Since July 1997, Graham & his friends have been releasing CYF zines whenever they feel like it, & the web version has been around since early 1999. We do reviews, interviews, & the occasional tribute-y spiel about a favourite artist or rant about what's on our minds. Contributions/trades are encouraged.

Electric Newspaper
come.to/Electricmusic

Firehorse
www.firehorse.com

Garv
www.garv.net

Gods of Music (formerly MP3 Reviewer)
www.godsofmusic.com
'Gods of Music' is dedicated to providing detailed, constructive and honest reviews for all bands / artists. We employ a sophisticated 6 point rating system which makes for a well balanced and helpful reference for all readers. We currently have 10 reviewers from all over the world and we generally review between 20-30 new bands each month.

Gravity Girl
people.enternet.com.au/~acarew

hEARd
www.ozemail.com.au/~hmag
Non-profit organisation promoting new music & youth culture in general. Covers all genres of music & accepts unsolicited material from both commercial distributors of independent & major labels as well as independent bands, management & unsigned bands, divided into categories, plus other free & 'at cost' services to the music community in general.

ILLUMINATI-Zine!
www.geocities.com/illuminati_ezine

Joyzine
www.joyzine.zip.com.au

juice dot net
www.juice.net
Online community with the latest in music, movies & lifestyle issues from Australia and internationally. Including radio and video streaming, MP3s, online shopping, cinema listings, trailers and chats.

bestmusiczines.com

Put up a beautiful display of your music related site for FREE!

Kill the Cod
www.geocities.com/TelevisionCity/Station/7421
We review all indie pop and rock, to be published both online and off- distributed throughout Australia.

Medea
Anna   medea@ozemail.com.au

Mediasearch
www.mediasearch.com.au

mono
www.mono.net

Mosh Editors
www.geocities.com/themosh_2000

MOZ Music
www.mozmusic.com
Popular music site with free promotion for indie & independent artists.

MP3.com.au
www.mp3.com.au

popcycle
www.geocities.com/SunsetStrip/Loft/8455

Sevenmag
www.sevenmag.com.au

slide show
www.vinylrevival.homepage.com
Would you like your new vinyl release reviewed? Keep getting ignored by those compact disc loving zines? Everything submitted to SLIDE SHOW will be reviewed within two weeks of receiving it. If you'd like to send you latest 7-inch, 10-inch, 12-inch or LP for review, please go ahead. Address parcels to PO Box 72 Westmead NSW 2145 Australia. If you are wondering...no, we don't review CDs.

Secrets of Home Theater and High Fidelity
www.hometheaterhifi.com/main.html

Smokin' Dog Zine
smokindogpress@hotmail.com
www.hotyellow98.com/smokindogpress
From the makers of Australia's legendary 'Smokin' Dog Press' zine. Read Interviews with worldwide indie acts and be interviewed! Send stuff to be reviewed! Updated weekly and advertised thoroughly in Oz. We will have a new URL at "www.sdp-online.com" starting in June, with every interview etc etc and will have a classifieds section for bands .... and more. We want bands to give us Mp3's as well so people can hear unknown stuff.

Warm Cola
www.warmcola.com

Asia

India

The Music Magazine
www.themusicmagazine.com/review.html

Japan

1audio
www.1audio.com

Catch that Beat!
www.mars.dti.ne.jp/~yayoi

Fish the Music.com
www.FISHtheMUSIC.com

NewMusicJapan.com
www.newmusicjapan.com

Waves Indie Club
www.blackblue.co.jp/err/dl.html

The Philippines

Spearmint Head
go.to/spearminthead
This Filipino girl loves indiepop. Popkids of the world unite!

Singapore

Beta
Chung
home2.pacific.net.sg/~ch_lee

Africa

South Africa

Amuzine
www.cd.co.za
SA music online magazine with news, reviews and concert details. And our associated online CD store, www.oneworld.co.za, selling SA music of all types, to the world.

G-String
www.gstring.co.za

Country Music

This section also contains roots, alternative country and rockabilly sites.

United States

Alt-Country
www.rockzines.com/altc/

alternativecountry.com
www.alternativecountry.com
alternativecountry.com..pretty much tells the story.....al-ter-na-tive coun-try (awl-tur-na-tiv kun-tree) n. 1.another musical option 2. a remaining choice 3. that which is no longer considered "country" because of the misappropriation of the term. 4. definitely more Billy Joe than Billy Dean, more Steve Earle than Sawyer Brown, more Wilco than Wade Hayes, more Lucinda than LeAnn Rimes, and much more Johnny Cash than Clay Walker!.... We review music, list radio stations that play real country music, we include news and information, and shortly there will be artist profiles and audio streaming

Bluegrass Magazine
206.100.237.27

bluegrass now
www.bluegrassnow.com

The Bluegrass Telegraph
www.bluegrasstelegraph.com
A monthly internet magazine devoted to bluegrass music. Stay informed with the latest news, reviews, and trivia.

Bluegrass Unlimited
www.bluegrassmusic.com

Blue Suede News
www.bluesuedenews.com
House Organ of the Church of Rock'n'Roll.

Country Chatter
www.countrychatter.com

Country Girl
www.steamiron.com/cgrrl

Country Review
www.countryreview.com

Country Standard Time
countrystandardtime.com
Your Guide To Roadhouse, Roots And Rockabilly.

CountryCharts.com
www.countrycharts.com/link.htm

Cowboys n Cowgirls
www.geocities.com/Nashville/6900

Cyber-Country
www.cyber-country.com

Cybergrass
www.banjo.com

Flatpicking Guitar
www.flatpick.com/Pages/Main/FPGMO-MainPage.html

Freight Train Boogie
www.freighttrainboogie.com
Features news and reviews of Roots music with an emphasis on Alt.Country or Americana music, including some Rock, Folk and Blues and everything in between.

Great Lakes Twang
www.geocities.com/Nashville/Stage/9596/gltwang.html
Promotion of Americana/Alt-Country bands in the Great Lakes region.

Grindstone Magazine
members.aol.com/grind55
Your Guide To Roadhouse, Roots And Rockabilly.

iBluegrass
www.ibluegrass.com

Independent Country Entertainer (ICE)
country-music-club.com/Independent-Artists/usa/current.html
The Independent Artists Directory at the Country Music Search Engine. Independent Country Entertainers get a free Web Page/Directory listing that is simple to use. Related resources include; Indie Artists News Magazine with Press Release Submitter, Country Music Banner Exchange, Free Country Classifieds, Free E-mail accounts, web site development and promotion advice plus an MP3 Directory and more.

Indie Tracker
www.indietrackermagazine.com

Made in America
www.madeinamericamusic.com

MandoZine
www.mandozine.com

Muledog Magazine
www.execpc.com/~muledog/magazine/magazine1.html

The Music Matters Review
www.mmreview.com

My Kind of Country
www.mkoc.com
Country music at it's finest from yesterday's legends, to the newest up and coming country singers and songwriters. Featured in Real Audio and video.

The Newgrass Site
www.cashiers.com/woodward

No Border Lines
www.noborderlines.com

No Depression
www.nodepression.net
A bimonthly magazine covering alternative-country music (whatever that is).

Old-Time Herald Online
www.mindspring.com/~oth

Original Cool
hometown.aol.com/OrigCool/ochome.html

Roadhouse Fever
www.roadhousefever.com

Rockabilly Central
www.rockabilly.net
Rockabilly Central is the ideal starting point in your search for rockabilly music. We have links to just about every rockabilly band and site out there, along with lots of tour dates, reviews press articles, photos, etc.

The Rockabilly Hall of Fame
www.rockabillyhall.com
Great rockabilly compliations and individual artrists, including Italy's world famous Dimaggio Bros. Label use available to rockabilly performers.

Rooted Magazine
www.rooted.com
An online journal of Texas music and art..

Rural Route Twangzine
www.twangzine.com/front.html

Twangin'
www.steamiron.com/twangin

Welfare Music
www.welfaremusic.com
Music with a twang. This is the online resource for all things alt.country. News, Interviews, links, MP3 downloads, and a great message board.

Who's Where in Bluegrass
www.angelfire.com/ct/bluegrassnewsletter

Women of Country
womenofcountry.com
The Internet's #1 Guide To Female Country Music.

Wrangler Gene & The Bunkhouse Gang
www.wrangler-gene-texas.com

Canada

Bluegrass Canada
www.cmpa.ca/pa1.html

Fiddler Magazine
www.fiddle.com

New Country Canada
newcountrycanada.com

Opry North
members.home.net/oprynorth
Canada's #1 site for everything country, dedicated to providing information and support for the artists and fun for the fans.

Finland

Southern & Rocking Music
www.sci.fi/~srmusic

France

Destination Country Music
www.asi.fr/plurielfm/pages/country/pages/country.html

Germany

Keep it Country
www.i-c-m-a-g.net
Online Magazine in german and english of the Independent CMA Germany, with CD Reviews, Stories about Singers, Songwriters, Bands etc.

Independent CMA
www.i-c-m-a-g.org
A non profit Organisation, which supports artists, bands etc. all over the world, with Charts, Online Voting, Internet Radio Show, and much more

Insurgent Country
www.insurgentcountry.com

The Netherlands

Alt Country NL
www.xs4all.nl/~bebisch
A Dutch website for music fans of Alternative Country, rootsrock and Americana.

Slovakia

Country Fest
www.countryfest.sk

Svonky
www.bluegrass.sk/zvonky/index.html

United Kingdom

Country Music Gazette
www.jdenterprises.co.uk/cmg

Country Music Ireland
www.countrymusicireland.com

Country Music People
www.countrymusicpeople.com

Country Music Plus
www.countrymusicplus.co.uk

JD Enterprises
www.jdenterprises.co.uk

North West Bluegrass News
www.nwbn.freeserve.co.uk
A non-profit British Bluegrass Magazine, hard copy and free online archive, with quality articles with photos, reviews, tablature, etc.

Southern Country
angelfire.com/sd/scountry
We are a country music magazine covering the British country music scene for the Southern half of the country, that is as far as the gig guide and club coverage is concerned. We carry advertising for events all over the UK and abroad, and have coverage for the same. As well as reporting on the live events, we carry album reviews, book reviews, readers letters, news, features, and articles on related subjects. We also sponsor the annual UK Country Radio Awards.

Australia

Country Goss
www.countrygoss.com.au

Country Grapevine
www.countrygrapevine.com

Country Music Review Page
www.ozemail.com.au/~fiddling

Hillbilly News
country-music-club.com/Independent-Artists/hillbilly/current.htm

Japan

Moonshiner
www.kh.rim.or.jp/~bluegras/MoonShiner/index.html

BEST SHEET MUSIC.com
your guide to the best sheet music, tab and lyric sites on the Internet!
www.bestsheetmusic.com

Dance Music

North America

United States

2c Magazine
www.geocities.com/SunsetStrip/Palladium/2457

A House of Techno & Electronic Music
www.house-of-techno.com/Eindex.html

Club Arena
Diggy diggy@online.ee
www.clubarena.com/

Dance Music Authority (DMA)
www.dmadance.com

drumnbass
www.drumnbass.com

etronik
www.etronik.com

Frequency
www.frequencyradio.com

groovefactory.com
www.groovefactory.com

HUGE!
Riverfront Plaza, Box 200562,
Newark, NJ 07102-0310, USA
i.am/HUGEzine
A very REAL look into the >NYC-based rave scene focusing on party kids themselves.

jungle kidz
www.jump.to/jungle_kidz
DnB/Jungle Site Displaying MC Samples, Dubplates, DJ Sets, DnB Reviews/Reports, Pics, and Artist Bios! Site based out of SF.

Ministry of Sound
www.ministryofsound.com

Pax Acidus
Larry Zoumas sloth@paxacidus.com
www.paxacidus.com
Pax Acidus is a techno literary website dedicated to the underground arts of site and sound.

The Selekta
www.selekta.com/

The Skinny
www.skinny.com

subsystence
www.subsystence.net

Vybemuzik
info@vybemuzik.com
www.vybemuzik.com

www.housemusic.com
www.housemusic.com
The website for house music on the web. Started by a dj for serious dj's and househeads, DJ Eldon has put together a site for dj charts, record label links, and reviews of new music.

Canada

Cognition
Andrew Duke cognition@techno.ca
Cognition/In The Mix, 1096 Queen St #123,
Halifax NS Canada B3H 2R9
techno.ca/cognition

BEST MUSIC BOOKS offers HUNDREDS of music books that can help to shape your career including *"How To Be Your Own Booking Agent and Save Thousands of Dollars"* by Jeri Goldstein and *"How To Promote Your Music Successfully on the Internet"* by David Neuve

Nocturnal
www.nocturnalmagazine.net
Covering the genres of house, garage, techno,trance, jungle, drum n bass, hardcore, hardhouse and progressive, Nocturnal has emerged as the complete guide to the music and the people that make Toronto the best place to party in the world.

Toronto Rave Connection
members.home.net/raver4life

Tribe Magazine
www.tribe.ca

Europe

Finland

Findance
www.findance.sci.fi

Music Mission
www.kauhajoki.fi/musicmission

France

Atome
www.atome.asso.fr

Dream Escape
www.dream-escape.org

Freakz Connection
perso.cybercable.fr/freakz

Hypertunez
www.hypertunez.com/english/ht/home.htm

New Forms
Florian Fossa florian@newforms.net
www.newforms.net

Speedfonk
listen.to/speedfonk

Germany

Motor
www.motor.de

Wicked World of Electronic Dance Music
music.city.de/wicked

Italy

THEVibes.net
www.thevibes.net

United Kingdom

[pheet]
www.pheet.f2s.com

Dance Central UK
www.dance-central.ndirect.co.uk

Drum n' Bass
www.drumandbass.co.uk

Drum n' Bass Arena
www.breakbeat.co.uk/

FLY Magazine
www.fly.co.uk

gaialive Radio Reviews
www.gaialive.co.uk/index.shtml

G-Club
www.g-club.net

In-Site Magazine
www.in-sitemagazine.com

M8 Magazine
www.m8magazine.co.uk/menu

mixmag
www.techno.de/mixmag

Mixology
www.mixology.co.uk

New Forms
www.new-forms.demon.co.uk

The NRG
www.the-nrg.co.uk

Australia

3D Music
www.threedworld.com.au

Spraci
spraci.cia.com.au/

TransZfusion
www.tranzfusion.net

Experimental Music

Experimental, Electronica, Goth, Ambient, Industrial, Avant Garde, New Age and Noise.

North America

United States

A Result of Most Dismal Procrastination
www.freespeech.org/akane

Aegri Somnia Vana
Michael Babcock   aesova@aol.com

Alchemie Ezine
www.goth.net/~alchemie
A place for goths to gather and share their dark rhythms.

almostcool.org
www.almostcool.org/
Updated weekly, this long-running site features a huge music review archive of independent and electronic artists.

Al's Review Archive
www.awrc.com/review

AmbiEntrance
www.spiderbytes.com/ambientrance
Covers ambient, electronic and/or experimental recordings.

Apocalypse
www.island.net/~jsmith

Asphyxia
Zoe Security   zoesecurity@hotmail.com

Assimilation
members.xoom.com/assimilate1/enter.html

Assumed Power Focus
www.overwhelmed.org/apf/

AsYlem Magazine
www.hallucinet.com/asylem

aural innovations
aural-innovations.com/

Auricle Electrozine
www.auricle.cc
Electrozine of aural culture. Monthly Web zine dedicated to creative independence in every genre.

AUTOreverse
www.AUTOreverse.net
We gladly review all DIY/self-released/ microlabel recordings of a non-commercial nature.

Avant Garde Times
www.angelfire.com/on2/AGT

Baba Luba
www.babaluba.com
Ambient, Electronic, Industrial, Dance & Experimental Music-CD, Vinyl, Cassette.

Base Asylum
members.tripod.com/~base_asylum/main.html

beamy
www.wwnet.net/~mikelod/beamy.htm

Bleeding Minds
Jessica Ocasio   jessica@bleedingminds.com
PO Box 520, Cranbury, NJ 08512
www.bleedingminds.com/zine/zine.html
An online zine featuring dark/gothic/punk/ industrial art, poetry and photography. I will also review goth, industrial or punk bands in the zine.

The Brain
www.brainwashed.com

Carpe Noctem
www.carpenoctem.com

The Catacombs
www.geocities.com/SunsetStrip/Club/3075

Chaos Control
www.chaoscontrol.com

Choler Magazine
www.choler.com

The Cimmerian
www.geocities.com/SoHo/Exhibit/4089
An intelligent and beautiful online music magazine aimed at exposing the latest and best releases in the gothic, ambient, and industrial genres.

CLOUZINE
www.angelfire.com/ab/clouzine

Computer Music Journal
mitpress.mit.edu/e-journals/
Computer-Music-Journal

Cool and Strange Music
members.aol.com/coolstrge/coolpage.html

Corpse in the Cupboard
www.geocities.com/SoHo/Lofts/2287

The Creative Musician's Coalition
www.aimcmc.com

Crying Clown
member.aol.com/CryClown/cry.html

Cyberia
Melpomene Whitehead
MelpomeneX@aol.com
Erik O'Brien SoulMgr242@aol.com

D.E.A.D. Webzine
www.geocities.com/SunsetStrip/Arena/1313

Damaged Transmission
www.angelfire.com/va/asbestos
A guide to music and movies.

Danse Assembly Music Network (DAMn!)
members.aol.com/DAMnet
3x yearly - 5,000 copies 2 colour cover b/w inside pages. Has advertising.

Dark Desire
www.nocturna.net/darkdesire
A website for the dark, obscure and romantic side of music.

Dark Velvet
www.darkvelvet.com

darkzine.net (formerly Shattered Dreams)
www.darkzine.net
darkzine.net is a dark/goth e-zine publishing fiction, poetry and artwork in the dark fantasy, horror and dark erotica genres. The zine also features reviews of current "dark" bands including but not limited to goth and industrial music.

Dead Angel
lonestar.texas.net/~monorecs
Ezine with wide variety of underground music reviews and interviews.

Decadence
David Ranford md2992@cnsvax.albany.edu

Deep Magazine
www.deepmag.com

Delirium Magazine
www.deliriummag.com
Webzine catering to music features, reviews and show listings.

Dewdrops
techmart.com/dewdrops

Die Forum
www.netherworld.com/~paisli

Digital Death
www.digital-death.org

Digital Intersect
www.digital-intersect.com
An experimental and electronic music quarterly print zine and distro.

Dirty Princess
www.geocities.com/~synthkatt

disquiet.com
www.disquiet.com

Distorted Silence (on the web)
www.jesusfreak.com/distortedsilence

Dominion Radio Reviews
auslander.hypermart.net/main.html

Digital Drive-Thru
stations.mp3s.com/stations/1/
digital_drive-thru.html

Eklectique
www.gothics.org/eklectique
A sarcastic zine catering to the Gothic/ Industrial scene.

electro@ge
electroage.lowlife.com

Electronic Musician
www.emusician.com

Electronic Surveillance
elektronicsurveillance.homestead.
com/home.html
A webzine dedicated to Electronic - Industrial - Experimental - Synth - Cybercore music. Includes interviews, images, reviews, and more... Will accept promos for review.

Electrozine
home.earthlink.net/~hrb39/electrozine.htm
A review/scene site for mainly artists of the Gothic/Industrial/Electro/Techno genres but all artist submissions are accepted and will be reviewed.

Esoterica
www.sexynexus.com/esoterra
Does interviews but not reviews.

Extreme Scene
www.users.interport.net/~velvet/bands.html

The Fading Halo
www.geocities.com/SunsetStrip/
Backstage/4979

False Prophet Campaign
fpc.hypermart.net

FIX Magazine
www.fix.com

Flesh and Wire
www.angelfire.com/id/rev
Australia's largest Industrial, Gothic & Darkwave Zine. Includes interviews, articles and reviews.

FLUX Europa
www.fluxeuropa.com

Frequency Fundamentals
24.3.95.46

Friends Like You
members.tripod.com/~friendslikeyou
Christian alternative music.

Giants Lore - Experiment IV
itsnova.mach.uni-karlsruhe.de/
~meiswink/giantslore

God Etcetera!
lynx.dac.neu.edu/s/skremen

Godsend Online
www.evansville.net/~tgodsend
Webzine covering electronic, experimental, post-industrial, noise, techno, and ambient sounds.

GOOD STUFF
listen.to/goodstuff

The Gothic Preservation Society
www.gothicpreservation.com
The GPS has been described as The Gothic Readers Digest....it's a monthly webzine dedicated to the darker side of life.

Gothic Topic
www.gothictopic.com
An online and offline publication covering news and music pertaining to the Gothic and Wiccan world.

Grave Concerns
www.angelfire.com/ny2/graveconcerns
An e-zine that is concerned with gothic, industrial, ethereal, synthpop, techno, and dark alternative/metal bands. At the E-zine you will find many interviews, reviews, and news of bands from these genres along with many other special features.

Graveside Terrors
members.tripod.com/~Todd_Myers
Website dedicated to music, reviews, cemetery photos, and other things of a dark nature.

Grinding Into Emptiness
www.emptiness.net
Underground reviews news and interviews: electro/noise/synthpop/industrial/et al."

Grooves Magazine
www.rain.org/~audio/grooves
Experimental electronic music only (think Aphex Twin/Alec Empire/Mu-Ziq).

Halana
www.halana.com
Welcomes esoteric sounds.

Hollow Ear
www.hear.com/hollow

The House of Three Ravens
www.darksites.com/souls/goth/threeravens
Featuring reviews and interviews: Gothic, Industrial, Ambient, Electronic, Ethereal and more. Online and print versions available!

Hypercult
www.hypercult.com

In Faction
infaction.8m.com
Independent magazine that covers electro, industrial and experimental music genres.

Inamoena Tempora
reciprocus.com/inamoena
A webzine dedicated to art (visual, aural, or otherwise) that explores the aesthetic of the dark corners of the subconsious.

Independent Reviewer - Ram Samudrala
www.ram.org

Independent Reviewer - Mark Weddle
www2.southwind.net/~markw/cdreviews

Industrial Az Fuck
www.half-asleep.com/industrial

The Industrial Bible
www.industrial-music.com/ib

The Industrial Information Station
dune.fionline.it/iis/kd2.htm

Industrial Mayhem
Tim & Svet   Birminghm6@aol.com

Industrial Nation
www.IndustrialnatioN.com

Infinity Complex
Jason Rodgers
electricmindwarp@hotmail.com
97 Intevale Rd; Wilton, NH 03086
Industrial, Punk, Radical Insanity, Discordian freakfest.

Innerviews
www.innerviews.org

inorganic.net
www.inorganic.net

Interface Magazine
www.interfacemagazine.com

Intransitive Recordings
www.visionload.com/intransitive
Improvised and electro-acoustic music. works by Richard Chartier, Roel Meelkop, Loren Boyer, Brume, Kapotte Muziek, nmperign, many more.

Juxtaposition
www.virtulink.com/immp/jux/j_index.htm

Killing Ground
www.geocities.com/SunsetStrip/Mezzanine/6567/intro.html

Lady Doom's
members.aol.com/LadyDoom

Last Sigh
www.lastsigh.com
Ambient, Noise, Industrial, EBM, Gothic, Power-percussion, Interviews, Reviews, Photos etc.

Late Train
www.latetrain.com

Legends Online
www.legendsmagazine.net/
Goth/Ambient/Techno/Industrial Reviews - 10 Years Running.

Leonardo Music Journal
mitpress.mit.edu/e-journals/Leonardo/lmj/sound.html
Accepts submissions for a yearly CD Compiliation.

LowLife
www.lowlife.com

Lunar Magazine
www.lunarmagazine.com

Midnight Voices
www.goth.net/~jeriko/frame.html

Music for a New Age
www.his.com/~fjp/music.html

Neo-Barbaric
www.fortunecity.com/roswell/spells/49/neobar.htm
Carnal H. Coitus chcoitus@hotmail.com
POB 144/ Ashville, PA 16613 USA
Paper & internet zine, DIY, all forms of extreme recording styles, reviews, interviews, cosmic combat comics, all underground, Ads free with submissions. Paper-$1.

The Nerd Den
www.angelfire.com/in2/nerd4life

Netmix
www.netmix.com

Neuralgia
members.tripod.com/~rasputina13/Neuralgia
Sick and twisted, dark and bizarre zine. Goth, industrial, etc.

Nikline Hillbight's zine
www.geocities.com/nodar_2000/NIKLINEHILLBIGHT.html
A new zine for unknown experimental artists.

NoiseWeb
noiseweb.com

nougat
www.nougat.com/index.shtml

Object A
www.object-a.com
Comprehensive coverage of underground culture featuring reviews, interviews, and profiles of gothic, industrial, experimental and electronic music, art, and writing.

Oklahoma Gothic
members.aol.com/oklagothic/main.html

Ongaku Otaku
www.charnel.com/ongaku
American based magazine that focuses on Japanese alternative music.

Opiate
www.minot.com/~slasher

Ornery Hipster
ornery_hipster@hotmail.com

Outburn
www.outburn.com

Panopticon
ezines.net/Panopticon

pjoe
pjoe.net

bestmusiczines.com
Put up a beautiful display of your music related site for FREE!

The Plague
www.the-plague.com

Progression Magazine
www.progressionmagazine.com
World's largest art-rock magazine. Display advertising available. Contact us

Psignalpath
noiseweb.com/psignalpath

Psychedelic Realm
www.psychedelic.com
An emphasis on electronic, experimental and unusual music.

Purist Online Magazine
members.xoom.com/puristzine

QRD
members.xoom.com/hrthrt
Reviews, stories, news, poetry and zombies.

Remote Induction
members.tripod.com/rem_ind
From quirky pop to experimental electronic music, an exploration.

The Reviews of The Almighty
www.princeton.edu/~abpurvis/radioshow/reviews/reviews.shtml

Rob's Page of Album Reviews
members.aol.com/kmfdm3/reviews.html
Album reviews for electronic music of all styles.

Seven
www.nezzwerk.com/seven

Shadowed Sky
www.cyberstage.net/shadowedsky/main_index.htm
Underground Gothic, Industrial, darkwave and etheral music, photography and art.

Sinkhole Experimental Music Magazine
www.sinkhole.net/magazine

Sistinas
sistinas.com

Site-Online
site.hypermart.net

Sonic Barrier
www.sonicbarrier.org

Sonic Envelope
www.sonicEnvelope.com

sonicdiscourse (formerly Rivets Magazine)
www.sonicdiscourse.net

spawning ground
www.azstarnet.com/~fishes

Stark Reviews
www.23x.com/starkview

StarVox
www.starvox.net
Bringing a gothic nation together.

Technotica.com
www.technotica.com

Terra Industria Magazine
www.terraindustria.com

Title Goes Here
stations.mp3s.com/stations/18/title_goes_here.html
Weekly newsletter for the electronic music community. Featuring reviews, tips, interviews, bios, and links to free software and samples.

Tronikzine
www.troniks.com/zine
Web-based zine + label always interested in hearing new and exciting experimental and electronic sounds.

Ujamaa's Ambient Experience
Eric Prindle   prindle@susqu.edu
www.susqu.edu/students/p/prindle/ambient/default.html
Exploring the ambient universe: reviews, interviews, news and more.

Ultra Pop!
users.erols.com/guerue/index2.html

Unit Circle
www.etext.org/Zines/UnitCircle

Veindance
www.veindance.com

the vision and the void
home.earthlink.net/~nitzer/

Voidstar Productions
www.tiac.net/users/deftlyd
Artistic collective featuring resources for electronic and experimental musicians including DJ Lists, Zine Lists, Music Review sites, Video Artists lists, discussion lists, and the web pages of Industrial, Ambiant, IDM, EBM, and Avant Garde artists involved in this site.

Voltage
www.voltage-zine.com

www.deathrock.com
www.deathrock.com

XLR8R
www.xlr8r.com

Zu Casa
www.zucasa.com

Canada

Another State of Mind
www.geocities.com/shawn_e_spermicide
An amalgamation of punk, hardcore, ska, rockabilly, surf, goth, garage mayhem. Articles, photos galore, bass tabs, news and gig and music reviews.

Chaotic Critiques
www.geocities.com/SunsetStrip/Palms/6031

Corridor of Cells
www.geocities.com/~zaraza_doom

Critiques de disques par Vincent Bergeron
members.xoom.com/altmuziq

earsay
www.earsay.com

Feedback Monitor
www.stainedproductions.com
Reviews/interviews of electronic and experimental music/arists.

Kortex
kortex.rapeculture.net
Industrial-EBM-Experimental-Noize-Electro Webzine in French & English.

Mote
Kelly Saldat-Brix Mote_@hotmail.com

raw42
www.raw42.com/

Rue Morgue
info@rue-morgue.com
www.rue-morgue.com
We review music releases (no demos) of horror related music; soundtracks, goth, dark electronica, horror themed punk, black metal, dark rock, ambient music and anything else. Theme is important, not necessarily content

Tentacles
www.yip.org/squid
Industrial Music E-Zine and Club Nights at Sanctuary, Toronto.

Wrapped in Wire Canada
www.wrappedinwire.com
Tons of reviews!

Mexico

Distortion Sekt
Otto Rios
www.geocities.com/SunsetStrip/Stadium/3733/DS.html

Urbe01
www.urbe01.com

South America

Argentina

Esculpiendo Milagros
www.eemm.com.ar

Brazil

Electronik Brazilian Musique
www.ebm.trix.net

Fiber Online
www.fiberonline.com.br
An electronic music community featuring interviews, reviews, forums, etc. Written in Portuguese.

Quintessence
www.swcp.com/mv/essence

Colombia

El Laberinto
members.tripod.com/laberinto1

Europe

Belgium

Darker than the Bat
www.proservcenter.be/darkerthanthebat
Independent organisation - goal : helping bands with promoting their music.

l'entrepot
users.skynet.be/entrepot

BEST MUSIC BOOKS has books on MP3's including *"The MP3 and Internet Audio Handbook"* by Bruce Fries, *"The Official Guide to MP3"* by Michael Robertson & Ron Simpson and *"MP3 Power!"* by Justin Frankel & Greely Sawyer
www.bestmusicbooks.com

De Kagen Kalender
Stefan kagan_kalender@hotmail.com
KAGAN, p/a Wim Troost, Geerdegemstraat 23, B-2800 Mechelen, BELGIUM
welcome.to/dekagankalender
Kagan focusses on wave-gothic-electro-industrial, including all the related styles. It has a weekly radio-show, a gig- and party-guide including reviews, a dj-team, parties and a web-site. Each promo is assured to get a review (on both KaganKalender and web-site) and will be played on radio-shows, if it suits within the music styles we focus on.

Seraphim
bewoner.dma.be/seraphim

SIDE-LINE
www.side-line.com

Uzine
www.dma.be/p/ultra
The web site is now only a contact point for the printed zine.

Finland

5HT
www.sci.fi/~phinnweb/5HT

Frantic
www.sci.fi/~cyberwar/Frantic.html

Freak Animal Magazine
www.saunalahti.fi/~fifteen/freak-animal

Megabaud
www.megabaud.fi

Sub-Fennica
www.kolumbus.fi/scorpius/
A Webzine focusing on the Dark Music genres: Electronic, Metal, Gothic and so on.

Subway Magazine
Henrik Wetterstrand
hwetterstrand@gnwmail.com

France

Darkface
www.multimania.com/darkface

Elegy
www.multimania.com/darkface/fanz/elegy.htm

etats limites
dust.net/elimites

Freakz Connection
perso.cybercable.fr/freakz

Obscure Depression
obscure.iFrance.com/obscure

Prémonition
www.premonition.com.fr/

Totentanz Webzine
www.multimania.com/totentanz
Dedicated to all forms of dark, industrial and gothic music. It features reviews, interviews, scene news as well as a calendar of concerts, parties and tours.

Utter Dark
www.geocities.com/utterdarkradio

Germany

ALPHAbeat
www.pixelhouse.de/alphabeat

Auf Abwegen
www.aufabwegen.de

Black Screen
www.blackscreen.de

Blackmagazine
come.to/blackmagazin

Bodystyler Magazin
www.textundton.com

Crossover
move.to/crossover
A non-commercial network for youth culture and music resources.

Die Willkuer
home.rhein-zeitung.de/~nettwill

Different Frequencies
www.fan-base.de/mags/differen.html

Eclipse
www.eclipse.de

e-lectric
www.e-lectric.de

Equinoxe
www.tu-chemnitz.de/~safa/equinoxe.htm

FAN BASE
www.fan-base.de

Gothic World
www.ritchies.de/gothicworld

Kato's Net Zine
userpage.fu-berlin.de/~carlosbc

Klangwald
www.klangwald.de

Kraftwerk
kraftwerkzine.cjb.net
Kraftwerk Zine is a strawberry in the cake the overman eats not only on birthdays and parties, but each and every day - every moment of his existence, awake and dreaming, always, always and forever.

MEMi
www.memi.com

The New Empire
www.newempire.com

Orkus
www.geocities.com/~orkus/

reclaim
www.reclaim.de

re.fleXion
www.re-flexion.de

Schrei
informatik.uni-bremen.de/~goecke

Schützis Page
www.geocities.com/SunsetStrip/
Vine/6186/index.html

Scope-X
www.scope-x.de
The alternative music and lifestyle center

Sigill
www.eislicht.de/eislicht

Surface
members.aol.com/surface3
We divided the homepage into a german and english part. Musical page about: Electro, Synthpop, Wave, Industrial.

synthetics
www.synthiepop.de

TranceForM
www.tranceform.de

Wrath
www.wrath.de

Zillo Musikmagazin
Kirsten Borchardt   asmodo@zillo-music.de
Georg-Ohm-Str. 5, 23617 Stockelsdorf,

Germany

www.netcity.de/zillo
Leading German magazine featuring mainly dark wave, alternative, industrial music.

Italy

Chain D.L.K.
dune.fionline.it/chaindlk

Ink Box
www.dune.fionline.it/inkbox

Modulazioni Industriali
members.xoom.com/modulazioni

Neural
a.ludovico@agora.stm.it

Suburbia
www.geocities.com/SunsetStrip/
Backstage/2592/SUBURBIA.HTML

Ver Sacrum
www.geocities.com/Paris/LeftBank/
1667/versacrum.html

The Netherlands

DFM
desk.nl/~dfm

Experizine
Robert@lookoutfgx.com

Forcefield Reviews
home.wxs.nl/~exiq/ED/home.html

The Fredscape Collective
www.fredscape.com/

Kagan
welcome.to/dekagankalender

Vital
www.staalplaat.com

Russia

Black Kobzar
Anton Shekhovtsov, pr. Nakhimova 7 kv. 3,
UKR - Sevastopol 99011, Ukraine
www.blackkobzar.newmail.ru
The Ukrainian Dark Site: gothic, folk, dark bands: interviews, reviews, reports featured.

Gothism
www.gothism.da.ru

Industrial Music Digest
www.vl.kharkov.ua/%7Eben

Russian Gothic Page
www.gothic.ru
Spain

The Black Box
dominios.net/theblackbox

gRASA
www.espacio3.com/grasa

Laylah
pages.whowhere.lycos.com/
entertainment/laylah
Spanish Gothic/industrial webzine. Music and literature.

Margen Magazine
www.arrakis.es/~margen
Progressive and new music magazine with a lot of interviews, dossier, reviews....

Necropolis
www.teleline.es/personal/sogonz/

Recorre el Submundo
www.geocities.com/SunsetStrip/Disco/2861/Darkness.html

Sweden

Casual Online (used to be Faith & Devotion)
home4.swipnet.se/~w-49526

Geisterfahrer Webzine
www.csd.uu.se/~s95ksj/home1.html
Exploring new music on the inner net.

Gothic.nu
gothik.nu
Reviews, mp3s, articles and NEWS. Music: goth, EBM, industrial, darkwave.

Prospective
www.prospective.nu

Release
Mikael Kahrle   release@swipnet.se
Box 7144, S-402 33 Gothenburg
www.releasemagazine.net
Music web magazine in English. Speciality: electronic, industrial, gothic, techno.

Wanted
members.xoom.com/moriensis/wanted/wanted.htm

ZEOLight
zeolight.framtid.nu

United Kingdom

4:33
Amir H. Nikoupour
four33.virtualave.net

Altair 5
www.collective.co.uk/altair5

Beat Freakery
www.beatfreakery.uk.com

Black Monday
www.blackmonday.co.uk

The Black Pages
welcome.to/the_black_pages

Compulsion
www.callnetuk.com/home/compulsion

cybase 23
www.demon.co.uk/cybase23

Fused
www.fused.com

Future Music
www.futurenet.com/futureonline

Goth is Goth
www.geocities.com/Paris/Bistro/9610

Guilfin
www.guilfin.org

Hard Wired
www.appleonline.net/kelcombe
A quarterly fanzine that is produced by a team of dedicated enthusiasts. We cover all forms of the alternative music genre - goth/EBM/Indie/Dance/Metal etc. Nothing mainstream makes it into our pages. For more info, visit our website.

Haywire
www.haywire.co.uk

Immerse
www.haywire.co.uk/immerse

The Milk Factory
www.themilkfactory.co.uk
Monthly site packed with altenative reviews on electronica, dance and quality pop. Come and see by yourself!

Misfit City
www.collective.co.uk/misfitcity
Eclectic, in-depth music reviews - anything good considered and covered.

MK ULTRA
www.mkultramag.com
News, reviews and interviews. Evil and funny. Definitely the darkest rock n' roll publication in the world.

Organ
www.organart.demon.co.uk

The Ptolemaic Terrascope
www.terrascope.org
Long-running fanzine reknowned for unearthing predominantly psychedelic/folk nuggets.

Rubberneck
www.btinternet.com/~rubberneck/

The Slaghuis
www.slaghuis.net
Gothic, Darkwave, Industrial Reviews & Radio Free Abattoir.

Synth Music Direct
www.synthmusicdirect.com/
Specialists in Eletonic music Distribution and retail sailes.

White Noise
www.burntweeny.freeserve.co.uk

The Wire
www.thewire.co.uk
Leading international monthly specialising in electronica, breakbeat, avant rock, free jazz, classical, global and beyond.

Wire Magazine
www.thewire.co.uk/

Australia

The Aether Sanction
www.goth.org.au

Blatant Propaganda (formerly aja)
www.teknet.net.au/~eye/mainset.htm

Blatant Propaganda
www.teknet.net.au/~eye/mainset.htm
Underground music reviews and suppressed information.

Dissonance
dissonance.space.net.au

EYE
www.teknet.net.au/~eye/mainset.htm

The Kronic Oscillator
clananalogue.org

Nadabrahma
www.users.bigpond.com/nadabrahma

Yippie Bean
www.warehouse.net/yippiebean

New Zealand

Gothic Underground New Zealand (G.U.N.Z)
gunclub20@hotmail.com
gunz.nitro.gen.nz
Music, arts and community resource site offering extensive underground networking, for all aspects of local subculture loosely defined as "dark.

BEST MUSIC BOOKS offers many directories that can help you promote your music
www.bestmusicbooks.com

Asia

China

Independent Reviewer - Olivier Petitpas
Olivier is working for various Chinese music magazines and they're looking for things to review in their pages. They want recordings, zines, whatever. Send them any kind of music from noise to techno and anything else.
China 10/F KamPing Building, 95 King's Road, North Point, Hong Kong, China
etoile@wongfaye.com

Japan

Digital Biscuit
Nogucci Harumi
MGH03372@niftyserve.or.jp

Songs From Torture Chambers
www.geocities.co.jp/Broadway-Guitar/4498

Hip Hop

United States

360 Degreez of Hip Hop
www5.50megs.com/hiphop
Ill hip hop site that contains Real Audio, a Store, Reviews, Release Dates, and More. Looking to add independent music.

88HIPHOP.COM
www.88hiphop.com
We offer our audience continuously updated current events, reviews, music, videos, happenings in the world of Hip-Hop, and an instant link to our homepage. The 88HIPHOP.COM Daily News keeps our audience coming back each and every day, hungry for the latest in Hip-Hop culture. 2 Minutes of Fame highlights unsigned, up-and-coming, and independent artists and companies.

Altrap.com
www.altrap.com
The main factor of altrap.com is to elevate and educate the hip-hop nation with mad precise views on hip-hop.

Apacalypse
apacalypse.8m.com

B-Boys.com
www.b-boys.com

BeatBandit.com
www.geocities.com/Hollywood/Club/8457
Have You Ever Seen Hip-Hop This REAL?

Black Hole
www.eyeofthehole.com
The new and growing zine reflecting the dynamics of urban music and culture.

Black Hole
www.tmottgogo.com
Washington artists only.

Blaze
www.blaze.com

Breaker Beats
mastayoda.iwarp.com
A Hip Hop site that reviews music that comes into the Hip Hop genre. The site strives to get the best underground Hip Hop/Rap acts know and recognised. Breaker Beats is willing to retail Underground music, if it is necessary. Breaker Beats receives about 1000 hits per month so the content posted is well spread around.

BX Factor
www.bxfactor.com/index2.html

Craig's State of the Union
pages.prodigy.net/andthem/home.html

Cyber Sturg
www.ewsonline.com/music

Cyber Vibe
www.cybervibe.com

The Cypha
www.cypha.com
Indie Hiphop/Rap Promotion, Real Audio, CD Compilations, Bios, Demos, Place To Battle, Freestyle Live.

DaveyD's Hip Hop Corner
www.daveyd.com/

Digital187.com
www.digital187.com

Down-South.com
www.down-south.com

drhiphop.com
www.drhiphop.com
Doctor Hip Hop dot come is the main source for Hip Hop and other music info on the net. We provide you with everything from news, reviews, pictures, chat's, freestyling boards, downloads and alot more. We are always willing to advertise for you especially if your a new and upcoming rapper or group we needs the world to see them or needs some nice beats to flow on.

DU $OLDIER$
www.dusoldiers.com

Ego Trip
www.egotrip.com/

Elemental Magazine
www.elementalmag.com

Exploit Da Network
www.exploitedmusic.com

GlobalHipHop.com
www.globalhiphop.com

GodsHipHop.com
www.godshiphop.com
We focus on Holy Hip-Hop emcees and groups. We'll post your music, pictures, and news about your group for free.

The Groove Spot
www.Tha-Real.com

Hip Hop Flash
www.gotchaopenradio.com
Radio and reviews.

Hip Hop Massive
www.den.net/shows/hiphopmassive

Hip Hop News Daily
www.geocities.com/Tokyo/Bay/3187

Hip Hop Reviewz
reviewzxl.com/

HipHopSite.com
www.hiphopsite.com

HMC
hellish1.tripod.com

Ill Crew Universal
www.illcrew.com/

Illtip
www.theilltip.com

Insomniac
PO Box 592722 Orlando, FL 32859, USA.
www.insomniacmagazine.com
Insomniac Magazine "The World's Only Hip Hop Industry Magazine." Tm Insomniac is a national publication that features the best in pure hip hop. Past covers include: Kool Keith, Slick Rick, Rakim, The Roots, Common, Black Moon and more. Insomniac supports indie releases and offers them the best ad rates in the business. Insomniac can also handle national radio promotions of your new release. If you have a quality hip hop release we can help get it play on radio stations nationally.

The Internet Ghetto Blaster
www.igb.com/

JDP
www.jdp.cjb.net
Website focusing on underground and independent hip-hop culture. Includes reviews, RealAudio archives, artist spotlights, area spotlights, and interviews

Loop Hole
www.loopholemagazine.com

Mad Rhythms
www.madrhythms.com
The entertainment magazine for the college audience.

Manhunt
www.manhunt.com
Hip-hop, r&b, news, interviews, reviews, song clips, etc.

mrblunt.com
www.mrblunt.com

Murder Dog
www.murderdog.com

Northwest Hip-Hop Underground
206hip-hop.8m.com

OHHLA
www.ohhla.com

oldschoolhiphop.com
www.oldschoolhiphop.com

PhillyHipHop.com
www.phillyhiphop.com

Platform Network
mail@platform.net
www.platform.net

Planet Rap Network
www.planetrap.net
We got full albums, singles, breakbeats, pictures, free e-mail, voice chat, and alot more...updated daily.

Pound Magazine
www.poundmag.com

Radio Rukus
remus.rutgers.edu/~imielin/radioruckus
A hip hop radio show and website in Central Jersey dedicated to showcasing creative true school and underground hip hop.

Rap Pages
www.rappages.com

The Rap Source.com
www.therapsource.com

Rapmusic.com
www.rapmusic.com
Check out our Underground Artist Section and submit your artist info and/or get on our Radio Show for free.

Rebirth Magazine
www.rebirthmag.com
An award-winning hip-hop e-zine featuring reviews, news, exclusive video and legal MP3, interviews, artist features, radio hosted by famous hip-hop artists, forums, and much more. Operates out of Chicago with offices in six countries, and also runs promotions, booking, management, publishing, graphic design, and distribution firms that cater to urban culture.

Soul-Session
www.soul-session.com
An online magazine established to advance the beauty and expression of a culture. The substance of this literary reflects hip hop consciousness with hopes of illuminating social problems on a grassroots level. Essentially, we are trying to build a community of people who are conscious of their surroundings and the state of hip hop. Please participate and check us out.

Support Online Hip Hop (SOHH)
www.SOHH.com

Tha Real
www.hiphopflash.com
A frequently updated website containing a lot of exclusive material.

Da Thunda Dome
www.ltvnet.com/domeproper.html

TMOTTgogo
www.TheGrooveSpot.com/home.htm

Triple-Bypass Magazine
www.triple-bypass.com

Underground Reviews
hiphop.simplenet.com/Underground
Underground hip hop reviews, Real Audio, and Online Store.

underground sound
www.ugsmag.com
We post/review submitted hip-hop mp3s & even have a feedback board on each artist's page.

Urban Ambiance Journal
www.uajournal.com
Music in the rhythm of life: reviews of independents alongside major-label.

Urban Beat
www.urbanbeat.com

Urban Earth
www.urbanearth.com

Wodie.com
www.wodie.com
The only unbias hiphop magazine.

Word of Mouth
www.aka.com/wordofmouth

Words of Wizdom
stations.mp3s.com/stations/0/wordz_of_wizdom.html

Canada

JACKHOUSE
c/o URBNET.com, PO Box 10617, 998 Bloor St. West, Toronto, ON, M6H 1L8
www.urbnet.com/Jackhouse
The Urban Entertainment Network: Online Urban Magazine, Web Development, Digital music delivery and rich media advertising solutions.

Mic Check
www.interlog.com/~miccheck

Tha Northside
go.to/northside-pov

Rewind
www.urbnet.com/Launch.html

France

Black Swing
www.blackswing.com

LeHiphop.com
www.lehiphop.com
A website dedicated to the world-wide hip-hop culture. We propose reviewz, interviewz, articlez, MP3, etc. French Staff ready to rock the hip-hop planet !!

Vivonzeureux
J.-C. Brochard / Pol Dodu
vivonzeureux@wanadoo.fr
perso.wanadoo.fr/vivonzeureux
100% optimistic hip-pop fanzine (in French and English)

Germany

Broken Silence
www.brokensilence.de

Rap.de
www.rap.de

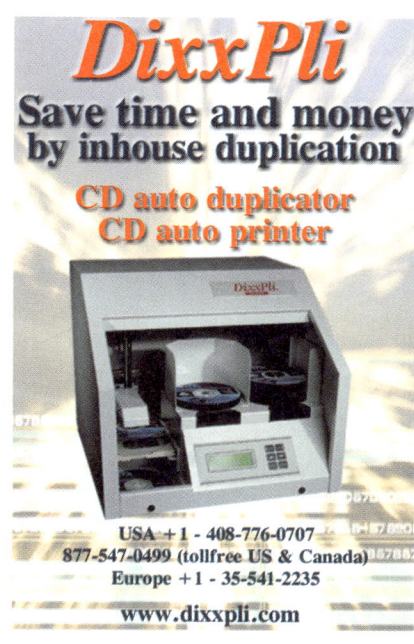

The Netherlands

Art12.com
www.art12.com
HipHop-News from Amsterdam Southeast. Interviews, reviews, reports, MP3's, grafitti and presents www.school-of-hardknocks.com the place to prove skills.

Spain

Hip Hop Flash
www.hiphopflash.com

Russia

Hip Hop Zone
hiphopinfo.da.ru

Sweden

backlashmagazine
www.araby-dalbo.com/users/1195/122/backlash

mokkamekka
www.mokkamekka.com/home

Street Zone
www.streetzone.com

svendetta.com
www.svendetta.com

Svenskunderjord
www.svenskunderjord.com
This the number one hiphopsite in Sweden in Swedish, mos def if you know what I mean?"

Undercover
www.graffiti.org/tranzit/undercover

Underground Productions
www.underground-productions.se

Switzerland

Cosmic Hip Hop
www.cosmichiphop.com
The biggest french speaking Webmag exclusively dedicated to Hip-Hop. Updated each week with at least 3 articles, music excerpts and much much more...

United Kingdom

Blues and Soul
www.bluesandsoul.co.uk

The Crate Estate
www.members.tripod.com/the_crate_estate
A web site that promotes the largely underrated Hip-Hop scene in the United Kingdom. Acts that submit their material are guaranteed a fair review and a lot of coverage on the site.

gunshotuk
www.gunshotuk.com

hiphopmusic.co.uk
www.hiphopmusic.co.uk
Representing underground hip-hop music and culture in the UK and the USA. Featuring news, reviews, interviews and much more.

spinemagazine.com
www.spinemagazine.com

UK Hip Hop Central
www.ukhiphopcentral.co.uk/

ukhh.com
2hip 2hip@ukhh.com
www.ukhh.com
We offer a great chance to gain exposure for all UK hiphop acts.

Y2Hiphop.com
www.y2hiphop.com

bestmusiczines.com

Australia

Bombhiphop.com
www.bombhiphop.com/menu.htm

Stealth
info@stealthmag.com
GPO BOX 666, SYDNEY NSW 1043, AUSTRALIA
www.stealthmag.com
Australia's premier hip hop magazine Points of interest: the magazine has developed from a basic zine to a full colour publication with a CD-Rom attached and with all content being mirrored with video stories at Kgrind.com. Types of Music covered: hip hop (not gangsta rap), soul, funk, drum'n' bass, r&b, reggae, dub, electronica, turntablism. Also graffiti & urban art, fashion, breakdancing, DJ-ing, education andsocial and political issues.

South Africa

Hip-Hop Headrush
www.hiphop.co.za
Covering global Hip-Hop culture from a South African perspective with news, interviews, audio, video, photo's etc.

Jazz/Blues/Folk Music

United States

Acoustic Guitar Central
www.acguitar.com

acousticmusician.com (formerly Music Alive!)
www.acousticmusic.com
Music Alive! is a gateway to information about folk and acoustic artists, venues, resources and CD reviews. The site contains links to the web sites of over 200 musicians plus the Folk and Acoustic Music Exchange; reviews of over 500 compact disks. All this and NO banner ads! It's all about the music.

All About Jazz
www.allaboutjazz.com
The premiere jazz & blues magazine/resource on the web.

allJaZZGuiTar
www.alljazzguitar.com
An Educational, Reference, and Resource Site for the Jazz Guitar Enthusiast!

Amazing Sounds
www.amazings.com/amaze.html
Amazing Sounds, on line since November 2nd., 1996, is an e-zine about electronic music, Ambient, New Instrumental Music, World Music, Electroacoustic, New Age, and other alternative genres. In Amazing Sounds you will find all the ingredients that can be found in conventional magazines (news, articles, interviews, a great amount of album reviews...), plus many others specifically belonging to the Internet environment: links to other webs, links to sound clips, links to some online shops. Amazing Sounds is also available in text format with e-mail distribution.

An Honest Tune
anhonesttune.com

Any Swing Goes
www.anyswinggoes.com
We are a publication that allows Indie CDs for review, primarily in the categories of swing, big band, jump blues, and rockabilly.

Blue Suede News
www.bluesuedenews.com
House Organ of the Church of Rock'n'Roll.

Blues & Rhythm
www.bluesworld.com/BnR

Blues On Stage
www.mnblues.com
A comprehensive blues guide featuring one of the largest review sections on the internet. Winner of the of the 1999 Keeping the Blues Alive Award for achievement for blues on the Internet.

The Blues Revue
www.bluesrevue.com

bluesreviews.com
www.bluesreviews.com

Blues Access Online
www.bluesaccess.com

Blues Bytes
www.bluenight.com/BluesBytes
A monthly blues CD review magazine.

the BLUES NEWS
home.earthlink.net/~thebluesnews

Cadence
www.cadencebuilding.com/Cadence/CadenceMagazine.html

CrossRoads
www.xrm.com
The acoustic, folk, roots & world music resource for radio, retail, labels & artists.

DownBeatJazz
downbeatjazz.tunes.com

Electric Blues
www.electricblues.com

Folk & Acoustic Music Exchange
www.acousticmusic.com/fame/famehome.htm

Independent Reviewer - Frank Matheis
www.frankspicks.com

Jazz Country
www.jazzcountry.com

Jazz Friends Review
tri-millenia.net/jfr

Jazz Guitar Online
www.jazzguitar.com

Jazz Now
www.jazznow.com

The Jazz Review
www.jazzreview.com

Jazz Times
www.jazztimes.com

Jazz USA
jazzusa.com

The Jazz Zine
members.aol.com/plabjazz
We are a jazz fan's website. Featured are CD and Jazz Book Reviews, articles on jazz greats, Jazz poetry, Short stories and the latest news from the jazz world plus much more. We are currently also doing liner notes for new jazz recordings.

The Jazzine
www.jazzine.com
An Online-magazine about Jazz and Blues.

Jazziz
www.jazziz.com

Jelly
www.jellyroll.com

Mudcat Café
www.mudcat.org/radio.cfm

MusicAmericana
www.musicamericana.com/

(musings)
www.geocities.com/SoHo/Square/6100/

Offbeat
www.offbeat.com

Pause Record
www.pauserecord.com
Dedicated to jam rock, jazz, bluegrass and amateur recording.

Rambles
www.rambles.net
An online cultural arts review magazine focusing on traditional/roots music.

Rootin' Around
www.rootinaround.com

Sing Out!
info@singout.org
www.singout.org
Quarterly publication covering a wide range traditional and contemporary folk.

Suncoast Blues Society
www.suncoastblues.org

TakePhiveJazz.com
www.takephivejazz.com
We maintain an extensive collection of jazz links, artist biographies, images, & discographies, jazz history, online radio, mp3's, album reviews, and essential recordings.

Canada

Les Amis du Blues – Magazine AB
www.clic.net/%7Eblues

Northern Journey Online - Canadian Folk Music Website
www.northernjourney.com/

Penguin Eggs
www.penguineggs.ab.ca

Real Blues Magazine
www.realbluesmagazine.com

Sound Bytes
members.tripod.com/~marketer
Jazz/Bluesy stuff.

Belgium

The Folk Pages
club.euronet.be/claude.calteux/

Finland

Blues News
www.dlc.fi/~bnews

France

Improjazz
perso.wanadoo.fr/improjazz/Garde.html

Jazz Hot
BP 405 - 75969 PARIS CEDEX 20 - FRANCE
perso.wanadoo.fr/jazzhot
Jazz Hot, la revue internationale du Jazz depuis 1935. Abonnez-vous/suscribe : 11 numéros par an/11 issues a year + supplément internet mensuel / + the monthly internet supplement + une petite annonce de 100 caractères/ + one classified advert of 100 caracters

Le Jazz
www.lejazz.simplenet.com

So What
sowhat.telecorporate.com
So What is the site of the only french FREE jazz magazine (since 1995) and we're listed yet as the third jazz magazine in France (beside Jazz Magazine and Jazzman). The site, provides informations, concerts dates, cd reviews and many articles about musiciens. Photos, pictures and links are available.

Germany

Jazz Thing
www.jazzthing.de

Blues News
www.blues-germany.com/news_gb.htm
Here you can find all about the blues in Germany. Links to bands, labels, agencies, magazines, blues clubs, festivals and many many more.

Norway

Jazz Scene
jazzscene.no

Sweden

Jazz4you
come.to/jazz4you

Jefferson Blues Magazine
jeffersonbluesmag.com

United Kingdom

Blueprint
www.blueprint-blues.co.uk
Britain's finest, foremost, independent blues magazine. Each month, Blueprint reports on the blues scene, with emphasis on what's happening in the UK. You can read about stars of the blues past and present, the latest CD releases, live blues as it happens, check out blues dates both home and abroad with full venue details, and get the lowdown and inside information on the music you like to hear.

Flyin Shoes Review
www.flyinshoes.fsnet.co.uk/flyinshoes/
The Oxford, England journal dedicated to the very best of songwriting, literature and fine art.

Folk Roots
froots@froots.demon.co.uk
www.froots.demon.co.uk

Australia

Jazz Views
www.ozemail.com.au/~fishergl

Mr. Blues Online Haven
www.zip.com.au/~mr-blues/index2.html

New Zealand

Jazz Online
www.jazz.co.nz
For New Zealand musicians only.

Metal

Heavy, Thrash, Grindcore, Death, Black, Doom, Speed, Progressive and Viking metal.

North America

United States

9fingers
www.9fingers.com

A Bullet Hole In the Face of Reality (ABHFR)
137.192.98.63/index800.html
I guarantee a review if you submit.

A Village of Underground Metal and People
www.geocities.com/SunsetStrip/Palladium/6235

Adrenalin
www.angelfire.com/wi/adrenalin
A 'zine promoting bands ranging from metal to the extreme.

All Out
members.aol.com/alloutfz
Interviews, Reviews, and AD Space also availiable.

antimtv
www.antimtv.com

Arcane Asylum
www.gl.umbc.edu/~ascott7/aa

Arrows of Malice
members.xoom.com/_XMCM/Grizzer/index.html

Ascendant Strains
members.aol.com/CWISNOM/ascendant.html

Asylum Magazine
www.hallucinet.com/asylum

Axeman's Metal Trade and Review
slaughter.net/disclocator/axeman
ON THIS SITE WE ACCOMPLISH TWO THINGS: 1. TRADE METAL CD'S/CD-R'S/DUBS & 2. REVIEW THE LATEST HEAVY METAL ALBUMS

BallBusterHard
www.ballbusterhardmusic.com
Glam Punk Cyber Pop Rock Glossy Music Fanzine/Magazine.

BANDINDEX
www.bandindex.com

Battle Helm
www.battlehelm.com
PO Box 175, Chaska, MN 55318 USA
Classic heavy metal publication taking it to the top!

Beyond Death
pages.infinit.net/jpmorin/beyond/beyond.htm

Black Metal Reviews
www.evilmusic.com/about/blackmetal.html

Black Promises
PO BOX 98072, PITTSBURGH, PA 15227

Black/Death/Doom Metal Reviews
user.cs.tu-berlin.de/~ducki/music/metal.html

BlackThorne
home1.gte.net/blckthrn/bt.html
Independent site dedicated to Black and Death metal.

Bleeders – MP3.com
stations.mp3s.com/stations/0/bleeders_digest2.html

Bludbawd
www.bludgawd.com

Burn the Sun
www.burnthesun.com/

Burning Remnants
come.to/burningremnants
For metal bands of any and all types...

Burnt Black
www.gurlpages.com/other/burntblack

Burnt Zine
400 Park Rd., Parsippany, NJ   07054-1737
www.msu.edu/user/ortegafr/burnt.htm
A personal/music zine put together by 3 kids in NJ. We write about whatever we feel like covering (cops to cheese) and review punk, ska, emo, and hardcore music. Contributions always welcome but only run if we like them.

Chaos Theory
www.dsrmusic.com/chaostheory

Chaotik Webzine
www.multimania.com/chaotik
One of the first two metal music webzines to be on-line on the web. We cover with news, reviews, interviews, samples the metal/hardcore scenes.

Christian Metal Resource
www.christianmetal.com/cmr
The encyclopedia of Christian metal.

Cold Coffin
www.geocities.com/SunsetStrip/2968

Corpse Gristle
www.corpsegristle.com

Cruor
www.geocities.com/SunsetStrip/Alley/7506

The Cynic's Dungeon
www.fortunecity.com/tinpan/4skins/212

Da' Core
www.da-core.com

Dark Blood
members.tripod.com/~darkbloodmag

Dead The E-Zine
www.afn.org/~sfr/dead/index2.html
Christian Death Metal.

Dead On Impact E-ZINE
XJoshX deadonimpact@hotmail.com
www.geocities.com/deadonimpact
Music Reviews for Metal, Hardcore and Emo. Picture section and anything received get played on U-Mass Dartmouth Radio show which will be broadcasted over the Internet soon!!!

DEADNOISE (formerly Neptune)
www.infernalhorde.com/deadnoise

Death Metal and Black Metal
www.anus.com/metal
Reviews of metal, grindcore, punk, thrash as evolving history. Contains involved reviews of MP3 samples tracklists covers. You can't buy anything - it's non profit.

Death Metal Killing Capacity
www.geocities.com/SunsetStrip/Garage/2227

Death Metal Reviews
www.evilmusic.com/about/deathmetal.html

Destroy Pop Music
hometown.aol.com//destroypopmusic
A cool website that does CD and MP3 reviews in all metal genres it has MP3 radio and band interviews.

Devil's Triangle
www.devilstriangle.com
The Metal zine for the Stalkers of Evil.

Diabolical Dismemberment
www.angelfire.com/vt/dismembered

Dimensi
www.geocities.com/SunsetStrip/Lounge/9018

Direct Action
members.tripod.com/DirectActionFanzine

Disinter
disinter666@yahoo.com
discorpse@aol.com
www.disinter.com/disrings.html

The Enchanted Castle
members.aol.com/darkmemory/index2.htm

Endemoniada
www.angelfire.com/ny3/ENDEMONIADA/intro.html
Mostly female bands, or bands with female members.

Enslain
members.aol.com/enslainmag
Reviews of death, thrash, black, grindcore, etc. metal bands.

Eternal Frost
PO Box 584, Conyers GA 30012-0584
surf.to/eternalfrost
Webzine supporting extreme culture and the extreme music/film underground.

Evilmusic Mail Order and Reviews
www.evilmusic.com/
Contains short, very readable reviews of MP3 samples tracklist cover and ability to buy.

The Fading Halo
www.geocities.com/SunsetStrip/Backstage/4979

FuBARM
www.fubarm.com

The Ghoul 'Zine
www.angelfire.com/ny/GhoulZine

The Goblin Cleaver
www.thegoblincleaver.com
A new black/death metal zine. It's free and available through Relapse, Blackmetal.com, Full Moon Prod, Abyss Prod, and many many more.

Grendel
internettrash.com/users/grendel666/main.html
A webzine whose focus is obscure or underground heavy metal and horror culture.

Grind Core
www.geocities.com/Paris/Rue/3914/goregrind.html

Hammerhead
hammerhead.hypermart.net

The Hard Rock Society
hardrocksociety.webjump.com

Hard Rock Universe
homes.acmecity.com/music/metal/399

Hard Times
www.geocities.com/SunsetStrip/Studio/5180

Harder Beat
harderbeat.com

Hardwire Daze
members.tripod.com/~kmon666

Headbanger's Delight
www.headbangersdelight.com
Bands interested in us reviewing their material let us know. We would be glad to help.

Heady Metal
headymetal.simplenet.com
The best way to hear progressive metal on the web.

Heavy Metal is the Law
go.to/powermetal

Heavy Metal Lives
Alan Christensen
webmaster@vanalan.zzn.com
redrival.com/metallives
Death,Black,Thrash,Traditional,Power Metal and more.

Hell Frost
www.hellfrost.com

HM Magazine
www.christianmusic.org/cmp/hmmag.htm
Reviews hard music projects for publication in national music magazine.

The Hooligan's Mosh Pit
www.geocities.com/SunsetStrip/Towers/9194

Ice Storm
members.aol.com/Albdamnd/ritual.htm

Ill Literature
www.illliterature.com
This long-running 'zine is considered to be one of the best as it covers an array of artists encompassing the entire heavy metal spectrum.

In Depth
www.indepthzine.com

Independent Reviewer - Paul Hanson
prhmusic@hotmail.com
I do freelance reviews and write for about 15 different websites. Send music to be reviewed. I prefer metal, but open to others.

Ironworx
www.geocities.com/Vienna/1845/ironworx2.html

Jeff's Pimp Rock Page
www.geocities.com/SunsetStrip/Venue/6236/pimp.html

Justin's Heavy Metal Site
members.tripod.com/~JustinHarvey

Khaos A.D.
www.khaosad.com

LARM!
members.xoom.com/larm666
THE FOURTH REICH OF REVIEWS: specializing in underground metal.

The Last Exit
www.geocities.com/SunsetStrip/Stage/1438

Locobands
www.angelfire.com/in/localbands

Lord Severance's Metal Domain
www.thesyn.com/lordseverance

Lord Xul's Archive
www.borg.com/~lordxul

loudnet
www.loudnet.com
Unique zine for black, death, thrash, metal, hardcore, grind, and more!

Loudside
www.loudside.com

Mad Puppy Metal Heaven
members.xoom.com/Rotweiler213/
homepg2.htm
News, reviews, and information on hundreds of metal bands.

Marc's Metal Reviews
www.geocities.com/%7esulinski/music.html

Mass Metal Zine
homepages.go.com/~massmetalzine/
home2.html

Metal Dreams
member.aol.com/mtldreams/main.html

Metal Edge
www.mtledge.com

The Metal Fanatix Home Page
members.aol.com/LEGION59

The Metal For Jesus Page
surf.to/theMFJpage
Your guide to Christian Metal. Contains plenty of info and addresses that you as band in this genre can have good use for.

The Metal Haven Zine
www.angelfire.com/wv/heavensmetal/zine.html

Metal Land
metalland.virtualave.net
This site features many unsigned and underground metal bands, as well as a few well known ones.

Metal Mad
www.metalmad.com
Metal Mad brings you the latest from the world of Heavy Metal. The latest Heavy Metal news, reviews, interviews, and of course the Metal Mad Babe of the Month. You will also find Metal wallpapers and winamp skins on the media page and a huge Houston section supporting local musicians and bands.

Metal Mafia
metalmafia.cjb.net
Underground death/gore/grind 'zine.

Metal Maniacs
www.metalmaniacs.com

Metal Meltdown
www.metalmeltdown.com
Metal interviews, radio, reviews, news, and pictures.

Metal Rules! Magazine
www.metalrulesmagazine.com
Accepts all unsolicited music for review!

Metal Sludge
www.metal-sludge.com
Rock's biggest and most controversial website!

Metallic Symphonies
www.onr.com/progress

Metalview
members.home.net/jtlam/Metalview.htm
Thorough Reviews/Contact info on all metal genres, signed or unsigned!

minusweb.com
minus.simplenet.com

Misery's Metal Hell
www.geocities.com/Hollywood/Hills/6648/miserys.html

Modern Music Magazine
www.modernmusicmagazine.com

Mourning the Ancient
www.mourningtheancient.com
Offering unique black and death metal interviews, poetry, dark medieval photography, samples and much more.

Mullet Mania Promotions
Brandon mulletmaniapromo@hotmail.com
www.mulletmania.com
We are a Free web promotion company who will do reviews of any metal hardcore and extreme music and we have interviews and band of the month

The Necronomicon
www.angelfire.com/pa2/marduk

Necrosis
www.necrosismag.com/

Night Ritual
nightritual.simplenet.com
Reviews all kinds of heavy metal.

The Noise Box
www.thenoisebox.com
Dedicated to the promotion of indie and signed bands, primarily in the metal, crossover, hardcore, industrial, and emo genres.

Nosebleed17
www.nosebleed17.com
Webzine with the latest news, album reviews, concert reviews, tour dates, interviews, and features MANY unsigned bands!

Now Meet Satan
www.cheezus.com/nowmeetsatan/

Paranoize
www.angelfire.com/la/paranoize
Southern hardcore/metal/punk fanzine. Reviews, interviews and more.

Pit Magazine
PO Box 9545, Colorado Springs, CO 80932
Attn: Underground Connection
www.pitmagazine.com

Planet-Noise
www.planet-noise.com

Rainbow Flame's Metal Domain
www.geocities.com/SoHo/Studios/2786

The Rat Hole
www.rathole.com

Remnants of Reezon
www.remnantsofreason.com/

Rock and a Hard Place Zine
www.rockhardplace.com
CD reviews, independent and imported Rock, Metal, and AOR.

ROCKNATION
www.rock-nation.com

Rupture
smub.st-and.ac.uk/jason_matthiopoulos/metal/ rupture.html
This long-running 'zine is considered to be one of the best as it covers an array of artists encompassing the entire heavy metal spectrum.

Satan Stole My Teddybear
www.chedsey.com
Your source for online reviews of metal, punk, industrial, ambient and more!

Satan's Mailbox
members.aol.com/SatansMB/box.html

Sea of Tranquility
www.seaoftranquility.org

Sense of Pride
members.tripod.com/blue_seven/Sense

SickHead Webzine
www.angelfire.com/oh3/sickhead

Sociopathic Despair
come.to/despair
Covers a variety of styles in heavy metal and hardcore and an array of libertarian/nationalist socio-political issues. Bands, record labels, and zines can send items for review to: P.O. Box 10025 Bowling Green, KY 42102-4825.

Soul Killer
www.soulburn3d.com

Souls of Black
welcome.to/soulsofblack.com

Sound420
www.sound420.com/home.htm

Sounds of Death
www.soundsofdeath.com

Thingy's Metal Reviews
www.execulink.com/~thingy/music.html

TotalDisaster
www.angelfire.com/ma2/totaldesaster

Ultimate Metal Guide (UMG)
www.silcom.com/~armann/metalmenu.htm
Your expert source for Metal reviews, ratings and information!

Ultimate Metal Reviews
www.metal-reviews.com

Unchain the Underground
P.O. Box 15, Stony Point, NY 10980 - USA
www.unchain.com
Web site featuring reviews and interviews related to all forms of extreme music. Unchain the underground receives, on the average, 3000 unique visitors a day.

Under the Corpse
members.xoom.com/UTCzine/home.html
Webzine features any heavy music, ranging from Internal Bleeding to Candiria to Indecision to etc...

Vibrations of Doom
members.spree.com/vibrations

Violated Rot
www.violatedrot.com

W3M3
w3m3.fortysecond.net

Wicked Promotions
www.wickedpromotions.com

Worm Gear
www.crionicmind.org/wormgear

www.deathrock.com
www.deathrock.com
Send your material for review and to be included in our index of related bands. I am also putting together an unnofficial site for bands that do not have any informative web presence or very little.

Canada

Blistering - Metal Heaven
www.blistering.com/
News, reviews, interviews, pictures, audio and more!

Cronic Disorder
www.cronic3.com
Speed/thrash/death metal band from North Carolina. MP3's, reviews, interviews, pics, and metal galore.

Loudweb — The Loud Music Network
3353 Credit Woodlands, Unit 151
Mississauga, Ontario, Canada, L5C 2K1
www.loudweb.net
The Loud Music Network is one of the most complete and comprehensive webzines on the Internet today focusing on the Metal scene. The site includes the latest news, reviews, interviews, a band index, and tons more. If you're in a band and in need of a website or help with promotion Loudweb may be just the site you're looking for. Check us out and experience loud music at its best, Loudweb style!

Mindspell
members.tripod.com/~mindspell

Obscure zine
come.to/coto
We cover: metal/grindcore/hardcore punk music and horror/cult movies. We are Satanicly based.

The Ontario Metal Pages
www.crosswinds.net/~daimonahnjeel

Vile Productions
www.vileprod.com
Reviews interviews and general underground band stuff and lot'o'links!!!!!!

Mexico

Black Souls Domain
www.angelfire.com/ak2/morborum/FrameDeControl.html

Blasfemia Diabolica
www.angelfire.com/az/azarak/

Death Dealer Birthday
members.tripod.com/~ddbirthday

South America

Brazil

Abhorrent
www.abordo.com.br/abhorrent

Alchemist Magazine
P.O. Box 251,
Campo Grande, MS, Cep: 79002-970

Dark Page
www.sidenet.com.br/darkpage

Heavy Metal Rock
hmrock.cjb.net

Megatherion Metal Page
www.geocities.com/SunsetStrip/Arena/6373

Metal World
zinemetalworld.cjb.net

Needle
brafin@africanet.com.br

Planetmetal
planetmetal@hydra.com.br

Renegade2K
www.renegade2k.com
Metal site specialized in all metal styles, including news, interviews, reviews, soundfiles and much more. Updated daily!

Roadie Crew
www.roadiecrew.com

Rock Brigade
www3.cafemusic.com.br/rockbrigade

Undermetal
welcome.to/undermetal
Home of true metal bangers. Reviews, releases, links and news of the Heavy Metal Underground scene.

Valhalla
Eliton Tomasivalhalla.magazine@mailexcite.com
www.valhalla.com.br
One of the most important Metal Magazines from South America.

Yell
yell@zipmail.com.br

Chile

Discordancia
www.discordancia.cl/espanol/index.htm

Grinder
web.interactiva.cl/~grinder

Metal Age
www.geocities.com/SunsetStrip/Towers/9793

Colombia

Carloncho.com
carloncho.com

Colombian Metal Web
www.truemetal.org/colombianmetal

Himnos Rituales de Guerra
listen.to/himnosrituales

Peru

Blackland
www.geocities.com/SunsetStrip/Arena/8051/blackland.html

Cuero Negro
www.geocities.com/Nashville/5262/index.html

Europe

Austria

Resurrection
www.resurrection.at

Belgium

Abla Zine
www.multimania.com/caddaric

Amon Lhaw
www.altern.org/amonlhaw
Amon Lhaw is a support site for Belgian Heavy Metal bands. It is also the home of the Belgian Metal WebRing.

The Black and Gothic Metal Site
www.crosswinds.net/~roan
Everything about Black and Gothic Metal: Honest CD Reviews and free music files of bands like Dimmu Borgir, Tristania, Cradle Of Filth, NightWish, Opeth and many more...

Carnage Zine
come.to/xnendex

Lugburz
www.dma.be/p/lugburz
A support site for Belgian Black & Death Metal bands.

Mindview
www.iad.be/mindview

Rock Report
home.pi.be/rockreport/

Undertow
www.angelfire.com/on/spincity
Goth too!

Denmark

Metalized
come.to/metalized

Finland

Aorta
members.tripod.com/aortazine

Eter
come.to/Eter-zine
A webmagazine focusing on music that is full of feelings - mostly metal.

Screen & Steel
www.geocities.com/SunsetStrip/Cabaret/7739

Tuska Webzine
T. Lahdelma tlahdelm@nic.fi
tuskawebzine.cjb.net
Interviews, reviews, etc. what a zine usually includes.

Whispering Leaves
www.dlc.fi/~olaitala

France

La Confrerie Des Bardes
www.confrerie.fr.fm/

Decibels
www.atinternet.com/isa/hardrock

L'Édition Métallique
www2.jonction.net/~jdan

The French Connection
home.nordnet.fr/~lbocquet
A free promotion metal site for any bands; It does reviews, interviews, but also distribution, contest....

The Metal Quest
www.multimania.com/demouron/quete.html
International underground metal/hardcore/punk music featuring interviews of famous and local bands, reviews, news and gig summaries.

Thrash N Blades
www.multimania.com/slayer

Germany

Ablaze
www.schlund.de/ablaze

Amboss
www.amboss-mag.de

Burnout
members.aol.com/~burnoutprd

Chaos
www.geocities.com/SunsetStrip/Backstage/6884

Cothurnus
www.cothurnus.de

Die Geister, die ich rief
www.geister-bremen.de

Eternity
eternitymagazin.de/

Fegefeuer
www.fegefeuer-webzine.de
News, reviews and interviews with underground and established Metal bands.

Forever Free
www.geocities.com/SunsetStrip/Alley/6677

Forever Metal
www.thats-metal.de
Nils Jordan's Empire Of Steel. Heavy/ Power/ Speed/ Thrash/ Progressive/ Epic/ Melodic/ True METAL and some Hard Rock Reviews and Interviews all over the place. Metal Forever!

Gut Fuck Magazine
members.tripod.com/BSBB

Heavy-Metal.de
www.heavy-metal.de

Invader
www.invader.de

Mayhem
www.mayhem.de

Metal District
c/o Patrick Weinstein
Schlaifhausen 135, 91369 Wiesenthau, GERMANY
www.metal-district.de
We are a German Heavy Metal Webzine and we review all styles of Metal, do many interviews, have a underground and demo-section and many more!

Metal Inside
www.metal-inside.de

Metal Online
metal-online.de

Moral Insanity
home.t-online.de/home/tsnoobs/index.htm

The Moshpit
www.moshpit.de

Powermetal.de
www.powermetal.de
Powermetal.de is a german online metal fan magazin. You can get much informations about metal and gothic bands, also reviews about concerts and cds and interviews. check it out!

Powertrip
www.powertrip.de

The Purgatory of Grief
www.pog666.de/
Webzine for Black/Death/Dark Metal and beyond.

Rock Hard Online
www.rockhard.de

The Sacred Metal Page
www.geocities.com/SunsetStrip/Stage/5007

Snakepit
truemetal.org/snakepit

Sweet Suffering
www.sweet-suffering.de

Tiefgang
www.tiefgang-online.de

The Underground Empire Metal Magazine
truemetal.org/ue

Unholy Terror
home.t-online.de/home/unholyterror-666

Vampster
www.vampster.com

Vönger
www.voenger.de

Greece

Altars of Metal
truemetal.org/altarsofmetal
German Metal/Rock/Gothic Music Magazine with Reviews, Tourdates, etc.

Frozen Hell
members.xoom.com/adenon
Bands and labels, send your stuff to Adenon Productions/Frozen Hell Zine for sure review within the pages of the zine and our website.

Headbanger's Pit
www.geocities.com/SunsetStrip/Loft/6427

Metal Invader
www.metalinvader.com

The Metal Zone
www.geocities.com/SunsetStrip/Studio/2643

Seventh Sign
users.hol.gr/~sevsign

Italy

Evil Surfer
www.evilsurfer.com

Italian Metal Kingdom
Mattia msalsi@tin.it
welcome.to/Italian-metal-kingdom
A resource that helps the Italian metal scene to be known by the rest of the world.

Oltraggio al Pudore
www.oltraggioalpudore.netfly.it

Lithuania

Edge of Time
www.mindcage.com/edge
Printed magazine and webzine dedicated to progressive and other metal.

Subzero
vejas.pit.ktu.lt/~voroneri

The Netherlands

Aardschok
www.aardschok.com

Martelgang
www.angelfire.com/va/martelgang
Dutch-written on-line MetalZine, includes reviews, news and interviews.

Metal Maidens
www.geocities.com/SunsetStrip/
Stadium/5238
The official web site to the magazine - is entirely dedicated to the females in (Hard)Rock and (Heavy)Metal.

Norway

Norway Metal
members.tripod.com/metalnorway

Scream
www.scream.no

Poland

Legion Magazine
www.nestor.minsk.by/lg

Masterful
www.masterful.art.pl

Rape Your Mind
www.rym.dr.pl

rock i metal po polsku
www.rockmetal.art.pl

Portugal

Abyss Magazine
welcome.to/abyssmagazine

Ancient Ceremonies
come.to/ac_zine

Dark Oath Magazine
members.tripod.com/DarkOathOnline

Honor Sanguine
alumni.dee.uc.pt/~pauloj/main.htm

SOS Radio
www.angelfire.com/mb/sosradio

Russia

Charon's Chronicles
www.enet.ru/win/digitalKenig/user/artscald/menu.html

Extreme Music News
nestor.minsk.by/emn

Konstantin's Metal Page
www.geocities.com/SunsetStrip/Towers/6266
Metal and Gothic RealAudio files. Album and gig reviews.

Russian Darkside
darkside.ekort.ru

Vae Solis
www.rusmetal.ru/vae_solis

Spain

Bloodcifery
www.cyberleku.com/bloodcifery

Heavy Weight
perso.wanadoo.es/yemi

Necromance
www.iedatos.es/user/necrom/intro.htm

Sweden

Alfgar
www.geocities.com/Area51/Chamber/2307

Amon
come.to/amonmag
A metal webzine, focused on all kinds of metal music. Reviews and interviews, updated once a week!

Apostasia
www.come.to/metal-storm
Apostasia is a webmagazine dedicated to all forms of dark music! MP3's, interviews with the leading bands, reviews, song talks, news etc.

Athnor
m1.910.telia.com/~u91002876/aindex.html

Cadla
listen.to/cadla

Fear Magazine
hem.passagen.se/fearmagazine

Gallery of Sin
come.to/galleryofsin

GL Productions
hem.passagen.se/lillie

Graveland
www.metalprovider.com/graveland

Heathendoom Magazine
come.to/heathendoom

Internet@Metal
www.rockt.nu/InternetMetal

Krig
home4.swipnet.se/~w-41767/krig

Lokes Hörna
w1.454.telia.com/~u45402340/zine.html

Metal Duck
hem.passagen.se/raffe666

Metal Law
members.xoom.com/westarr/metal

Mysticism
hem1.passagen.se/thyrfing/mysticism.htm

Prospective
www.prospective.nu

Punishment
snap.to/punishment

Scythe
welcome.to/scythe

Swedish Metal
www.metalprovider.com/swedishmetal/

Swedish Metal Inquisition
www.satan.nu

Therold's Music Reviews
stud.sb.luth.se/~roglas-6
Passionated music lover from northern Sweden.

Switzerland

The Renewal
home.balcab.ch/renewal

Swiss Metal Factory
www.metalfactory.ch

United Kingdom

Attitude
burieddreams.com/attitude/webzine
Scottish rock / metal webzine. News, reviews, interviews, release dates etc.

Backbone
www.backbone.freeserve.co.uk

Black Velvet
www.blackvelvetmagazine.com

Butchered
members.tripod.co.uk/butchered

Death to Dead Things
www.users.globalnet.co.uk/~ianweb

Epigram for the Last Straw
www.progmetal.net

Friday 13th Zine
pages.hotbot.com/fan/friday13th/main.html
The zine has been on the metal scene since 1988, and I have interviewed some really cool bands such as slayer, judas priest, pantera, dream theater, scorpions, motorhead and metallica just to name a few. I am totally dedicated to the underground scene, but I try to ad 1-2 big names too. The last 5 copies have come with a full colour cover.

Lykos
Sam Wright mccu8sw2@fs2.ee.umist.ac.uk
18 Limefield Terrace, Levenshulme, Manchester, M19 2ED, UK
www.cryogen.com/lykos
Website, fanzine and free newsletter combined. Underground and mainstream metal. All styles, from death to heavy. Interviews, reviews, free email, etc.

Metal Hammer
www.metalhammer.co.uk

Powerplay
www.powerplaymagazine.co.uk

Real Rock
www.absolute68.com/real_rock.htm
As well as the Web Site which covers: Guitar Based Music, mainly Heavy Rock and Indie but also Alt Country and other genres, we also run a small gig promotions company .

Stormbringer
website.lineone.net/~derekdaniel

Terrorizer
www.terrorizer.co.uk

Vomit Noise
www.geocities.com/SunsetStrip/Show/3569
Extreme Music Zine: Grind/Noisecore, Power Electronics, Digital Hardcore, Harsh Noise, Power Violence, Crust, Sludge, Brutal HC, Industrial, EBM & other wierd & extreme genres.

Australia/New Zealand

AUSMETAL
www.ausmetal.net
Australian-based heavy metal music site.

Digital Death
www.digital-death.org
Online Metal Ordering and underground artist promotional services.

Loud & Heavy Magazine
www.loudandheavy.com.au/

Loud! Online
www.geocities.com/SunsetStrip/Stage/4599

Musically Incorrect
www.netstra.com.au/~aslukic
Australia's only Heavy Metal Publication. Bringing you the best the world has to offer and more.

QUIDDITY ZINE
members.tripod.com/~QUIDDITYZINE
For all things Black, Death, Thrash...

thegatesofhell.org
www.thegatesofhell.org
Metal reviews, MP3's, band hosting and web site creation.

Venomous Magazine
www.ausmetal.net/hod

vis nox (formerly Nihilum)
www.ausmetal.net/visnox/

Western Front
www.wf.com.au

Wreathe of Thornes
www.wreatheofthorns.com/
Christian metal magazine.

Asia

Singapore

Dawn of the Apocalypse
home1.pacific.net.sg/~pbjm1

Africa

South Africa

The Crusader
members.smartnet.co.za/~lunatic

Progressive Rock

United States

AOR Heaven
www.aorheaven.com

JamBands.com
www.jambands.com
An on-line web zine devoted to improvisational music.

Music Street Journal
www.50megs.com/msj

ProgNaut's Home
www.geocities.com/SunsetStrip/Mezzanine/2281

Prog-Net
www.prog.net

The Space of Carlos Tavares
www.geocities.com/SunsetStrip/9815/sctavares.htm

Zoltan's Progressive Rock Page
www.geocities.com/SunsetStrip/Arena/1282

Brazil

AORsters
www.aorsters.com

France

Acid Dragon
perso.club-internet.fr/acidrago/ad2.htm

Germany

Die Ultimative Review Page - DURP
www.durp.com

The Netherlands

The Dutch Progressive Rock Page
www.dprp.vuurwerk.nl
One of the leading Internet magazines on progressive rock.

iO Pages
io.net4u.nl

Sweden

First Light
www.geocities.com/SunsetStrip/Balcony/6435/meny.htm
The goal of my site is to promote progressive rock to the wider public and help both bigger prog bands and indie prog bands reach the masses.

United Kingdom

Acid Attack
freespace.virgin.net/martin.jones10/info.htm

AOR Basement
www.ifb.co.uk/~aorb
Specialist music review site for both signed and unsigned bands.

Bathtub of Adventures
www.btinternet.com/~archimedes
U.K based - Interested in reviewing Progressive / Psychedelic / Improvisational music genres.

Eleusis
www.eleusis.freeserve.co.uk/music

Progression
www.progression.co.uk
World's largest art-rock magazine. Display advertising available. Contact us!

Rock Haven
www.rockhaven.co.uk

Punk

Punk, Ska, Hardcore, Emo, oi

North America

United States

(em)zine
Jered   pressure@spiritone.com
Twice a year, two color cover, punk/HC zine, better than 97% of zines out there.

10 THINGS Jesus Wants You To Know
www.10things.com/10things
Punk rock, reviews, columns, news, and much more!

3rd Arm Electricity Zine
www.3AE.com

A Different Kind of Greatness
adkg.com
*Indie, emo, punk, etc.
email john@adkg.com for info.*

A Smaller Footprint
www.asmallerfootprint.com

Agent 1904
www.crosswinds.net/~a1904zine

Amish Drive By
www.geocities.com/SunsetStrip/Stage/5375

Anarchist Barbie Doll
www.anarchistbarbiedoll.com

Anesthesia
www.anesthesia.8m.com/

Annoyance
www.annoyances.com/zine.html

Artificial Life
come.to/aflifezine

As the World Burns
Dan Disturbeddandisturbed@hotmail.com

Attention Deficit Disorder (ADD)
James Macklem addzine@gte.net

The AU Zine
www.angelfire.com/nj2/au

Autohypnotic Online (formerly Happy Boy)
members.tripod.com/sighnus

Backseat
backseat.simplenet.com

Bad Idea From the Start
Arthur the Omnipotent
arthurpeewee@hotmail.com
Opinionated highschool geeks run zine a la 'Big Brother Skateboarding', but about anything. We are short on resources and are in need of any help at all.

Bast
www.bastmagazine.com

Bizzare Ink
goldfish.central.netaxs.com/~hrea/bizarreink

Blank Generation
www.blankgeneration.com
We review garage, power pop, and '77 style punk rock.

Blank Page
www.angelfire.com/ca4/blankpage

Blasphemour Webzine
www.blasphemour.com

Body Count/FEM-UH-NIST Zine
www.gurlpages.com/zines/unitedgirlfront

Bored and Violent
Silas Bored bored@ticon.net
A whole bunch of cheapshot comix. Punk rock theme.

Brace Face
Evan WinikerTandomRask@aol.com
A zine with incredibly innovative ideas. All submissions are welcome!

California Hardcore
www.truestrength.com/cahc

Carbon 14
www.c14.com

Case Maker (is now "Make Room!")
home.austin.rr.com/makeroom

Chicken IS Good Food
chickenisgoodfood.com

Chipp'd Teeth
www.geocities.com/SunsetStrip/Bistro/7265

Chord Magazine
www.chordrecording.com/

The Chronic Masterbator Ezine
www.geocities.com/SunsetStrip/Vine/6996

Co2toxics.com
www.co2toxics.com

BEST MUSIC BOOKS offers many directories that can help you to promote your music including *"The Musician's Atlas 2000", "The Recording Industry SourceBook", "The 2000 Songwriter's Market", "Music Directory Canada"* and *"The Film and Television Composer's Resource guide"*

Common Ground
www.geocities.com/forceofhabit123/
CommonGround.html
An online zine that will review any metal/ hardcore/punk/ska CD's or Demo's, and much more.

Common Ground Record's Zine
www.internettrash.com/users/
cgprod/choose.htm

Concrete Rhythm
clix.to/crzine

The Continental Magazine
www.dblcrown.com/contmag.html

Corn 'Zine
www.cornzine.com
Covering hardcore, punk, ska, indie, emo, etc. since 1994.

Cornflake Overdose
www.angelfire.com/mi2/
cornflakeoverdose/cod1.html
Punk & Horror zine....with a growing underground cult status.

crackmonkey
www.freespeech.org/crackmonkey
crackmonkey motto: everything sounds better when it's free!

Crank Magazine
www.crank.com

Croakroom Records - The Zine
come.to/croakroomrecords

Crust as Fuck
www.streetpunk.com/crustasfuck

Dead Inside
Travisvaruker13@yahoo.com
A small zine political musical and open to anything. I'm also starting a record company - Fat Bastard Records. To any unsigned bands, I'd be happy to release your music.

Deadbeat (Florida)
www.geocities.com/~deadbeat

Deadwinter
come.to/deadwinter
Reviews for mostly emo/indie/hardcore type stuff, also poetry, editorials, interviews, etc.

Decapolis
decapolis.com
Decapolis was founded in the summer of 1999 by Conrad Tolosa (ex-guitarist/s ongwriter from the band Ghoti Hook). The site covers just about everything from Music, and Movies, to Faith and Literature. If you have a label or a band and you would like Decapolis to review your material please contact our Music Reviews Coordinator Tom Bastian at Tommy@Decapolis.com.

Decoy
punkska.osiriscomm.com

dedkitty
dedkittyzine.onweb.cx

Delusions of Adequacy
www.adequacy.net/index2.html

Dilapidated Zine
PSC 76 BOX 6389, APO AP 96319-6389
www.angelfire.com/pa/dilapidatedzine
More entertaining than a monkey on Ritalin.

Dilemma Fanzine
Christine XdilemmaX@aol.com

Disjointed Thoughts, Paranoia?
www.angelfire.com/oh2/dtp/enter.html

Does It Need A Title?
www.angelfire.com/ca/punkiskaworld/

DogPile Punk and Ska Reviews
3464 Heatherstone CT,
Orlando, FL 32812, USA
www.geocities.com/Area51/Comet/3658
DogPyle is made up of Punk and Ska CD reviews and interviews and articles.

Do Wrong
doowrong.hypermart.net/

Driver's Side Air Bag
www.dsazine.com

Drunk Tank
144 Whittington Dr.,
Lafayette, LA. 70503, USA
It's mostly about the Lafayette,LA local scene and Mystic Fix(my band). But we also do reviews of CD's, tapes, etc. Feel free to send stories and artwork also.

East Coast Grindcore
www.geocities.com/BourbonStreet/
Bayou/7055/grind.html

East Coast Hardcore
www.hardcorewebsite.net/

The East Side Mag: A Zine
members.tripod.com/~EastSideMag

Easy Life Ska Zine
members.tripod.com/~SkaGirl/easylife.html
Covering ska and related subcultures - all materials welcomed!

Elvis Ain't Dead
members.xoom.com/elvisaintdead/
contents.htm

The Emo Pussies Project
www.yahtzeen.com/emopussies/

Engine
Matt Average   engine98@earthlink.net

EUGENE fanzine
Mark Borders eugenezine@hotmail.com
Interviews, comics, paper airplanes, pinball games and punk rock. Good toilet literature!

Excessive Force
Jacqui nola_xx@yahoo.com
Local compilation zine, columns, reviews, local news scene zine.

The Excuse
Django Bohren theexcuse@hotmail.com
Music and entertainment reviews, interviews and more...

FASTMUSIC
www.fastmusic.com/

Fat Lip Zine
Dave   L79P@aol.com

Fend For Yourself
www.fendforyourself.com

Finger Lickin' Good
fingerlickingood.cjb.net

Firefly Meanzine
www.angelfire.com/biz3/hellkitten13

Flipout!
www.gurlpages.com/music/stupor/
flipout.html
Zine from NY. Contains a lot of writing from our talented staff: STUPOR, T.G. Clown, prehistoric as whole, Fungus Amongus, Portia, tick, and Brittany! YAY.

Floor Spazz Zine
floorspazz.cjb.net/

Forbidden Planet
www.seas.upenn.edu/~vlm/forbidden.html

Four Fourty Fanzine
members.tripod.com/four40

Freedom Energy
www2.hawaii.edu/~smiyakaw/zine.htm
Punk rock zine from Hawaii with madness for your brain.

Friction
1117 Patunia St NW,
Hartville OH 44632, USA
members.aol.com/xxfriction/index/
friction.html
Reviews independent/DIY music from all genres. Both print and Web published.

Frigid Ember
frigidember.com

Gashcream
surf.to/gashcream

The Gauntlet
www.thegauntlet.com

GotPunk.com
www.gotpunk.com
Monthly webzine devoted to the punk scene including reviews, opinion and lots more.

Gray Noise
www.skapunx.net/~punx101

Guillotine
WendyGuillNYHC@aol.com
A hardcore, punk music and subculture magazine.

Happy Goat
www.geocities.com/timing0933

hardcoremusic.com
www.hardcoremusic.com

HeartattaCk
www.ebullition.com/hac.html

The Hive Zine
members.tripod.com/~hivehxc/main1.htm

Holy Bullshit Webzine
hbswebzine.8m.com/index3.html
HardCore/Death Metal/Metal-Core/atheism and everything in between. You will crap in your scary black jeans.

Holy Titclamps/Queer Zine Explosion
www.holytitclamps.com/
Only reviews recordings with queer content.

Hotdog Amerika
www.angelfire.com/il2/hotdogamerika

House of the Rising Punk/Mikhail's Punk Album Reviews
www.punkrock.org

I Dunno
www.sonic.net/~mpaglia/zine
We are God's gift to the Internet. Bow to us.

If I Were to Die In My Sleep
www.geocities.com/Athens/Stage/9825

I'm Like Yeah
www.imlikeyeah.com

In Effect
www.ineffect.f2s.com/

init
www.geocities.com/SunsetStrip/Palladium/4248

Inkablore
www.angelfire.com/il2/inkablore

Instant Magazine
www.instantmag.com/

Invisible Youth
www.invisibleyouth.com
A site updated monthly, contains art, articles, reviews of literature, movies, and music (punk, hardcore, metal, ska, emo, indie, rock, whatever), and has contests. Always accept review submissions from anyone.

Ivy's Ska Universe
www.geocities.com/CapitolHill/Senate/1193

Jesse Average's Punk/Zine Homepage
members.tripod.com/~Finx79

Klusterfuct
surf.to/klusterfuct
A personal zine with poetry, articles on life, artwork and humor. Cost: $1

Know Shit
www.angelfire.com/ny/pdrob

Leavenworth Times
the11worth@hotmail.com
Hardcore and Punk related topics and reviews.

Listless
internettrash.com/users/listless

The Little Playmate
surf.to/lilplaymate

Louder Than Words
acornweb.com/ltw

Make a Change
www.geocities.com/SunsetStrip/Cabaret/2843
The zine that asks why not make a change? Props to the hardcore, punk, etc scenes.

MAXIMUMROCK N WRESTLING
www.dclink.com/mrw

Moma Was a Saint so I Shot Her
Jay Reatardreatard1@yahoo.com
Rock n roll and the hatred of people put to paper.

Mtska.com
www.mtska.com

The Noisy Popsicle
www.geocities.com/SoHo/Village/7495

The Old Punk's Web Zine
home.earthlink.net/~emerson7/oldpunks.htm
Since January 1997. World's largest punk and new wave web zine.

On the Rag
www.ontherag.net

Outcast and Martyred
outcastandmartyred.tripod.com
An Escape From Those That Persecute You. Christian Punk for the Soul!

OxPx
members.tripod.com/~MADKATTER/zine.html
Since 1994, everything underground and more! Comix, Stories, & interviews!

pastepunk
www.pastepunk.com

The People's Punk Page
stations.mp3s.com/stations/4/peoples_punk_page.html

Pennsylvania Hardcore
pa215hxc@voicenet.com
members.tripod.com/~pahxc
PA style hardcore and philly graffiti.

Phreak Zine
surf.to/PhreakZine.com
A monthly e-zine featuring Ska, Punk, Rock, Alternative, Grunge, Hardcore, and tons more local, Underground, Mainstream and Indie Bands. PhreakZine is absolutely free of charge!!!

Pink Shoelace
SSaen@aol.com
Everything your mama wants to know about punk/ska/oi.

Pisspunk's Pit
www.geocities.com/SunsetStrip/Amphitheatre/5535

The Pit
www.gainsay.com/the_Pit

Poppunk.com
www.poppunk.com

Primal Chaos
www.primalchaosonline.com/

The Probe
www.proberecords.com

Psychobilly Homepage
www.wreckingpit.com

PSychopathiC PunK
www.angelfire.com/me2/punkstart

Punk & $ka Magazine
www.geocities.com/SunsetStrip/Lounge/8312

Punk and Ska Archive
P.O. Box 493, Botsford, CT 06404
members.tripod.com/~voodooglowskulls
Directory of PUNK and SKA stuff on the Internet. Thousands of links. Contains reviews,tabs,band info, chat room,message board,tour dates,news,and much more. Check It Out!

Punk and Ska Review
www.geocities.com/SunsetStrip/Balcony/8991

Punk Fiction
www.punkfiction.com

Punk Interview Resource
punk.acornweb.com

The Punk Page
www.thepunkpage.com

Punk Zine
Michael Motrecords@aol.com
Indie based magazine about expression. Humor, news, music, film, etc. We review all forms of media and except contributions. Ads and classifieds are cheap!

punkplanet.com
www.punkplanet.com

punkROCKS.net
www.punkrocks.net

Retrogression Magazine
www.retrogression.com
A weekly ezine covering radical politics and underground music.

.the.robots.are.revolting!
www.therobots.zzn.com
.trar!z. covers all types of music, and offers more than any print zine can, free e-mail and downloads.

Rock n Roll Outbreak
www.peladorecords.com

Rockit Zine
www.angelfire.com/ny/rockitzine

Rude and Reckless
www.angelfire.com/pa/rudeandreckless

Rude International
www.rudeinternational.com

Rudenet
www.rudenet.com

Running With Scissors
www.genderdoctor.com/rws

Scatter Brain Gutter Spazz Fanzine
www.geocities.com/SunsetStrip/Booth/2686
Scatter brain gutter spazz is a political punk fanzine that's trying to save the world through awareness.

Scorpion Zine
Willona Sloan wsloan1@erols.com

Selfish Satan
Amiselfishsatan@webtv.net
A punk rawk fanzine that's laced with social - politikill personal writing, & a shitload of reviews!

shotgunblast
come.to/shotgunblast

Sic Boy Federation (formerly (sic) Heavy Metal zine)
sicmusic.cjb.net

Sick's Degrees of Agitation
www.extreme-music.net/

Ska Au Go-Go
go.to/SkaAuGoGo
We are a free newsprint zine focusing on music and art.

ska nj ska
skanjska2000@home.com or
skanjska.cjb.net
A great site for any type of music consisting from ska.punk.emo.hardcore.etc... I can have your review up within two weeks of recieving material. Check it out. Also I have the biggest show page in Jersey so if you want your show up let me know too.

Ska, Punk and Other Junk
www.geocities.com/SunsetStrip/Palms/2015

SKAb Pickers
www.smartlink.net/~nivek/skab.htm

Skank Punk City
members.aol.com/buthead51/zine.html
Christian Punk.

Skaville.com
www.Skaville.com

skinheads.net
www.skinheads.net

Skratch
www.skratchmagazine.com

SlutWhoreBitch
www.gurlpages.com/zines/girrrlie
An independently owned and edited zine by a riot grrrl.

Small Town Minds
www.angelfire.com/tx2/smalltownminds
Clever punk/alt/ska ezine with reviews and random stuff.

So Far No Good
tinpan.fortunecity.com/blondie/195

So Fuckin' What?
www.geocities.com/SunsetStrip/Diner/2604

Social Napalm
www.geocities.com/Pipeline/Ramp/3598/SNhome.htm

Someone say...Punk??!!!
www.angelfire.com/sc/apageofpunk

Spank
www.geocities.com/spankfanzine
Featuring interviews, photos, ordering info, and a listing of every band who has appeared within our pages.

Sparechange Magazine
www.sparechangemagazine.com/

Spill the Blood Ezine
www.crosswinds.net/~gringozine/

Spool Pigeon
Heathheath@anchormen.com
Dedicated to chronicling the vibrant, widespread cassette culture. Concentrating on independent, tape-only releases from around the world.

Stand Your Ground
punkmusic.com/syg

Starve
www.geocities.com/SunsetStrip/Amphitheatre/6380

Status Magazine
www.statusinc.com/magazine.html

Stolen Goods
www.jesusfreak.com/stolengoods
Christian Punk.

stomp ezine
www.stompzine.com

Stomp it Up
TedStompzine@aol.com
Political/personal & music zine, loving most anything in the underground.

Stutter
surf.to/stutter

Suburban Voice
Al Quint   alellen@shore.net
Long-running 'zine covering punk, hardcore, garage and other aggressive musical forms.

summer*salts
www.summersalts.com/

Sweet Amerika
www.lostchildpub.cjb.net
5021 Shepherd Road.
Cincinnati, OH 45223, USA
Politikill/Punk rock zine, website. Always looking for submissions and review material. Anything from (political) pop punk to anarchopunk to crust to grindcore.

Tastes Like Chicken
Mike Tounian   Chewyska@aol.com
A ska punk zine with an emo-core twist.

Ten - Forty Four (formerly Down Syndrome Barbie)
www.downsyndromebarbie.com/

TESTicle PRESSure
www.testicle.com
Punk Hemp Psychedelia Music Comix Art Politix & Anti-Corporate Indieness.

Theory X Fanzine
www.geocities.com/SunsetStrip/Stage/6673/theoryxfanzine.html

rhepunkpage.com
www.thepunkpage.com
Your best source for punk rock on the web, period.

The Trouble With Normal
Boone Stigall ttwn@hotmail.com
Just your typical underground music and sociopolitics zine.

truepunk.com
truepunk.com

UnitedPunks.com
www.unitedpunks.com

Unusual Discharge
Bob Shane Germs152@aol.com
Psycho cut + paste w/ a crust/thrash/ hardcore/peacepunk angle.

UPRISING!
Rob Gorczycauprising@email.com
Features local and national acts. Distribution of 1000 throughout the US and overseas. Can't wait to hear from you!

Urban Guerrilla Zine
Jay JAYUNIDOS@aol.com

The Vegetable Inside Us All
Anneduchess@unm.edu
Per-zine whose editor isn't afraid to laugh herself.

Velocity NYC
www.velocitynyc.com

The Vicious Circle Voice
members.tripod.com/~XstraightonviewX

Vision On
Steve Lee stevevisionon@hotmail.com
Self opinionated bollocks with plenty of humour.

The West Coast is the Best Coast!
SteveDNSSSTEVE@aol.com
Basically about the hardcore / punk / pop punk scene in the west coast. Sometimes with music in the east coast too.

Wipe Your Eyes and Face the Day
www.freeyellow.com/members5/jweihs

Would You Like Some Zucchini?
members.aol.com/SKAnita

The Writ
members.tripod.com/writ
PUNK ROCK AND OTHER SHIT!!!

www.detroitska.com
www.detroitska.com
The Detroit Music Scene's Webtrash.

X-Tra
Lisa and PeteXrecords@aol.com

X-Zistance Zine
www.geocities.com/SunsetStrip/Plaza/1957
An online zine on punk rock, hardcore, etc.

XDark Violence of the HeartX (formerly XPhoenixX's XhardcoreX XpageX)
www.geocities.com/SunsetStrip/Vine/2855/index.html

Ya'kuz'a Magazine
www.yakuzamag.com

Canada

Attirude!
members.tripod.com/Attirude

La Binouze
lunatik.net/binouze

Caustic Truths
www.caustictruths.com
A small independent zine which focuses on punk, hardcore, garage, and other noizy music.

Ctrl-Alt-Del
www.user.dccnet.com/krysko/

Dead Herring
deadherring.a-zone.org

Fist City
Rob Ferraz fistcity@ican.net
A humourous, somewhat twisted look at music, culture, and life.

Flex Your Head
flexyourhead.vancouverhardcore.com
Hardcore and punk online. Reviews, audio samples, photos, program and local scene information, interviews, links, and more.

Folk-ME-faster
Johnny Sizzle johnnysizzle@hotmail.com
206 Elgin Street, Room #204,
Sudbury, Ontario, P3E 3N5, Canada.
For heavy and fast sounding folk. The artists of CDs that I really like will get an interview by me and have an article written solely on themselves.

FUCKIN EH! Zine
www.geocities.com/canadianpunkeh

Mental Zine
www.angelfire.com/me/mentalzine
We review, interview all types of crazy, catchy cool music.

Moral Minority
www.reject.org/punk

Punk Fiction
www.knowhow.com/punkfiction
Zine focusing on the punk scene/politics/ music/fun etc. Punk/HC/ska bands and publications send stuff in for review.

Raw Energy
rawenergy.passport.ca

Rude Moods
www.skaville.com/rudemoods/main/main.html

Senseless Ramblings
Candace Mooerscamooers@hotmail.com
Personal rants, punk, politics, pix, interviews, columns & much more. $1 or 2 Canadian stamps in the mail.

SOAp 'N Sp1Kes
www.soapnspikes.com/

World Wide Punk
www.worldwidepunk.com
Anti-racist, feminist, D.I.Y., and punk. Reviews indie rock, hardcore, electronic and everything in-between.

Mexico

Parafernalia Del Subsuelo
Miguel Angel Valladares
kitsch@sdm.net.mx
PDS is about punk and hc mainly with interviews, articles, columns and reviews (not mainstream shit!).

Puerto Rico

Boricuas Bestiales
Javier Tous boricuas@caribe.net
Ska, Reggae, Oi!, Punk 'zine in Spanish with a 2,000 copy run on newsprint format.

South America

Argentina

Fatzine Zine
(Fat) Nicolas Dacunto fatzine@email.com
Suipacha 2602 (2000)Rosario,
Santa Fe, Argentina
Breaking The Rules Distro.

Hazlo Tu Mismo
Fred hazlotumism@hotmail.com
Oriented towards punk/hc/emo music and its politics. 1000 printed, out every 3 months.

Natural Mystic
Chechonmzine@yahoo.com
Hardcore punk zine, newsprint, subculture, ideas, counterinformation.

No Pasaran
Huevoupthefukingpunx@hotmail.com
Dedicated to punk, ska, oi!, h.c. and other rebel sounds of all the world. It also has articles of history, anarchism, comix, literature, reviews of zines and music.

Brazil

Firestarter
www.firestarter.com.br

HardCore Scene
www.geocities.com/SunsetStrip/Villa/1353

Needle Fanzine
Frederico Finelli & Juliana Ribeiro
needlezine@hotmail.com
Each issue of Needle has 60-70 pages, more than 100 reviews of stuff, interviews, notes and ads.

Planeta Hardcore
home.openlink.com.br/rodalves

Trapilho
come.to/trapilho

Underpress
mpgodinho@yahoo.com

URBANzine
www.geocities.com/Baja/Canyon/4210
Third world underground...reviews, links and some other stuff...

Velocidade Burlesca
www.geocities.com/SunsetStrip/Mezzanine/4214

Chile

Discordancia Miticos (DMS)
discordancia.miticos.cl/dms

Europe

Belgium

Beta Webzine
www.mediaport.org/~beta/
Our site deals with a wide variety of styles: Mainly emo but also a lot of punkrock, oldschool and newschool hardcore, chaos... Be openminded is our motto!'

Brussels Hardcore Page
www.brusselshardcore.net

Punk Updates
users.skynet.be/punkupdates
Punk Updates is a site that focuses on keeping a very up to date chronological list of all upcoming and recent punk releases. Also a good percentage of records are reviewed by the Belgian webmaster. Bands are free to send in stuff for reviewing or to put up links. If provided, mp3's will be posted. Upcoming releases will also be posted on punknews.org by the same webmaster.

False Identity
www.geocities.com/SunsetStrip/Mezzanine/9540

Nameless
www.zewoc.com/nameless

Teenage Warning
www.ping.be/ska-ntwerpen/teenage.htm

Wanted Dead or Alive
The Lonesome CowboyBS248718@skynet.be
Zine about all the good things in live, like Sex, Punk and Rock'N'Roll.

Bay Island Records, Inc. an independent record label dedicated to new original music!
www.bayislandrecords.com

Denmark

Deadbeat
hjem.get2net.dk/deadbeat
Reviews, interviews and features on all kinds of trash. The leading truckstop on the net for everything rock´n´roll, Punk, surf, trash, garage etc. Also out in print!

Finland

15tCrew - Kovaydin zine
www.saunalahti.fi/~fifteen

The Finish Punk Guide
dlc.fi/~pvallin

Sue
koti.icenet.fi/~sue

Toinen Vaihtoehto
dlc.fi/~pvallin/tv

France

Broken Ear
www.multimania.com/brokenear

Earquake
members.xoom.com/earquake/earquake.htm

Evil Area
www.zewoc.com/nameless/evilarea

Frigid Ember
frigidember.com

Izmobil
www.jetty.org/izimobil

Kill...What?
www.ultranet.com/~killwhat/html
The most American French fanzine. In French and distributed all over France, Quebec, Switzerland and Belgium.

L'Oreille Cassee
www.multimania.com/brokenear/oc.html

Pogo
www.chez.com/pogo
A French fanzine, label and mail order catalogue. POGO means For Wide Openned Ears which also means that we are interested in nearly all kind of music.

right through
www.rightthrough.org/

RunkpOckeR
www.geocities.com/Paris/2513
Covers independent hardcore and punk and reviews music & print.

Scream
perso.club-internet.fr/nocomply

Sounds
hey.to/sounds

Starsixtynine
www.multimania.com/starsixtynine
French zine dedicated to music (from hc to emo) and other topics (from social themes to comix stuff).

Wardance
www.wardance.net/

Worst
www.multimania.com/worst

Xtatic Noise
www.citeweb.net/xtatic

Germany

Ben Zine
Stefan Jonas   proud_to_be_loud@gmx.net
Four times a year, including tons of reviews, interviews, political/personal stuff. We like hardcore, oi, punk, ska, swing, emo, power-violence and crust.

Benzine
Timo SchliepSubversiv_Radio@gmx.de
Punk,HC,Ska Fanzine, Stuff will also be played in the Subversiv Radioshow. Contact us for our Tape-Sampler.

Cowpox
www.cowpox.de
German punk, ska, indie e-zine & fanzine.

Doc Mac Rock
Markus Brillertwww.docmacrock.de

elektrotot
www.planet-interkom.de/elektrotot

Enough
www.punkrawk.de/
A non-profit DIY punk/HC/Ska/Indi E-Zine for the Scene!

Interpol Times
www.stormloader.com/scenepolice/main.html
Fanzine, printrun of 2.500, featuring all kinds of music: HC, punk, emo, noise, garage, crap, etc etc. comes out twice a year, 100 pages! with a special topic every issue!

Ox Fanzine
www.punkrawk.com
Germany´s biggest punk rock & hardcore zine

Pandora
scorchedearthpolicy.de/Pandora/Pandora.htm

Schenkelklopfer
www.schenkelklopfer.de

Stupid Over You
mitglied.tripod.de/Stupid

Useless Earlyripes
Mitch Seisermitchuseless@t-online.de
The trashy German 60's, Garage, Punk, R'n'Roll & Power Pop Monster!

Hungary

The Hungarian Punk Page
angelfire.com/ok/HungPunk
Get reviewed both in English and Hungarian & discover this scene.

Italy

AAA Punk Rock
www.geocities.com/SunsetStrip/Stage/6852

Hey Hey Punkrockers
members.tripod.com/hhpr

Parco Dio
Paolo Nardi nardi_paolo@hotmail.com
Punk rock and pop punk oriented 'zine with interviews, columns, reviews of Italian and world wide punk records! ITALIAN WRITTEN!!

Spread Out
www.geocities.com/SunsetStrip/Palladium/7846

SThINK
www.sthink.com

Vida underground e-zine
www.vida.it

W il Punk Rock
utenti.tripod.it/WilPunkRock

The Netherlands

Mr. Hardcore #1
www.stack.nl/~edwinhe

Russia

Knives N Forks
Dmitri Ivanov knivesnforks@usa.net
Mail: Russia, 195009 St.Petersburg, p.o.box 30
www.chat.ru/~k_and_f
Punk rock hardcore ska fanzine, 4 issues out. People can send us music & zines for review.

Spain

El diario de Peter Punk
www.fortunecity.com/victorian/louvre/218/index0.htm

SLAM ZINE
Sergio Sainz slam_zine@yahoo.com
C/Islas Canarias N°23,
09006 Burgos, SPAIN
A hardcore zine in Spanish. 6 issues released. Good paper (like magazines) $1 ppd, and lots of interviews with all styles of hardcore bands!

Sweden

A Message to You
w1.871.telia.com/~u87102493

Backlash
hem1.passagen.se/backlash

Chaos is King
www.come.to/chaosisking

Feeble Bastard
hem1.passagen.se/skitlass

Glitz Zine
www.glitzine.com

Illdisposed
illdisposed.just.nu

Switzerland

evil
www.multimania.com/evilzine

Stagedive
www.stagedive.ch

United Kingdom

Armed with Anger
www.awa.ndirect.co.uk/

Clean Shaven
Pete Flynn pete@badmusic.net
9 Beech Way, Oakdene Road, Godalming,
Surrey GU7 1QG, U.K.
An array of reviews and opinions, covering a rather tidy range of the musical spectrum. And then some more. Something for all the family.

collective
www.geocities.com/SunsetStrip/7727/reviews.html

Dancing Penguin
www.dancingpenguin.com/

Dirty Dog
Nick Spit NMetherell@aol.com

ENZK
www.angelfire.com/wi/enzk

Fracture
www.seanchai.dircon.co.uk
5,000 circulation free fanzine covering punk, hardcore and the rest.

Happy House
www.cert.demon.co.uk/hh

KONTROL
www.kontrol.freeuk.com

TROLL on line
www.troll-zine.freeserve.co.uk

Yugoslavia

Floskula
www.banjaluka.org.yu/floskula

Australia

A Slice of Stale Pizza
www.ozemail.com.au/~crust
Indie, emo, punk, etc - email john@adkg.com for info.

Bastard Child
www.angelfire.com/ga/bczine

Crew Zine
www.activate.8m.com

Living a Lie
livingalie.itgo.com/

Long Gone Loser
c/o Damo, PO BOX 18, Modbury North,
S.A. 5092, AUSTRALIA
Interviews, Reviews and articles with it's main focus on all aspects of great rock n roll punk and those many cool things that rock n roll rides along with (Hot Wheels cars, scalectrix sets, cars, videos etc.) Put out two or three times a year. Price $1 p.

Pee Zine
come.to/peezine

Purple Monkey Dishwasher
come.to/purplemonkeydishwasher
A perverse look into everyday life. Music and zine reviews, taboo subjects, interviews with the weird and bizarre, articles on personal thoughts and whatever. Price = $1 plus stamps for postage or zine trade (if the zine's actually a good zine, not some crappy poetry zine).

Sphagnum Nagasaki
Evan Smith comradeev@hotmail.com

Asia

Indonesia

Tigabelas Zine
arian13tigabelas@end-war.com
Thrash, Crust, Grind, HC and punk. It is all written in Indonesian.

Malaysia

Dungpeople (formerly Blasting Concept!)
dungpeople.port5.com/

Broken Vision
Jimbo and Jeryzon
www.geocities.com/SunsetStrip/
Palladium/8727/main.html

Raincitiers
Ahmad Zahid boylovesemo@hotmail.com
Punk, satanism, alcoholism, murder, suicide, debauchery - It's all here.

Snootchie
Kaisersoze acidreaders@hotmail.com
090103 Taman Sri Rampai,
Setapak Jaya, 53300 Kuala Lumpur,
Malaysia.
A Malaysian underground zine cover from local and the underworld... we try to combine art with music.

Solidaritas
Najib Anuar solidaritas@mailcity.com

The Philippines

Mutilated News
www.geocities.com/SunsetStrip/
Exhibit/3347
One of the oldest International DIY PUNK/HC fanzines here in the Philippines. Doing our shit since 1988. Send your stuff to review for our next issue.

Respire
Howell A. Casacop
Casacop@Lgn.Pworld.Net.Ph
A semi-annual hardcore zine but it doesn't mean that there are limitations, all submissions are welcome!!!

Thought Market
Agee Linan agee72@hotmail.com
Punk, ska, emo, hardcore, indie rock and occasional metal stuff. Mostly caters to the local filipino kids, so half of the stuff is written in the local language.

Turkey

Disgust
disguast.org

BEST MUSIC BOOKS has books on MP3's including *"The MP3 and Internet Audio Handbook"* by Bruce Fries, *"The Official Guide to MP3"* by Michael Robertson & Ron Simpson and *"MP3 Power!"* by Justin Frankel & Greely Sawyer

World Music

The African Recording Review
www.rootsworld.com/rw/feature/afriregi.html

Afro Disc
www.rootsworld.com/rw/feature/afrodisc.html

Afrojazz
www.afrojazz.com
This site is dedicated to all fine musicians, especially from Cuba.

BOOM! Online
www.boomonline.com

Brazil Online
brazilonline.com/musicp.html

Ceolas
www.ceolas.org/ceolas.html

The Contemporary Latin Music Review
www.geocities.com/SouthBeach/Sands/4404

The Deep Blue Page
users.compulink.gr/micmic
Brazilian acoustic and classical guitar.

Flamenco World
www.flamenco-world.com

frontera
www.fronteramag.com
English-language magazine chronicling the U.S. Chicano/Latino music explosion.

Jah Radio's Reggae Pages
paradigm.uor.edu/users/doktor

Kevin's Celtic and Folk CD Review's
www.surfnetusa.com/celtic-folk

'LA'Ritmo.com
www.laritmo.com
Straight from Nueva York, 'LA'Ritmo.com acts as a bridge between the Latin music community and the Net.

MusicScotland.com
www.musicscotland.com

NAPRA Music Reviews
www.napra.com
napraexec@rockisland.com

Picadillo
www.picadillo.com/musicidx.html
Always looking for new Latin music.

Reggae Review
quatec.com/reggaereview
A free, monthly publication commited to covering local, national and international Reggae, African and Caribbean music, culture, politics and more. The REGGAE REVIEW is also the premier Reggae music publication on the Internet.

The Reggae Source
www.reggaesource.com

The Reggae Web
www.reggaeweb.com

RootsWorld
www.rootsworld.com

Regional Publications

North America

United States

Arizona

Arizona Metal
www.coffinz.com

LiNK Music
www.linkmusicaz.com

The Spawinng Ground
www.azstarnet.com/~fishes

California

OC Weekly
www.ocweekly.com

Rock City News
Los Angeles
www.rockcitynews.com

Zero Magazine
www.zeromag.net

Florida

Coffee Stain
www.coffeestain.com

Locals Online
www.localsonline.net
Covers the south east US.

Georgia

Atlanta Music Scene
www.atlantamusicscene.com

Southeast Performer
PO Box 5915, Atlanta, GA - 31107-0915
Covers the south-east USA.

Hawaii

Aloha Joe
www.alohajoe.com

Illinois

Chicago Metromix
metromix.com

Chicago Reader
www.chireader.com

ChicagoGigs.com
www.Chicagogigs.com

Indiana

Noise
www.enoise.com

Iowa

Icon
www.iconquest.com

Kentucky

BRAT
www.brat.org

Louisiana

Offbeat
www.offbeat.com

Massachusetts

24-7
Boston
www.dlclive.com/247.html

Boston Phoenix
www.bostonphoenix.com

Boston Soundcheck
www.bostonsoundcheck.com

Soundwaves
www.swaves.com
New England area.

Michigan

Current Magazine
www.ecurrent.com

Detroit Free Press
www.freep.com

Detroit Metro Times
www.metrotimes.com

DetroitMusic.com
www.detroitmusic.com

Local Beat
www.oakland.edu/~fyvincen/LocalBeat

The Review
www.review-mag.com/homegrown.htm
Accepts cd and cassette submissions for consideration for review.

THE BUZZ! NEWS
Ed Childress and Jana
JamiesonTHEBUZNEWS@aol.com
406 W. Washington, Jackson MI, 49201

New York

Aquarian Weekly
www.theaquarian.com
Covers the area of New York, New Jersey and Connecticut

Long Island Voice
www.livoice.com

Village Voice
New York City
www.villagevoice.com

North Carolina
www.localsonline.net
South-East US Bands.

Ohio

Cosmic Hermit
stop.at/chp
Many services for bands in and around Ohio.

Out of Order
listen.to/outoforder
Central Ohio region.

The Village Buzz
www.bright.net/~sruiz
All the cool with the n/e ohio music scene.

Oregon

Oregon Live
www.oregonlive.com/ent/music

Pennsylvania

Groove Lingo
Philadelphia
www.groovelingo.com

Sound Effect Digital Magazine
www.ncsweb.com
If your recording is less then perfect don't worry about it. Sound Effect supports any talented bands or individuals willing to expose their music.

Texas

Houston Press
www.houstonpress.com

Washington

Pandemonium Online
seattlesquare.com/pandemonium
Covers the north west US.

Washington DC

Hometown Groove
home.digitalcity.com/washington/hgroove

Snap Pop!
Gina Espositoregina@snappop.com
PO Box 2812 - Sterling, VA - 20167-2812

Canada

Canadian Musician
www.canadianmusician.com
Showcases unsigned Canadian acts in showcase section.

CMB (Canadian Music Biblical Faith)
www.chazm.com/cmb

canmusic
www.canmusic.com

Muskrat Music
members.tripod.com/hackep
Canadian music only; reviews limited; news/tour dates preferred.

SEEN.COM (Soundbytes CD Reviews)
director@seen.com
www.seen.com/entertain
The Synergetic Education Entertainment Network - an E-Magazine & Communications Design company dedicated to bringing people and ideas together since 1997 - Publisher : Karla Ingleton.

West Coast Music Review
wcmr.com

Quebec

Voir
www.voir.ca

South America

Brazil

The Indie Place
indieplace@hotmail.com

Europe

Finland

Sisubeat
www.5r.com/sisubeat

Germany

CrossOver
www.crossover-agm.de/crossover
The AGM - network for youth culture.

The Netherlands

Gun
jump.to/gun

United Kingdom

British Rock
www.britishrock.co.uk
Great for news and information on the best UK rock bands of today.

British Unsigned Rock Band Site (BURBS)
www.burbs.org.uk
BURBs offers promotion, airplay, world sales, reviews and lots more!

Higher Than the Sun
members.tripod.com/arsed

Irish Music Magazine
mag.irish-music.net

Nightshift
nightshift.oxfordmusic.net/

Rabble
www.cheese.org/rabble

Rainsound
Scotland
www.geocities.com/SunsetStrip/Studio/9230/rainsound.html

Wiseacre
www.wiseacre.clara.net/music

Australia

Alternative Melbourne
www.mediasearch.com.au

Broken Pipe
www.omen.net.au/~elhornet

Bubblehead
members.iinet.net.au/~cartman2/

I-94 Bar
www.ozemail.com.au/~cregan1

Pig Meat
www.pigmeat.cjb.net/

Shine
www.shine.net.au/shinemag

XPress Magazine
www.xpressmag.com.au

The Indie Link Exchange
A new free and easy way to promote your website!
www.indielinkexchange.com

Section Two:
Radio Stations that are Willing to Play Independent Music

In my experience, sending music to a station without first contacting them is a waste of time and money. I suggest that you try and get in touch with a DJ that has a show catering to your musical style. This will dramatically increase the possibilities of getting airplay.

Mainstream

The majority of these stations have shows that caters to every genre of music – Pop, Rock, Folk, Jazz, Various Metals, Punk, Goth, Industrial, Electronic, Hip Hop, Country, Blues etc.

North America

United States

Alabama

WEGL
Auburn University
wegl.auburn.edu

WLJS
Jacksonville State University
www.jsu.edu/92j

WVUA
University of Alabama
www.newrock907.com/

Alaska

KCHU
Valdez
www.alaska.net/~kchu

KHNS
Haines
www.wcl.org/khns/services.html

KMXT
Kodiak
www.ptialaska.net/~kmxt

KSUA
University of Alaska Fairbanks
www.uaf.edu/ksua

KTNA
Talkeetna
www.ktna.org
Asking for material.

Arizona

KAMP
University of Arizona
kamp.arizona.edu

KASR
Walter Cronkite School of Journalism
www.asu.edu/studentprgms/orgs/theblaze

Katrina's Music Zone Radio Show
P O Box 857 Tempe, AZ 85280-0857
Katrina Alliason katrina23@mailcity.com
www.musiczone-online.com
A weekly college radio show specializing in independent releases in eclectic genres.

KFMA
Tucson
www.kfma.com

KXCI
Tucson
www.kxci.org

Arkansas

KABF
Little Rock
www.aristotle.net/kabf

KDRE
Little Rock
www.lick965.com

"*Please* let me hear my music on the radio!"

...GAVIN is listening.

GAVIN will mail your CD, picture, and bio to <u>any</u> group of radio stations reporting to <u>any</u> trade publication charts in <u>any</u> format for less than it would cost you to do it yourself.

Call Lou Galliani at 805-542-9999 *NOW*.

gavin

KUAF
University of Arkansas
www.kuaf.com/

California

Bryan Farrish Radio Promotion
airplay@radio-media.com
13111 Ventura Blvd., Suite 204, Studio City, CA 91604
Phone: 818-905-8038
www.radio-media.com
I'm an indie record promoter offering Signed and Unsigned-band promotion packages which obtain airplay for bands and labels on both commercial and non-commercial radio stations.

DMX
Los Angeles
www.dmxmusic.com

Green Witch Radio
San Francisco
Pam Long pamlong44@hotmail.com
415-826-8742
www.greenwitch.com
We are a multi-channel (commercial free) site based in San Francisco and we are huge supporters of independently produced music.

Indy Hits
www.indyhits.com

KALX
University of California Berkeley
oms1.berkeley.edu/kalx/

KAPU
Azusa Pacific University
kapu.apu.edu
Advertising for submissions.

KAUR
Augustana College
inst.augie.edu/~kaur

KAZU
Pacific Grove
www.kazu.org

KBAC
Santa Fe
www.kbac.com

KBHU
Black Hills State University
www.bhsu.edu/kbhu

KCBL
Sacramento
www.sacramento.org/stations/kcbl

KCIA
California Institute of the Arts
shoko.calarts.edu/~kcia

KCPR
California Poly State University
www.kcpr.org/

KCR
San Diego College
kahuna.sdsu.edu/kcr

KCRH
Chabot College
www.kcrh.net

KCRW
Santa Monica
www.kcrw.org

KCSB
Santa Barbara
www.kcsb.org

KCSC
California State Univeristy
www.csuchico.edu/kcsc/index2.html

KCSF
San Francisco City College
hills.ccsf.cc.ca.us:9878/~dnagle

KCSN
California State University - Northridge
www.kcsn.org

KCSS
California State University Stanislaus
student.csustan.edu/kcss/

KCXX
San Bernadino
www.x1039.com

KDNZ
University of San Francisco
dons.usfca.edu/~lagrpa00/kdnz
Plays the next hitmakers in urban, dance and alternative.

KDVS
University of California at Davis
www.kdvs.org/
Eclectic free-form radio, lots of noisy stuff.

KECC
El Camino College
www.elcamino.cc.ca.us/KECC
Requesting music.

KFMB Jen's Jukebox
San Diego
Jen sewell@kfmb.com
www.histar.com

KFRR
Fresno
www.newrock104.com/

KFSR
California State University Fresno
www.csufresno.edu/MCJ/kfsr-fm.htm

KHUM
www.khum.com
A locally owned station based in Northern California that plays tons of indie stuff.

KITS Soundcheck
San Francisco
www.live105.com/

KKUP
Cupertino
www.KKUP.com
Community radio - diverse music programming in several genres including jazz, blues, reggae, classical, electronic, World, folk, country, bluegrass and Latin.

KMUD
Redway
kmud.org

KOZT
Fort Bragg
www.mcn.org/a/kozt

KPCC
Pasadena City College
www.kpcc.org

KPFA The Bonnie Simmons Show
Berkeley
www.kpfa.org

KRFH
Humbolt College
www.humboldt.edu/~krfh

KSCR
Los Angeles
www.usc.edu/dept/student-affairs/KSCR

KSCU
Santa Clara University
www.kscu103.com

KSJS
San Jose State University
www.ksjs.org

KSMC
St. Mary's College
fermat.stmarys-ca.edu/~ksmc

The Indie Link Exchange
A new free and easy way to promote your website!
www.indielinkexchange.com

KSPC
Pomona College
www.kspc.pomona.edu

KSSU
California State University - Sacramento
www.csus.edu/asi/KSSU

KSUN
Sonoma State University
www.sonoma.edu/ksun

KUCI
University of California
www.kuci.org

KUSF
The University of San Francisco
www.kusf.org
A highly eclectic, underground college/community station that is very selective but welcomes vinyl, cd or DAT submissions of all genres.

KVMR
Nevada City
www.kvmr.org

KWOD
Sacramento
www.kwod.com/front.asp

KXLU
Loyola - Marymount University
www.lmu.edu/stuaff/kxlu/kxlu.htm

KXST
San Diego
www.sets102.com

KYDS
El Camino High School - Sacramento
www.sacramento.org/voice

KZSC
University of California Santa Cruz
kzsc.ucsc.edu/

KZSU
Stanford University
kzsu.stanford.edu

Moon Radio
Cypress
www.moon-radio.com

Music Spotlight Radio Show
www.musicspotlight.com/msrsfree.htm
FREE RADIO AIRPLAY in live weekly one-hour broadcast on KCLA in LA and Hollywood with Internet simulcast. We do offer free radio airplay WITHOUT having to be a member of our web site. We also offer optional additional benefits and exposure for those who do wish to join the site and there is a minimal fee for building their page in the site and making their music available on their page. NO ONE PAYS for FREE RADIO AIRPLAY and they do not have to join the site to be included in our Music Spotlight Radio Show!! For information and submission instructions visit our website.

NetRadio.com – Alternative Country
www.netradio.com/channels/altcountry

Radio DX
Sacramento
www.oe-pages.com/ARTS/Rock/radiodx

Radio Free Monterey
Montery
www.radiofreemonterey.org

Radio Free World
Joey Latimer
www.radiofreeworld.com
Broadcasts shows made up of nearly half indie music 24 hours/day via Real Audio live stream.

Rock-it Radio
Ventura
www.palmsradio.com/main.html

SF Liberation Radio
San Francisco
Richard Edmondson
www.slip.net/~dove

Colorado

KCSU
Colorado State U
KCSUfm.com

KDNK
Carbondale
www.kdnk.org

KDUR
Ft. Lewis College
www.kdur.org

KEPC
Pikes Peak Community College
www.ppcc.cccoes.edu/dept/kepc

KFMU
Steamboat Springs
www.kfmu.com

KGNU
Boulder
www.kgnu.org

KMSA
Mesa State College
mesa7.mesa.colorado.edu/~jhargrav/kmsa

KRCC
Colorado College
www.krcc.org

KSRX
The University of Northern Colorado
www.univnorthco.edu/ksrx
The University of Northern Colorado's Only Student Run Radio.

KTCL
Denver
www.ktcl.com

KVCU
University of Colorado
www.colorado.edu/StudentGroups/KVCU

KXPK
Denver
www.thepeak.com

Connecticut

Amazon Radio Show
Bridgeport
www.wpkn.org/wpkn/amazon
Welcomes music from women everywhere, all styles.

The Jon and Dave Show
The Jon & Dave show c/o Jon Michno, 110 Lu Manor Drive, Fairfield, CT 06432
ThapopeJon@aol.com
A bitchin new radio show in CT, The Jon & Dave Show on Tuesdays 6-8pm on 88.5 WVOF. Bands and labels get in touch - we wanna play your stuff!

WCNI
Connecticut College
oak.cc.conncoll.edu/wcni

WESU
Wesleyan University
www.wesleyan.edu/wesu/

WHUS
The University of Connecticut
whusfm.saup.uconn.edu
Please send us your music!

WPKN
University of Bridgeport
www.wpkn.org/wpkn

WQAQ
Quinnipiac College
go.to/wqaq/

WRTC
Trinity College
www.wrtcfm.com

WSAM
U of Hartford
200 Bloomfield Avenue, W. Hartford, CT 06117
wsam@mail.hartford.edu
phone: 860-768-4238

WWUH
Hartford University
uhavax.hartford.edu/~wwuh/welcome.htm

WXCI
Western Connecticut State U.
www.wcsu.ctstateu.edu/wxci/homepage.html

Delaware

WVUD
University of Delaware
www.wvud.org

Florida

M4 Radio
Sanford
Banzai (Lance J. Stinson)
www.m4radio.com

Spotlight On Musicians
www.theband200.com
Please send material!

WBUL
University of South Florida
www.ctr.usf.edu/wbul/

WERU
Embry-Riddle Aeronautical University
www.db.erau.edu/campus/student/weru

WMNF
Tampa Community College
www.wmtx.com

WOWL
Florida Atlantic University
www.fau.edu/student/wowl

WPBZ
Smith College
www.buzz103.com

WPRK
Rollins College
www.rollins.edu/wprk

WUFI
Florida International University
www.fiu.edu/%7Ewufi

WVFS
Florida State University
www.wvfs.fsu.edu

WVUM
University of Miami
www.miami.edu/wvum

WWRR
www.wwrr.net
The World Wide Radio Renaissance features a playlist of Independent Florida bands exclusively. The seven hour show is produced weekly.

Georgia

WMRE
Emory University
www.emory.edu/WMRE

WRAS
Georgia State University
www.gsu.edu/~www885/
The 100,000 watt voice of Georgia State University.

WREK
Georgia Tech
cyberbuzz.gatech.edu/wrek

WUOG
University of Georgia
www.uga.edu/~wuog

Hawaii

KTUH
University of Hawaii
ktuh.hawaii.edu/md@ktuh.hawaii.edu

Idaho

KUOI
University of Idaho
kuoi.asui.uidaho.edu

Illinois

Flames Radio
Chicago
www.flamesradio.com

WDBX
Carbondale
www.wdbx.org

WEFT
Champaign-Urbana
www.8am.com/weft

WESN
Illinois Wesleyan University
www.iwu.edu/~wesn

WHPK
University of Chicago
humanities.uchicago.edu/orgs/whpk

WKDI
Northern Illinois University
www.niu.edu/npr/wkdi
New site under construction at:
www.wkdi.org/

WLUW
Loyola University
www.wluw.org

WMCR
Monmouth College
www.wmcr.org

WNTH
New Trier High School
nths.newtrier.k12.il.us/activities/
media/%7Ewnth/html/Intro

WNUR
Northwestern University
www.wnur.org

WOUI
Illinois Institute of Technology
www.iit.edu/~woui

WPCD
Parkland College
www.parkland.cc.il.us/wpcd

WQCY
Quincy
www.wqcy.com

WQUB
Quincy University
www.quincy.edu/wqub

WZND
Illinois State University - Normal
www.its.ilstu.edu/wznd
Rock and Hip Hop.

Indiana

WBKE
Manchester College
www.manchester.edu/wbke

WCCR
Purdue University
expert.cc.purdue.edu/~wccr

WCRD
Ball State University
www.tcom.bsu.edu/wcrd/

WEAX
Tri State University
www.tristate.edu/organ/WEAX/
weaxopen.htm

WFHB
Indiana Univeristy
www.bluemarble.net/~wfhb

WISU
Indiana State University
wisu.indstate.edu

WIUS
Indiana University
www.indiana.edu/~wius

WMHD
Rose-Hulman Institute of Technology
5500 Wabash Avenue,
Terre Haute, IN 47803
phone: 812-877-8350

WMRH
Purdue University
expert.cc.purdue.edu/~wmrh

WRFL
West Lafayette
expert.cc.purdue.edu/~wrfl

WUEV
University of Evansville
www.evansville.edu/~wuevweb

WVFI
University of Notre Dame
www.nd.edu/~wvfi

Iowa

KBVU
Buena Vista University
edge.bvu.edu

KRUI Lo-Fi Lounge, The Weekend Showcase
University of Iowa
www.uiowa.edu/~krui

KSTM
Simpson College
www.simpson.edu/studentlife/
studentactivities/88.9_kstm.htm
Website contains only the station's e-mail address.

KURE
Iowa State University
www.stuorg.iastate.edu/kure

KWAR
Waverly
www.wartburg.edu/kwar

The Underground Radio Show
Sean Duregger scduregger@yahoo.com
1540 220th St., Garner, IA 50438
kzowunderground.8m.com
The Underground was set up to give North Iowa bands a chance to be heard, and it grew from there. Sean D. featured new alternative independant bands from across the nation and world every Monday night!

Kansas

Internet Radio Free Kansas
Witchita
www.tafcommedia.net/music.htm
Internet Only webcaster focusing on Alternative, Classic and Progressive Rock music. Chosen by Rolling Stone Magazine as "one of the coolest stations on the Web," April 15, 1999.

KJHK
University of Kansas
kjhk.ukans.edu

Worldwide Radio.com
Topeka
www.cosmicradio.com/

Kentucky

WFPK
Louisville
www.wfpk.org

WNKU
Northern Kentucky University
www.nku.edu/~wnku

WRFL
University of Kentucky
www.uky.edu/StudentOrgs/wrfl

WRVG
Georgetown College
www.wrvg-fm.org

Louisiana

KLSU
Louisiana State University
klsu.stumedia.lsu.edu

KNLU
University of Louisiana
knlu.nlu.edu

KNSU
Nicholls State University
listen.to/theedge

KNWD
Northwestern State University
vic.nsula.edu/knwd/

KSCL
Centenary College
personal.centenary.edu/~kscl
A non-commerical station managed and operated by the students of Centenary College. Promoting independent artists and record labels is our top priority.

KXUL(formerly KNUL)
University of Louisiana
kxul.com

LICK FM
Munroe
members.tripod.com/hawkfm

WTUL
Tulane University
www.tulane.edu/~wtul

Maine

WBOR
Bowdoin College
www.bowdoin.edu/~wbor

WCDQ
Sanford
www.wcdq.com

WHSN
Husson College
www.nescom.org/whsn/
Looking for jam bands/hippie rock.

WMHB
Colby College
www.colby.edu/wmhb

WMPG
University of Southern Maine
www.wmpg.org

WRBC
Bates College
www.bates.edu/people/orgs/wrbc

WUMF
University of Maine
violet.umf.maine.edu/~wumf

Maryland

WFWM
Frostburg State University
www.wfwm.org

WHSR
Johns Hopkins University
www.jhu.edu/~whsr

WKHS Nobody's Bizness
Worton
www.delanet.com/~zorak/wkhs.htm

WMUC
University of Maryland
www.wmuc.umd.edu

WRNR
Grasonville
www.wrnr.com

WSMC
St.Mary's City
www.wsmc.org

Massachusetts

BCR
Babson College
radio.babson.edu

Face the Music Radio Show
Worcester
www.splusnet.com/wcuw/facethemusic
Syndicated lesbian/feminist music program.

Radio Shanghai International
West Somerville
home.earthlink.net/~shanghaii
Advertising for submissions.

WAMH
Amherst College
www.amherst.edu/~wamh

WBRS
Brandeis University
www.wbrs.org

WBTY
Bentley College
web.bentley.edu/students/c/creight_eric

WCFM
Williams College
wcfm.williams.edu

WCUW
Worcester
foxy.net/foxy-wcuw.html

WECB
Emerson University
pages.emerson.edu/organizations/wecb/

WERS
Emerson College
pages.emerson.edu/organizations/wers

WGBH
Boston
www.wgbh.org/wgbh

WJUL
University of Massachusetts
www.uml.edu/misc/WJUL

WMBR
Massachusetts Institute of Technology
wmbr.mit.edu

WMFO
Tufts University
www.wmfo.org/

WMHC
Mt. Holyoke College
www.mtholyoke.edu/org/wmhc

WMUA
University of Massachusetts
wmua.org/

WMWM
Salem State College
wmwm.star.net

WNEK
Springfield College
Shanon Plaquet Splaquet@wnec.edu
Please send material!

WNRC
Nichols College
Michael Kowlenko kowalemg@nichols.edu
Please send material!

WOZQ
Northampton
sophia.smith.edu/org/wozq/

WRBB
Northeastern University
www.dac.neu.edu/wrbb

WRSI
Greenfield
www.wrsi.com

WSHL
Stonehill College
WSHL, 320 Washington Street,
Easton MA 02357
www.stonehill.edu/WSHL

WSMU
University of Mass/Dartmouth
www.des.umassd.edu/wsmu.html

WTBU
Boston U
www.bu.edu/com/wtbu/home2.html

WXPL
Fitchburg State College
falcon.fsc.edu/~wxpl

WXRA Outer Limits
Winston-Salem
Marcia Gan
www.wxra945.com

WXRV
Haverhill
www.wxrv.com

WZBC
Boston College
www.bc.edu/bc_org/svp/st_org/wzbc

WZLY
Wellesley College
erythrea.wellesley.edu/wzly/

Michigan

DMCR/WUDM
Detroit Mercy
listen.to/dmcr

Impact FM (formerly WDBM)
Michigan State University
whfr.hfcc.net

WCAL
Calvin College
www-stu.calvin.edu/wcal

WCBN
University of Michigan
www.wcbn.org

WHFR
Henry Ford College
whfr.hfcc.net

WIDR
Western Michigan University
www.widr.org

**WKHM AM Ed Childress'
Friday Night Show**
Jackson
www.wkhm.com
To book a spot on this 1/2 hour show, call Jana Jamieson at 517-787-8526.

WLSO
Lake Superior State University
www.lssu.edu/wlso/

WMHW
Central Michigan University
www.bca.cmich.edu/modern_rock_91.htm

WMRB
Massachusetts Institute of Technology
wmbr.mit.edu

WMTU
Michigan Technological University
wmtu.mtu.edu

WNMC
Northwestern Michigan College
www.nmc.edu/~wnmc

WPHS
Warren Cousino High School
www.wphs.com

WRHO
University of Detroit Mercy
newton.hartwick.edu/~wrho

WRKO
University of Detroit Mercy
www.udmercy.edu/personal/wrko

WUPX
Marquette University
longyear.acs.nmu.edu/~wupx

WXOU
Oakland University
www.oakland.edu/~wxou/

WYCE
Grand Rapids
www.wyce.org

Minnesota

IJIR
St. Paul
www.strangecloud.com/IJIR

KAXE
Grand Rapids
www.kaxe.org

KBSB
Bemidji State University
www.fm90.org

KFAI
Minneapolis
www.kfai.org

KJNB
Saint John's University
www.kjnb.org

KMSM
Montana Tech
sweetgrass.mtech.edu/kmsm

KMSU/SMSK
Minnesota State University
www.mankato.msus.edu/dept/kmsufm

KQAL
Winona
wind.winona.msus.edu/~www_kqal

KQRS
Minneapolis
www.92kqrs.com

KSTO
St. Olaf College
www.stolaf.edu/stulife/orgs/ksto

KUMM
University of Minnesota
www.mrs.umn.edu/~kumm
Hard alternative music.

KUOM
University of Minnesota
www.cee.umn.edu/radiok

KVSC
Saint Cloud State University
www.kvsc.org

The Musical Transportation Spree
Minneapolis
www.scc.net/~critter/mts
Prefers home recordings.

Radio Free Minnesota
www.angelfire.com/mn/UltrasonicRadio

WMCN
Manchester College
www.macalester.edu/~wmcn

WVOE
www.nwc.edu/students/wvoe.htm

Mississippi

WMSV
Mississippi State University
www.wmsv.msstate.edu

WUMS
University of Mississippi
www.olemiss.edu/orgs/wums

WUSM
University of Southern Mississippi
www-dept.usm.edu/~wusm/wusm2.html

Missouri

KCLC
Lindenwood College
199.217.137.67/~kclc

KCOU
University of Missouri
tiger.coe.missouri.edu/~kcou

KDHX
St.Louis
www.kdhx.org/
Asking for submissions.

KDLX
Northwest Missouri State University
www.nwmissouri.edu/~KDLX

KMNR
University of Missouri
www.umr.edu/~kmnr

KNSX - MCM Radio
St.Louis
www.93x.fm

KTRM
Truman State University
www2.truman.edu/ktrm/

KWJC
William Jewell College
www.91-9.com

KWUR
Washington University
kwur.wustl.edu
Student-run multi-format station of Washington University in St. Louis. Any material for airplay should be sent to: KWUR 90.3FM, Box 1205, 1 Brookings Drive, St. Louis, MO 63130

Music Monster
Highlandville
musicmonster.net

Montana

KBGA
University of Montana
kbga.org

KCFV
Florissant Valley College
www.stlcc.cc.mo.us/fv/kcfv

KGLT
Bozeman/Helena/Livingston
www.montana.edu/wwwkglt

Nebraska

Action Radio
Nebraska
www.angelfire.com/ne/actionradio

KDNE
Doane College
webcast.doane.edu

KWSC
Wayne State College
www.wsc.edu/academic/humanities/iomr4.htm

New Hampshire

Radio NHC
New Hampshire College
www.nhc.edu/radionhc

WDCR
Dartmouth College
www.dartmouth.edu/community/broadcast

WFRD
Dartmouth College
www.wfrd.com
Mostly rock.

WKNH
Keene State College
members.tripod.com/~WKNH

WPCR
Plymouth State College
mindwarp.plymouth.edu

WSCS
Colby-Sawyer College
Jacob Jarvela   jjarvela@colby-sawyer.edu
Please send Indie music!

WUNH
University of New Hampshire
wunh.unh.edu

New Jersey

RADIO 500
Sicklerville
www.c500.com/radio500.htm

WBZC
Burlington County College
staff.bcc.edu/radio/

WCPE
Union County College
www.angelfire.com/nj/wcpe

WFMU
Jersey City
www.wfmu.org
The country's longest running freeform radio station.

WGLS
Rowan University of NJ
www.rowan.edu/elan/wgls/homepage.htm

WHTG
Ashbury Park
www.fm1063.com

WNTI
Centenary College
www.wnti.org

WPRB
Princeton University
listen.to/wprb
Long live free-form radio!

WRLC
Livingston College/Rugers University
www.lycoming.edu/orgs/wrlc

WRNU
Rutgers University Neward
pegasus.rutgers.edu/~wrnu

WRPR
Ramapo College of New Jersey
ultrix.ramapo.edu/~wrpr

WRSU
Rutgers University New Brunswick
www.wrsu.org

WSOU
Seton Hall University
wsou.shu.edu/
Mostly hard music.

WTSR
College of New Jersey
www.trenton.edu/~wtsr

New Mexico

KRUX
New Mexico State University
www.nmsu.edu/Campus_Life/
KRUX/public_html

KTEK
New Mexico Tech
www.nmt.edu/~ktek

KUNM
The University of New Mexico
kunm.unm.edu

New York

High on the Air - The High Times Radio Hour
www.highontheair.com/
Syndicated show.

KSLU
Saint Lawrence University
it.stlawu.edu/~kslu/kslu.html

Rock n Roots Radio Show
Ann Sternberg and Thomas Boyd
www.rocknroots.com
bluesjazzrockworldcountryr&bfolk music from the 1920s through the present. Syndicated show in 52 US markets and 60 Australian markets.

WAMC
Albany
www.wamc.org

WBAI
New York
www.wbai.org

WBAR
Barnard College
www.columbia.edu/cu/wbar
We play everything that's quality.

WBER
Monroe College
wber.monroe.edu

WBIM
Bridgewater State College
3009 Broadway, NY, NY 10027 T: 212.854.6538   F: 212.854.7826
www.bridgew.edu/wbim/

WBNY
Buffalo State University
ipa.buffalostate.edu/~jciesla/wbny.html

WBSU
SUNY Brockport
www.acs.brockport.edu/~wbsu

WCDB
University of Albany
www.albany.edu/~wcdb

WCOT
SUNY Utica
www.sunyit.edu/~wcot

WCVF
SUNY Fredonia
www.fredonia.edu/sa/fredoniaradio/

WDST   The Indie Flux Show
Woodstock
www.wdst.com

WDVL
Fredonia State University
www.fredonia.edu/sa/fredoniaradio/

WDWN
Cayuga County Community College
www.cayuga-cc.edu/telcom

WEDG
Buffalo
www.wedg.com

WEXR
Monroe Woodbury High School
mw.k12.ny.us/schools/high/wexr/radio.html

WFNP
SUNY New Paltz
www.newpaltz.edu/wfnp

WFUV
Fordham University
www.wfuv.org

WGFR
Adirondack Community College
www.wgfr.org/htmlindex.html

WHPC
Nassau Community College
www.sunynassau.edu/dptpages/
whpc/whpc.htm

WHRW
SUNY Binghampton
www.whrw.org

WICB
Ithaca College
www.ithaca.edu/radio/wicb

WITR
Rochester Institute of Technology
www.modernmusicandmore.com

WJFFEmotional Rescue
Jeffersonville
www.wjffradio.org
Emotional Rescue is a weekly, 90 minute music show covering rock, pop, R&B, Soul, Blues, Indie, Folk, Celtic, World, Contemporary Native American and more. There are theme shows and regular mixes from the host. All world music, the 2nd Wednesday of every month.

WLIR Left of Center
Garden City
www.wlir.com

WNTC
Clarkson University
radio.clarkson.edu

WNYO
SUNY Oswego
www.oswego.edu/~wnyo

WNYU
New York University
www.wnyu.org

WQKE
Plattsburgh State University
wqke.iscool.net

WRCM
Manhattan College
www.geocities.com/CollegePark/
Dorm/5106

WRHU
Hofstra University
www.hofstra.edu/Communities/
frame.html?bounce=/SOC/wrhu

WRPI
Rensselaer Polytechnic Institute
www.wrpi.org

WRUB
SUNY University at Buffalo
wings.buffalo.edu/wrub

WRUC
Union College
wruc.union.edu/

WRUR
University of Rochester
www.cif.rochester.edu/sa-org/WRUR

WSBU
St. Bonaventure University
www.wsbufm.net/

WSGU
SUNY at Geneseo
onesun.cc.geneseo.edu/~wgsu

WSUC
State University of New York
wsuc.cortland.edu/

WUSB
SUNY Stoneybrook
www.wusb.org

WVBR
Ithica
www.publiccom.com/web/wvbr

WVKR
Vassar College
wvkr.fm.net

WXPA
Brentwood Public School District
www.88x.net

North Carolina

NCIR
Newberry College
www.newberry.edu/ncir

WASU
Appalachian State University
www.acs.appstate.edu/~wasu

WKNC
North Carolina State University
wknc.org

WQFS
Guilford College
www.guilford.edu/wqfs

WSOE
Elon College
www.elon.edu/wsoe

WVOD
Manteo
www.wvod.com
Global Radio is an eclectic new music show broadcast from the Outer Banks.

WWCU
Western Carolina University
www.z91.com

WXDU
Duke University
www.wxdu.duke.edu

WXYC
University of North Carolina
www.wxyc.com
Supporting independent music since 1977.

WZMB
East Carolina University
www.studentmedia.ecu.edu/wzmb/index.htm

Ohio

ACRN
Ohio University
www.acrn.com

Doctor 13 Radio
Cincinnati
w3.one.net/~dr13/dr13.htm

KBUX
Ohio State University
kbux.ohio-state.edu

Radio Freakency
Cincinnati
home.fuse.net/doc_diablo/tripodindex3.html

Radio U
Westerville
www.radiou.com
We have Indie Night Tuesdays 11pm-12:00 (part of our 11th Hour series each weeknight). We also play some indie groups during our normal rotation.

WBGU
Bowling Green State University
www.wbgufm.org

WBWC
Baldwin-Wallace College
www.bw.edu/~wbwc

WCBE
Columbus
www.wcbe.org
WCBE is one of the best Public Radio stations in the US, and has a few specialized shows to which you may wish to send your CDs.

WCSB
Cleveland State University
wcsb.org

WCWS
College of Wooster
www.wooster.edu/wcws

WGXM
University of Dayton
www.udayton.edu/~flyer-radio/flashed.htm

WJCU
John Carroll University
www.jcu.edu/wjcu/schedule.htm

WLHD
Ohio University
wlhd.east-green.ohiou.edu

WMCO
Muskingum College
muskingum.edu/~wmco

WMSR
Miami University
miavx1.muohio.edu/~wmsr

WOBC
Oberlin College
www.oberlin.edu/~WOBC

WONB
Ohio Northern University
www.onu.edu/wonb

WOXY
Oxford
www.woxy97x.com
97X, The Future of Rock and Roll.

WRUW
Case Western Reserve University
radio.cwru.edu

WSTB
Streetsboro High School
www.889vrock.com/home.htm

WWCD Independent Playground, Acoustic Coffee House
Columbus
www.cd101.com

WWSU
Wright State University
www.wright.edu/studentorgs/wwsu/

WXUT
University of Toledo
members.tripod.com/~PunkandSka/wxut.html

Oklahoma

KOCC
Oklahoma Christian University
www.oc.edu/kocci

KRSC
Rogers State University
www.rsu.edu/krsc/fm

WIRE
University of Oklahoma
wire48.ou.edu

Oregon

Area 54 Radio Show
The Dalles
www.area54.com

Indie Pop Radio
Portland
indiepopradio.com

KBVR
Oregon State University
osu.orst.edu/dept/kbvr

KEOL
Eastern Oregon State College
www.eosc.osshe.edu/~keol/keol.html

KLC
Lewis and Clark College
www.lclark.edu/~klc

KNRQ Thumbs Up or the Finger, Q After Dark
Creswell
www.nrq.com

KPSU
Portland State University
www.kpsu.org
Portlands only college radio with everything from indie, hip hop, punk, jazz, cajun, electronic and talk..

KRVM   New Music
Eugene
www.krvm.com

KSLC
Linfield College
www.linfield.edu/kslc

KTEC
Klamath Falls
www.oit.edu/~ktec

KWVA
University of Oregon
gladstone.uoregon.edu/~kwva

The Morning After Show (TMAS)
Portland
www.pdxnet.net/bands

Pennsylvania

WAIP Micah's Homegrown Grooves Show
Pittsburgh
843 Western Ave - Apt 3 -
Pittsburgh, PA 15233
Looking for a wide variety of music including jam, groove, fusion jazz, bluegrass, zydeco, blues, reggae, funk, and more.

WBUQ
Bloomsburg University
orgs.bloomu.edu/wbuq/

WCCB
Clarion University
comdept.clarion.edu/orgs/wccb

WCLH
Wilkes University
wilkes1.wilkes.edu/~wclh

WCYJ
Waynesburg College
waynesburg.edu/wcyjfm.html

WDCV
Dickinson College
omega.dickinson.edu/~wdcv

WDIY
Bethlehem
www.wdiyfm.org

WEHR
Penn State
www.clubs.psu.edu/wehr

WERG
Gannon University
moose.erie.net/~werg

WFNM
Franklin & Marshall College
www.fandm.edu/campuslife/
organizations/WFNM/wfnm.html

WFSE
University of Pennsylvania
hydra.vax.edinboro.edu/cwis/wfse

WIXQ
Millersville University
www.wixq.com/

WKPS
Penn State University
www.clubs.psu.edu/wkps

WLRC
Lycoming College
www.lycoming.edu/orgs/wrlc

WLVR
Lehigh University
www.Lehigh.EDU/~inwlv

WMUH
Muhlenberg College
www.muhlenberg.edu/cultural/wmuh

WNTE
Mansfield University
mustuweb.mnsfld.edu/studorgs/
wnte/indexnj.htm

World Café
University of Pennsylvania
www.xpn.org/sections/world_cafe.html

WPPJ
Point Park College
www.ppc.edu/~wppj

WPTC
Pennsylvania College of Technology
www.pct.edu/wptc

WPTS
University of Pittsburgh
www.wpts.pitt.edu

WQHS
University of Pennsylvania
www.wqhs.org

WQSU
Susquehanna University
www.susqu.edu/orgs/wqsu-fm

WRCT
Carnegie Mellon Univeristy
www.wrct.org

WJRH
Lafayette College
www.lafayette.edu/~wjrh

WKDU
Drexel University
www.wkdu.org/

WRKC
Kings College
www.kings.edu/wrkc

WRSK
Slippery Rock University
wrsk.homepage.com/

WSYC
Shippensburg University
www.ship.edu/~wsycfm

WUSR
University of Scranton
academic.uofs.edu/organization/wusr

WVBU
Bucknell University
134.82.6.10/wvbu

WVYC
York College
www.ycp.edu/wvyc

WXAC
Albright College
www.geocities.com/SunsetStrip/Venue/4075/frame.htm

WXLV
Lehigh Carbon Community College
www.wxlvfm.com

WXPN
University of Pennsylvania
xpn.org

WYBF
Cabrini College
www.cabrini.edu/~wybf

WYEP
Pittsburgh
www.wyep.org

WZBT
Gettysburg College
www.gettysburg.edu/~wzbt

Rhode Island

WBSR
Brown University
www.brown.edu/Students/WBSR

WJMF
Bryant College
web.bryant.edu/~wjmf

WQRI
Roger Williams University
wqri.rwu.edu

WXIN - Ricradio
Rhode Island College
www.ricradio.org
Ricradio.org is the internet carnation of WXIN-FM, Rhode Island College Radio in Providence, RI. We play all formats of music, both commercial releases and underground. If you need more info check out our web site.

South Carolina

WCNW
www.wncw.org
Broadcast over several frequencies in the Carolinas and Tennesse.

WSBF
Clemson University
wsbf.clemson.edu

WUSC
University of South Carolina
wusc.sc.edu/

South Dakota

KAOR
University of South Dakota
www.usd.edu/kaor

KSDJ
South Dakota State University
www.geocities.com/SunsetStrip/Vine/3879

KTEQ
South Dakota School of Mines and Technology
www.sdsmt.edu/student_orgs/kteq

KDDX New Music Spotlight Show
Spearfish
www.biffs.com

Tennessee

Radio Free Nashville
www.rfnash.org
Non-profit organization establishing community radio in Music City. Heavy focus on indie artists.

WEVL
Memphis
wevl.org
No calls, please; send CDs only to: Box 40952, Memphis TN 38174.

WFSK
Fisk University
www.wfsk.org

WMTS
Middle Tennessee State University
www.mtsu.edu/~wmts

Writer's Block Radio Show
Karen E. Reynolds   SoundAd@aol.com
SoundAdvice, RE: Writers Block, PO Box 18157, Knoxville, TN 37928
Weekly radio show dedicated to the promotion of the independent performing songwriter.

WRVU
Vanderbilt University
wrvu.org/

WRVW
Nashville
www.1075theriver.com

WTPL
Tusculum College
wtpl.tusculum.edu

WUTK
University of Tennessee
sunsite.utk.edu/newrock

WUTM
University of Tennessee
www.utm.edu/~wutm

Texas

dAISY rADIO
Dallas
www.daisyradio.com

KACV The Indie Hour
Amarillo College
www.kacvfm.org

KANM
Texas A&M University
kanm.tamu.edu

KCXR
El Paso
www.kxcr.org

KFAN
Fredricksburg
www.texasrebelradio.com

KGSR
Austin
www.kgsr.com

KNON
Dallas/Ft. Worth
www.knon.org

KOOP
Austin
www.koop.org

KPFT
Houston
www.kpft.org

KSAU
Stephen F. Austin State University
www.sfasu.edu/aas/comm/ksau

KSHU
Sam Houston State University
www.shsu.edu/~rtf_kshu

KSRC
Sul Ross State University
www.sulross.edu/~finearts/ksrcrad.html
Broadcasts internally on the cable system to the dorms, offices,etc. 7-24, and broadcasts on the local fm station KALP 92.7, Th./F/Sat. pm from 8-11.

KSYM
San Antonio College
www.accd.edu/sac/rtf/ksym.htm
Your only Alternative.

KTCU
Texas Christian University
www.ktcu.tcu.edu/ktcu

KTRU
Rice University
www.ktru.org/ktru.html

KTXT
Lubbock
www.ttu.edu/~ktxt

KUT/KUTX
University of Texas
www.kut.org

KVRX
University of Texas/Austin
www.utexas.edu/students/kvrx/index2.html

KWBU
Baylor University
www.baylor.edu/~Telecomm/KWBU/KWBU.html

Lone Star Radio
Dallas
www.lonestaradio.com

Planet Radio Network
Euless
www.planetradio.net

The Show That Fell To Earth
University of North Texas
www.kntu.unt.edu
Alternative music.

Spank Radio
Dallas
www.spankradio.com
We broadcast the newest innovative and underground music 24 hours a day.

ZUT
Austin/San Angelo
www.kut.org

Utah

KRCL
Salt Lake City
www.krcl.org

KSUU
Southern Utah University
www.suu.edu/ksuu

KZMU
Moab
www.kzmu.org/
Always on the cutting edge of fine new indie music.

Vermont

WEQX Download
Manchester
www.weqx.com

WGDR
Goddard College
www.goddard.edu/wgdr

WIUV
Castleton State College
www.csc.vsc.edu/WIUV91.3

WRMC
Middlebury College
wrmc.middlebury.edu/

WRUV
University of Vermont
www.uvm.edu/~wruv

WVTC
Vermont Technical College
www.vtc.vsc.edu/clubs/wvtc

WWPV
St. Michael's College
personalweb.smcvt.edu/wwpv

Virginia

Free Radio Oregon Hill
Richmond
Scott Burger burp@mindspring.com
P.O. Box 14738 Richmond, VA 23221
Dedicated to playing a diverse mix of music that is not heard on the regular fm dial.

WDCE
University of Richmond
www.student.richmond.edu/~wdce

WEBR
Fairfax
www.fcac.org/webr

WGMU
George Mason University
wgmu.gmu.edu

WMWC
Mary Washington College
1701 College Avenue, Box WMWC,
Fredricksburg, VA 22401
Phone:540-654-1710

WNRN
Charlottesville
wnrn.cstone.net

WTJU
University of Virginia
wtju.radio.virginia.edu

WUVT
Virginia Tech
www.wuvt.vt.edu

WVAW
Virginia Wesleyan College
www.vwc.edu/wwwpages/wvaw/wvawonln.htm

WVRU
Radford University
Star Shoemaker
www.runet.edu/~wvru

WXJM
James Madison University
www.jmu.edu/wxjm

Washington

AMPT Radio
Seattle
www.amptradio.com
Nationally-syndicated show mixing music with social and political issues.

F.U.C.C. Radio
www.sleepbot.com/fucc

KAEP
Seattle
www.1057thepeak.COM

KAOS
Evergreen State College
www.kaosradio.org

BEST SHEET MUSIC.com your guide to the best sheet music, tab and lyric sites on the Internet!
www.bestsheetmusic.com

KASB
Bellevue High School
listen.at/kasb

KCMU
University of Washington
www.kcmu.org

KCWU
Central Washington University
www.cwu.edu/~kcwu

KGRG
Green River Community College
www.kgrg.com

KNDD
Seattle
www.kndd.com

KSER
Lynnwood
www.kser.org

KTKNG Internet Radio
www.ktkng.com
Seattles only "Internet only" radio station.

KUGS
Western Washington University
www.kugs.org

KUPS
University of Puget Sound
diver.ups.edu/~kups

KWRS
Whitworth College
www.whitworth.edu/KWRS/

KZUU
Washington State University
www.wsu.edu/~kzuu

West Virginia

WVBC
Bethany College
www.bethanywv.edu/Academics/
Departments/Communication/wvbc

WVWC
West Virginia Wesleyan
www.wvwc.edu/c92/

WWVU
West Virginia University
www.wvu.edu/~u92

Wisconsin

Jam Jar Indie Music Show
University of Wisconsin Oshkosh
John Neuenfeldt
eddiewilson1@hotmail.com
www.wpr.org/schedule/wrst.htm

KUWS
University of Wisconsin
staff.uwsuper.edu/commarts/kuws

WBCR
Beloit College
www.beloit.edu/~wbcr

WBSD
Burlington High School
www2.wi.net/~wbsd

WIPZ
University of Wisconsin Parkside
www.uwp.edu/clubs/wipz

WLFM
Appleton
www.wpr.org/schedule/wlfm.htm

WMMM
Madison
www.1055triplem.com

WMSE Midnight Radio
Milwaukee School of Engineering
www.wmse.org

WMUR
Marquette University
www.mu.edu/stumedia/wmur

WORT
Madison
www.netphoria.com/wort
Listener sponsored community radio with diverse programs supporting independent artists.

WRFW
University of Wisconsin River Falls
www.uwrf.edu/wrfw

WRST
University of Wisconsin Oshkosh
www.wpr.org/schedule/wrst.htm

WSRI
University of Wisconsin Eau Claire
Jennifer Schwarz
132 Davies Center - Eau Claire, WI – 54702
College Station Dying for Material..

WSUM
University of Wisconsin Madison
wsum.wisc.edu

WSUP
University of Wisconsin Platteville
vms.www.uwplatt.edu/~wsup

WSUW
University of Wisconsin Whitewater
students.uww.edu/Stdorgs/wsuw

WWSP Grand Dad, Acoustic Revival
University of Wisconsin Steven's Point
www.uwsp.edu/stuorg/wwsp

Washington DC

WRGW
George Washington University
www.gwu.edu/~wrgw/

Canada

Alberta

Cellular Pirate Radio
Banff
www.irational.org/radio/radio90

CJSR
University of Alberta
www.cjsr.com

CJSW
U of Calgary
www.cjsw.com

CKUA
Edmonton
www.ckua.org
CKUA is Canada's oldest public broadcasters, and maintains a diverse and ecclectic program through their 17 transmitters and also online via Real Audio

British Columbia

CFMI Rock 101
Vancouver
Robin Larose
www.rock101.com

CFOX
Vancouver
Trace Ventura
www.cfox.com

CFUV
University of Victoria
cfuv.uvic.ca

CIRX
Prince George
www.themaxfm94.com
If we get a release that is worthy of airplay, then we are generally fair and supportive of the artists.

CITR
Vancouver
www.ams.ubc.ca/media/citr/citr.htm

CJSF
Simon Fraser University
www.cjsf.bc.ca

CKMO
Camosun College
ckmo.camosun.bc.ca/

Radio Escapade - CBC
Vancouver
Various hosts.
www.radioescapade.com

Radio Ethos
Strathroy
www.radio-ethos.com

Radiosonic - CBC
Vancouver
David Wisdom - Leora Kornfeld
www.radiosonic.com

Special Projects (CBC)
Vancouver
David Hawkes dhawkes@cbcradio2.com

New Brunswick

CHMA
www.mta.ca/chma

CHSR
University of New Brunswick
www.unb.ca/web/chsr
Infusing the minds of South Western Ontario listeners with radio that requires thought for 18 years.

CJPN
Benoit Locas
www.centre-sainte-anne.nb.ca/radiocom/radio.htm

Newfoundland

CHMR
Memorial University of Newfoundland
www.mun.ca/munsu/chmr/

NNUR
D.Edwards
www.geocities.com/Area51/Rampart/5931

Nova Scotia

CFXU
St. Francis Xavier University
cfxu.stfx.ca
University station with a wide variety of shows.

CKDU
Dalhousie University
is2.dal.ca/~ckdufm/

CKJM
Cheticamp
w3.franco.ca/arc/ckjm/

CKNA
Natashquan
www.chebucto.ns.ca/~cormier/ckna.html

Ontario

CFBU
Brock University
www.cfbu.niagara.com

CFFF
Trent University
ivory.trentu.ca/www/tr

CFMU
McMaster University
www.msu.mcmaster.ca/services/cfmu/

CFNY
Toronto
www.edge102.com

CFRC
Queens University
info.queensu.ca/cfrc

CFRU
University of Guelph
www.uoguelph.ca/~cfru-fm

CHRI
Ottawa
chri.ca
Christian Music.

CHRW
The University of Western Ontario
www.usc.uwo.ca/chrw

CHRY
York University
www.yorku.ca/org/chry

CHUO
University of Ottawa
aix1.uottawa.ca/~chuofm/about.html

CINN
Hearst
www.franco.ca/cinnfm

CIOI
Mohawk College
www.mohawkc.on.ca
What college radio should be!

CIUT
University of Toronto
www.campuslife.utoronto.ca/groups/ciut

CJAM
University of Windsor
www.uwindsor.ca/cjam

CJLX
Loyalist College
cjlx.loyalistc.on.ca/

CKCU
Carleton University
www.ckcufm.com/

CKDJ
Algonquin College
www.algonquinc.on.ca/ckdj

CKLU
Laurentian University
www.cklu.isys.ca/
A funky little station supporting indie music in Sudbury.

CKMS
watserv1.uwaterloo.ca:80/~ckmsinfo
Non-profit, campus/community radio station at the University Of Waterloo.

CKWR
Waterloo
musicdiscoveries.com/charts/radio/ckwr.html

Krankit Radio
Paris
www.krankit.com

Sugar Coma Radio Show
University of Guelph
www.uoguelph.ca/~cfru-fm
Sweet sugary tunes and candy give aways.

vibe radio
Toronto
sr5.xoom.com/viberadio/vibe

Quebec

CFAK
U of Sherbrooke
www.cfak.qc.ca/

CFLX
Sherbrooke
members.tripod.com/~cflx/

CFOU
Trois-Rivieres
rage.uqtr.uquebec.ca

CHAA
Longueuil
www.chaamf.qc.ca

CHGA
Maniwaki
www.chga.qc.ca

CHYZ
Université Laval
www.ulaval.ca/rcl

CIBL
Montreal
www.cibl.cam.org

CISM
Université de Montréal
www.cismfm.qc.ca

CJMQ
Bishops University
cyniska.ubishops.ca/cjmq
A campus/community radio station with a mandate to broascast a whole range of different musical genres- everything from classical, country and jazz to punk, ska, hardcore, ambiant and metal.

CKRL
Quebec City
www.ckrl.qc.ca

CKUT
McGill University
www.ckut.ca

Sunnymead Internet Radio
Waterloo
www.sunnymead.org

Saskatchewan

CFCR
Saskatoon
www.lights.com/cfcr

The Wolf
Regina
www.thewolfrocks.com

Mexico

Radio Univesidad
Universitaria en Mexico
radiouni.uat.mx

XHUG
Radio Universidad de Guadalajara
server.radio.udg.mx

Internet Radio and Syndicated Shows

2kool4radio
www.2kool4radio.com
We're 2Kool4Radio – home to the eclectic, eccentric and electric. Hear the best in alternative, indie, punk, hip hop, loungecore, and tons more.

369shoutcasters
www.thirdroad.com/369shoutcasters

A Boy and His Pet Heart Internet Radio Show
escape.angband.org/abahph

Acoustic Electric Radio Show
members.aol.com/folkdude/acouecle.html

Alan Haber's Pure Pop Show
www.purepop.com

The Anti-Elitist Radio Show
subrealsongs.com/antielitist
Internet radio show/review webzine for DIY artists and bands.

ArtistLaunch.com
www.artistlaunch.com

Batanga.com
feedback@batanga.com
2007 Yanceyville St., Greensboro, NC 27405, USA, attn: Programming
www.batanga.com/en/default.asp
Plays alternative Hispanic music like rock, hip-hop, ska and techno on multiple Internet channels.

Behind the Vinyl Curtain
www.rantersworld.net/

Boombox Radio
boomboxradio.com

Choice Radio
www.choiceradio.com
Multi-formatted internet broadcaster. Format genres include rock, hip-hop, urban, dance, alternative rock, rock, classic rock, classical, top 40, new age, jazz and latin. Accepting all independent and unsigned music.

Christian Pirate Radio
www.christianpirateradio.com

Cosmic Radio.com
www.cosmicradio.com

Cybro Radio
Larry Lowe cybroradio@juno.com
www.cybroradio.com
Internet Radio Station Broadcasting Blues, R&B, Jazz, Big Band, Swing, Cajun and Gospel music, from the USA.

Ductape Radio
www.ductape.org

EyeQRadio
www.eyeqradio.com

F.A.K.E. Radio
fakeradio.com

Fem Frequency
www.broadcast.com/shows/femfrequency
Featuring an alternative/progressive mix from rocker grrls, punk, metal & goth bands, and more — all fronted by women from around the world. You'll also hear global divas and the best in trip-hop/dance-trance.

The Femme Fatale Show
nwez.net/femmefatale
Mondays, 6-10 pm pst, nwez.net, nwez live. -A live internet radiovision show featuring 80-90% indie artists: female artists; modern/alternative artists; folk/singer/songwriter artists. Interactive live chat/audio and video streaming/frequent guest interviews&performances.

G27 Radio
g27.org
Accepts only MP3s for airplay consideration.

GetSigned.com Radio
www.getindie.com/indexlowhigh.cfm

Girl Power Flower Hour
www.girlmedia.com/girlbands/sounds.htm
GirlMedia's GirlMusic, website for only female musicians. Girl band listings as well as appearance on the radio show.

gogaga Internet Radio
www.gogaga.com/dyn/MRN
GoGaGa Brand Radio, the Internet1s first freeform eclectic radio station, features an interesting mix of diverse music that listeners are unlikely to find anywhere else. GoGaGa comes from outside the mainstream, offering listeners a delightful and refreshing alternative to the bleak selections offered on most commercial radio stations.

GoGirls Radio Show
www.gogirlsmusic.com

The Groovesite
www.groovesite.com

Groundwaves.com
groundwaves.com

I Write the Song Radio Show
www.lyricalline.com/show/

Independent Radio Network
www.irncast.com

Indie Online Radio Live
www.iorlive.com
An online radio station broadcasting exclusively indie music. All musicians/bands get in rotation immediately.

indieport.com
www.indieport.com/index.php
indieport.com (independent music portal), currently carries: 1. the weekly indieport.com program 2. Lord Litter's TAPDEPARTMENT from Berlin, Gemany 3. SAMPLICATIONS electronic/dance music mix.

IndieSonic Radio
www.indisonic.com/newweb/radio.cfm

Internet College Radio
des2.sw.cc.va.us/wsvc

iZoe
www.izoe.com
Christian station.

Joe's Blue Plate Special
www.joesgrille.com
Syndicated radio show.

K-JOEL Radio
www.kjoelradio.com

live 365.com
www.live365.com
The global Internet community where users can create and listen to independent audio broadcasts. It provides an outlet for independent musicians to broadcast to a worldwide audience.

localstation
www.localstation.com

Music Choice
www.musicchoice.com
Submit music for review to this muzac type service.

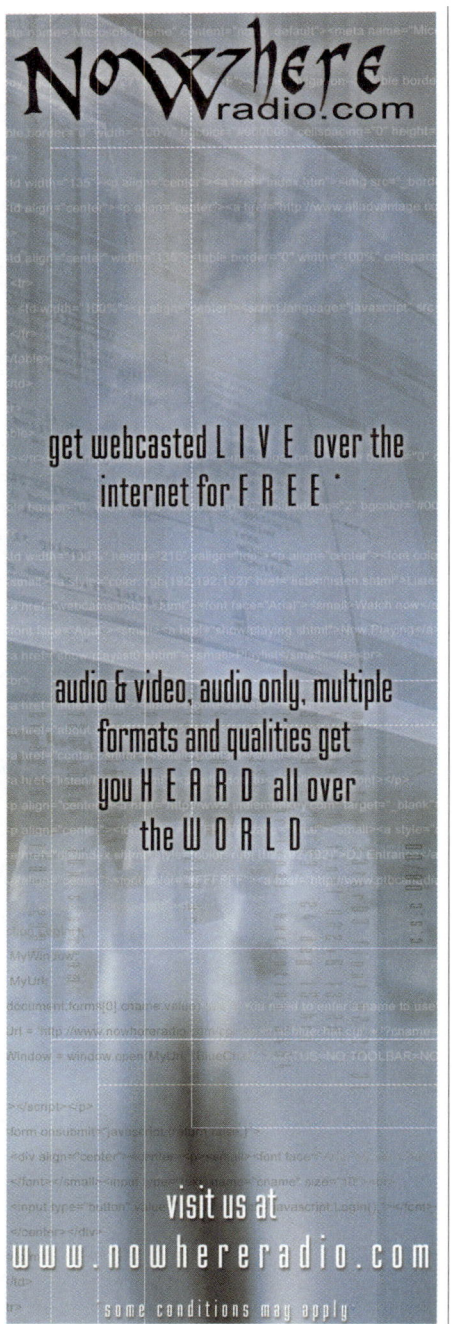

Net Rock
netrock.foxservers.com
Solicits Indie MP3s (Rock Only).

NetRadio.com
www.netradio.com

NewWaveRadio
www.newwaveradio.com

No Pigeon Holes Radio Show
Don Campau
www.kkup.com
Syndicated show. Don is a great supporter of Independent music.

NoWhere Radio
www.nowhereradio.com
We are the newest internet radio station out there, and our intent is to present to you the music you've never heard from the worlds best internet artists. Not to mention the many shows we've got planned for you!

NWEZ LIVE
nwez.net/welcome.htm
An internet entertainment network— featuring live radiovision with both audio and video streaming and live interactive chat rooms. Streams on realplayer, windows mediaplayer, and broadband. Schedule includes a wide variety of shows: some specializing in indie artists; some in alternative & modern rock; some in electronica & dance; one in hip-hop; one in blues; one in doo-wop; one in loud rock; one in a dr.dimento-type format; one in 'horn' music and a few in the talk/lifestyle format. NWEZ LIVE reports to CMJ. We accept indie submissions—by cd/video/mp3—info at: nwez.net/pages/unsigned.htm NWEZ LIVE specializes in indie artists, resulting in many indies charting on our CMJ charts NWEZ LIVE has an e-commerce site which sells indie artists that have been added to our roster.

The Pseudo Online Network
pseudo.com

Pirate Radio Network
102.1FM, P.O. box 16456,
Tampa, FL 33687
www.ldbrewer.com/pirate
We will play any indie sent to our submission address. We also sell and set up pirate radio statons.

Pulse Radio
www.stl-pulse.com
Providing Internet radio, MP3 downloads, a web page with photos, and a concert calendar for the next generation of musicians.

Quake Radio
www.quakeradio.com

Radio Anarchy
www.radioanarchy.net
www.radioanarchy.net plays the best of independent music "all the bleedin' time". It's all about the music.

Radio Deadly
www.radiopromo.com

Radio Girls
Submissions: PO Box 13164-3164, Albany, NY 12212, USA
MP3 Site: stations.mp3s.com/stations/9/radio_girls.html
WRPI Site: www.tripleccorral.com/wrpi/audio/g60sec.ram
Join hosts Corley Roberts and Valerie DeLaCruz as they feature a variety of musicians with live performance and spinning discs "of music we like" on WRPI's Radio Girls radio show every Sunday morning from 8-10am at 91.5fm in Troy, NY. You might hear an indie artist discovered on the internet played next to some Motown as the girls get down. Their combination of acerbic banter, irreverent wit and shameless self-promotion mixed in with great music has earned them a "Best Local Radio Programming" nod from Metroland Magazine. You never know who you might hear, and listeners regularly call in for information on artists they've never heard.

Radio IUMA
www.iuma.com/IUMA-2.0/brew

Radio Lightning
Phone: 1-888-682-8492
www.radiolightning.com

Radio Morgue
www.mfwinzlow.com/realaudio
Internet Radio For Unsigned Bands From Around The World!

Raw Radio
www.fims.uwo.ca/radio/

RealNetRadio.com
www.realnetradio.com/

The Rising Radio Station
www.thirdroad.com/369shoutcasters/
The Voice for Women in Music. Women need airplay? Contact rising@thirdroad.com

Risque Radio
Tam! risqueradio@netscape.net
www.risqueradio.com

Rude Radio
ruderadio.com

Soundclick Radio
www.soundclick.com

Spike Radio
www.spikeradio.com

Spinner.com
www.spinner.com

Static Radio - Irieman
www.geocities.com/SunsetStrip/2063/STATIC.html

Static Radio - Votraspace Media
members.tripod.com/staticradioxm/main.html

StompTech Core Productions
Ben Steimle admin@stcp.net
www.stcp.net
Management Internet Radio Production WebHosting

theindependentartist.com
www.theindependentartist.com
"Uniting Your Alternatives." Website, print magazine, tv show, live events, productions, Artist affiliate programs, indie-Artist catalogue, community.

ThePublicRadioStation.com
www.thepublicradiostation.com

Three Angels Broadcasting Network (3AB)
www.3abn.org

Tunes.com
www.tunes.com

Universal Buzz
www.universalbuzz.com
Submit your live shows.

unsignedacts.com radio
www.unsignedacts.com

Virtual Radio "The Street"
www.vradio.com

VR Radio
Michael Anthony fmyshow@hotmail.com
(215)258-2260
615 Market Street, Perkasie, PA. 18944
www.vrradio.com
VR Radio specializes in playing unsigned and independent artists of every genre from all over the world!. Funk to punk, rap, rock, reggae, jazz, pop, country, bluegrass, new styles too. NO CENSORSHIP. We play your music the way you intended it to be heard! VR Radio promotes and interviews the bands we play. If you'd like to set up an interview, please call us or include a contact number for your band.The most unique radio station in the world!

WASP Radio
Harold Martin mable99@mindspring.com
www.waspradio.org
Please send material!

WCAZ 2000
cazmedia.com/wcaz2000

Wiredplanet
www.wiredplanet.com/

The Witching Hour Radio Show
www.your-game.com/intradio

Women In Music
www.womenonair.com
Women in Music with Laney Goodman is a nationally syndicated public radio show with over 70 markets throughout the States, via the Public radio Satellite and an international audience online at Broadcast.com at:www.broadcast.com/shows/womeninmusic.

Women's Independent Music Show (W.I.M.S.)
diane@dianeward.com
www.wims.ws/
An Internet Radio show, hosted by Diane Ward, that showcases Independent female artists from around the world.

Womanrock Radio
womanrock.com/

www.com
radio.www.com

XeRadio
www.Multientertainment.com

Zero 24-7 Web Radio
www.Zero24-7.org

South America

Brazil

Brasil 2000
www.brasil2000fm.com.br/cgi-bin/index.pl
Everything from Reggae to Death Metal.

Ipanema FM
www.ipanema.com.br

Chile

Radio Usach
Universidad de Santiago de Chile
www.radio.usach.cl

Colombia

Univalle Radio
uv-stereo.univalle.edu.co

Europe

Austria

FM4
Linz UniversityAustria
fm4.orf.at

Freier Rundfunk Oberösterreich (FRO)
www.fro.at

Orange 94.0 - Free Radio in Wien
Wien
www.orange.or.at

Radio 1476
Mittelwelle Polycollege
www.polycollege.ac.at/1476

Radio Oberösterreich
Linz
radio-o.orf.at

UniRadio Salzburg
University of Salzburg
www.sbg.ac.at/ipk/uniradio

Belgium

Belgischer Rundfunk
Eupen
www.brf.be

Galaxie Radio
Belgium
www.multimania.com/nyto/nyto/page0002.htm

Planete Indie
Etalle
planeteindie.ctw.net
Europe's leading indie show, more than 250 collaborators worldwide.

Radio 101
radio101.de/radio101/links-e.htm
Free (some people call it "pirate") radio station in Germany and Belgium.

Radio Aktief
www.radio-aktief.com

Radio Campus
Bruxelles
come.to/radiocampus

Radio Canteclaer
Deinze
www.canteclaer.be

Radio Hellena
www.hellena.net/

Radio Katanga
home.planetinternet.be/~katanga

Radio Panik
www.10pm.org/radiopanik

Radio Scorpio
www.starspawn.com/foob/scorpio

Radio Tcheuw Beuzie
Frasnes-lez-Anvaing
www.altern.org/tcheuwbeuzie

Roots FM
user.online.be/sk001101/rootsfm.htm

RUN - Radio Universitaire Namuroise
Universitaires Notre-Dame de la Paix
www.fundp.ac.be/~run/index2.html
Student Radio in Namur, Belgium.

URgent Radio
University of Ghent
urgent.rug.ac.be

Croatia

Radio Student
Zagreb
www.fpzg.hr/radio_student

Denmark

Odense Student Radio
www.iastar.dk/osr

Station 10
Norresundby
www.station10.dk

Universitetsradioen
Nalle Kirkväg
www.uradio.ku.dk

Radio Østsjælland
www.lokalradio.dk

XFM
Denmark Technical University
www.xfm.dk

Finland

Atomi Radio Show
surf.to/atomi
A brand new cool indie radioshow in Turku Finland.

Radio Extrem
Helsinki
www.yle.fi/extrem

Radio Robin Hood
www.radiorobinhood.fi/rrh

France

Alternantes FM
Nantes/ Trignac
www.naonet.fr/guest/alternantes/accueil.htm

Campus Grenoble
www.radio-campus.org/grenoble/

Canal B
Rennes
www.rennet.org/cyber/canalb/home.htm

FMR la french independant radio libre
www.radio-fmr.net

Le Biplan
www.chez.com/biplan

no problemo web radio
www.noproblemo.com

Oxygen FM
Pamiers Cedex
www.altern.org/oxygenefm

PANX Radio
panx.net/panxradio

Radio 666
Saint Clair Cedex
www.radio666.com

Radio Alpine Meilleure
Hautes-Alpes
perso.wanadoo.fr/jb.oury/RAM.htm

Radio Bip
Besançon
www.bip.id-net.fr

Radio Bulle
Paris
www.multimania.com/radbulle

Radio Campus Besançon
www.chez.com/radiocampus

Radio Campus Clermont-Ferrand
perso.wanadoo.fr/radiocampus-clermont

Radio Campus Lille
www-radio-campus.univ-lille1.fr

Radio Campus Orléans
www.univ-orleans.fr/EXT/RADIO_CAMPUS

Radio Campus Paris
www.multimania.com/radioet

Radio Canal Sud
rafale.worldnet.net/~canalsud

Radio Clin d'oeil Alma
Sophia Antipolis
www2.ac-nice.fr/radio

Radio Grenouille
Marseilles
www.lafriche.org/grenouille

Radio Pluriel
www.asi.fr/plurielfm/index1.htm

Radio Primitive
Reims Cedex
perso.wanadoo.fr/primitive/sommaire.html

Radio Pulsar
www.radio-pulsar.org

Radio Vallée Bergerac
www.cetoucom.com/radio-vallee

RCT
Villeurbanne
www.radio-rct.com

Soleil FM
Crau Cedex
www.provnet.fr/SOLEILFM

Germany

ALPHAbeat Radio
DJ Ottic
www.pixelhouse.de/alphabeat/radio.html

Bayerischer Rundfunk
Sabine Bankhofer
www.br-online.de

Campus-Welle Köln
Universität zu Köln
www.uni-koeln.de/studenten/cwk

Doc Rock Show
Wuppertal
www.infomusic.de

elDOradio!
University of Dortmund
www.eldoradio.uni-dortmund.de

Freies Radio für Stuttgart
www.stgt.com/frs

Frequenz B
Berlin
www.freespeech.org/frequenzb

FRITZ Radio
Potsdam
www.fritz.de

HSF Studentenradio
Ilmenau
www.hsf.tu-ilmenau.de

ju: N ai
Magdeburg University
www.uni-magdeburg.de/uniradio

K2R Radio
www.radiok2r.de

Lord Litter's Radio Show
www.LordLitter.de
1. syndicated indie-radioshow across Europe, all styles, 2. regularly updated infowebsite, 3. solo music; rootsy Country-Folk, 4. Pub Rock; Litter & The Lazy Sleepers.
A. The idea is to present the whole true networking-indie-underground, so send whatever you produce with this attitude in mind ... from "traditional" music to "unconventional" experiments.
B. When I receive material, I try to react immediately, telling you what will happen with it (which is basicly airplay eurowide, spreading news via e-mail newsletters 'n Litter's Netnews website), also trying to send personal recommendations etc.
C. If I REALLY NEVER hear from you again (even after sending playlists that include your material) I'm not THAT much interested to receive more material. This is NOT a pure promo thing .... there is definitely the spirit of networking/communication involved.

cheerz 'n have a great day !

Offener Kanal Oldenburg
www.okol.de

Offener Kanal Osnabrück - OK Radio
www.ok-radio.com

QUERFUNK
Karlsruhe
www.querfunk.de

Radio C.T.
Ruhr-Universität
www.radioct.de

Radio Dreyeckland
www.failsafeproduction.com/rdlmusik
Non-commercial, musically almost mainstream-free, politically left wing and has been so for more than 20 years.

Radio DU mich auch
Duisburg
www.uni-duisburg.de/RADIO

Radio Flora
radioflora.apc.de

Radio Internationale Stadt
orang.spc.org

Radio Rheinwelle
rheinwelle.wiesbaden.de

Radio SIRUP
Siegen
www.avmz.uni-siegen.de/ugh-si/d/others/student/sirup

RadioActiv
Mannheim
www.uni-mannheim.de/radioaktiv

uniRadio Berlin-Brandenburg
www.uniradio.de

Universität
Tübingen
www.uni-tuebingen.de/uniradio

Whiskey Soda Alternative Music Show
www.whiskey-soda.de

Greece

Rhodes Radio
Rhodes University
www.rhodes.aegean.gr/radio.htm

Hungary

Tilos Rádió
tilos.hu

Italy

NovaRadio
novaradio.fol.it

Radio Beckwith Evangelica
web.tiscalinet.it/rbeonline

Luxembourg

Eldoradio
Dortmund
www.eldoradio.lu

Radio ARA
www.ara.lu

Radio LRB
Lëtzebuerg
www.ara.lu/front/klecksi.htm

Malta

Radju ta
Msida
www.vol.net.mt/unirad

The Netherlands

3FM
www.omroep.nl/radio3

Alternative Radio RATAPLAN
www.rataplan.com

Amstelveen Lokaal
musicdiscoveries.com/charts/radio/amstelveen.html

B92
helpB92.xs4all.nl

PopScene Radio
www.popsceneradio.8m.com
Dutch indie radio show. Every Tuesday between 21:00 and 23:00 hrs. You can also listen to PopScene via realaudio. BE MAD FOR IT AND LISTEN TO POPSCENE!!!!

Radio Drienerlo
vcd.student.utwente.nl

Radio Netherlands
www.rnw.nl

St. Radio-TV Borghende
Borne
www.tref.nl/midden-twente/borghend

Tracks Online Radio Show
www.tracksonline.com

Norway

Radio Nova
Oslo
www.radionova.no

Radio Tango
www.radiotango.no
Hard Alternative.

Studenten Radioen i Trondheim
www.stud.ntnu.no/studorg/radion

Studentradioen i Bergen
studentradioen.uib.no

Studentradio'n i Trondheim
www.stud.ntnu.no/studorg/radion

Poland

Radio Akademickie
Krakow
rak.uci.agh.edu.pl

Portugal

Rádio Universitária do Minho
www.rum.pt

Romania

Radio Galaxy Clar Obscur
Emanuel Focsan opaque@email.ro
bld.Tudor Vladimirescu no.1, Bloc C1, scara 1, etaj 4, ap.16
Drobeta Turnu Severin 1500, Romania
My show is called Clar Obscur and is based on modern 'leftfield music' of all generes, from drum'nbass to noise, from pop-punk to ambient, from electro-dance to post rock.

Slovakia

Ragtime Radio
Bratislava
www.ragtime.sk

Slovenia

Radio Mars
Maribor
www2.arnes.si/~mbrmars

Radio Student Public Institute Ljubjana
www.radiostudent.si

Spain

Pititako Irratia
Bizkaia
members.xoom.com/agur/pititako.html

Radio PICA
Barcelona
www.gracianet.org/pica

RADIO Q.K.racha
Asturies
www.naranco.com/radio

Secretos Bien Guardados Radio Show
Jesús Castillojlc00008@teleline.es
Pop, rock, post-rock, folk, new country, techno, trip-hop, house, downtempo, electronic, etc...

Sweden

benno Radio
www.benno.com

Mick 102
University of Umeå.
www.mick102.nu

Radio AF
Lund University
radio.af.lu.se

Rocket 95.3 FM
Stockholm
www.rocket.fm
"Rock radio in Stockholm and on-line in Real Audio". We play rock from all over the world, especially from US, UK and Sweden. Also, primarilly local, unsigned bands.

Stadsomroep Arnhem
www.staradio.gq.nu

Starshine Radio
www.lls.se/~jal/fr/star.html

Wrekin' Radio International
ourworld.compuserve.com/homepages/wrinternational

Switzerland

Frequence Banane
Lausanne
fbwww.epfl.ch

Radio Lora
swix.ch/lora

Radio Lora Live!
www.pda.ch/pdalora.html

United Kingdom

BCB Radio
Yorkshire
www.bcb.yorks.com

beatscene.co.uk
www.beatscene.co.uk

Clare FM
Clare
www.clarefm.ie

Downtown Radio
Northern Ireland
www.downtown.co.uk

Flirt FM
National University of Ireland
www.flirtfm.nuigalway.ie/history.html
Galway's student radio station with diverse music policy.

Franklin College Radio
Grimsby, S.Humberside
members.aol.com/Fcradio/radio.htm

Fresh Air FM
University of Edinburgh
www.freshairfm.co.uk

Imperial College Radio
Imperial College
icradio.su.ic.ac.uk

Indie Unite
London
www.indieunite.com

interFACE Pirate Radio
London
interface.pirate-radio.co.uk

Jimmy Possession's Radio Show (SBN)
www.geocities.com/sunsetstrip/backstage/1472
Band demos, unreleased tracks and (as yet) undiscovered bands from all over the world.

jockrock radio
www.vacant.org.uk/jockrock/jockrock.html

John Peel's Radio Show
www.bbc.co.uk/channel

Kick FM
West Berkshire
www.kickfm.co.uk

Passion FM
Blackpool
www.pasion.demon.co.uk

Phantom FM
Dublin
www.phantomfm.com

Pirate FM
www.piratefm102.co.uk

RAD SPC
bak.spc.org/radio

Radio Warwick
University of Warwick
www.raw.warwick.ac.uk
The Best in Student Radio!

RamAir
University of Branford
www.ramairfm.co.uk

rare FM
University College, London
www.ucl.ac.uk/~uczxrad

SomaCity
www.somacity.com
A new underground entertainment site dedicated to promoting the best new talent in music and film. Each week the site will feature a small selection of new artists who we think deserve exposure.

Souvlaki
www.geocities.com/SunsetStrip/Frontrow/6323
Alternative rock, industrial, indie and dance music and lifestyle zone.

Split Shift Radio
www.idea.org.uk/splitshift

Storm FM
www.stormfm.co.uk

Student Broadcast Network (SBN)
www.sbn.co.uk

Sub City Radio
Glasgow
www.subcity.freeserve.co.uk

Supanova Radio
www.supanovaradio.co.uk
Our jocks specialise in: Punk, Stoner, Psych, Progressive, Folk, Metal, Indie.

SURE
Sheffield
www.shef.ac.uk/sure

totallywired
mimi mimi@festivalradio.com
www.totallywired.co.uk
Radio show and website, on Surf 107.2 , Brighton - MP3's, streamed web show content -leftfield indie - alternative + unsigned bands.

UKCR
University of Kent
www.su.ukc.ac.uk/services/ukcr

University Radio Bailrigg
Lancaster University
radio.lancs.ac.uk

URB
Bath
www.bath.ac.uk/~su9urb

URN
Nottingham University
urn.su.nottingham.ac.uk

Webair
Salford University
hexie.memtech.salford.ac.uk/music2/webair

Weekend Rush Radio
London
www.weekend-rush.com

Wire FM
www.wirefm.com

BEST MUSIC BOOKS offers HUNDREDS of music books that can help to shape your career including *"How To Be Your Own Booking Agent and Save Thousands of Dollars"* by Jeri Goldstein and *"Guerilla Marketing"* by Bob Baker.
www.bestmusicbooks.com

XFM
London
Claire Kember
xfm.co.uk

Xpress FM
Cardiff University
xpressradio.co.uk/

Australia – New Zealand

Australia

2BBB Community Radio
2bbb@midcoast.com.au
PO Box 304, Bellingen, NSW 2454, Australia
www.2bbb.midcoast.com.au
Broadcasting to the mid-north coastal area of NSW including Dorrigo, Nambucca, Bellingen, Urunga, Thora and Kalang. 2BBB-fm has a commitment to Australian music throughout its programming, with a special Australian Music Breakfast on Tuesday mornings. The North Coast Music machine on Friday afternoons highlights musicians from the NSW north coast from Newcastle to the Queensland border, and includes touring bands from outside the region. The station is also interested in organising gigs for bands in Bellingen. Performers can send their cds to the station for guaranteed airplay.

2BOB
Taree NSW
www.amws.com.au/media/2BOB-info.html

2MCE
Bathurst
www.csu.edu.au/2MCE

2NCR
East Lismore
2ncr-fm.hypermart.net/

2NUR
Newcastle
www.newcastle.edu.au/cwis/ra

2RDJ FM Contact!
Burwood North
crash.tig.com.au/~andrew/contact.html
International Indie/alternative/new wave pop, broadcast across Australia. Demos too.

2RRR
Sydney
www.2rrr.org.au

2UNE
University of New England/Armidale
2une.une.edu.au
Student Radio Station in Northern NSW, other-than-mainstream music.

2UUU FM
Nowra
www.shoalhaven.net.au/jukebox

2XX
Canberra
www.2xxfm.org.au/
Send promo material care of - PO Box 1327 Woden 2606 Australia.

3CR
Victoria
home.vicnet.net.au/~threecr

3MU
Monash University
yoyo.cc.monash.edu.au/groups/3MU

3RIM
Mowbary College, Victoria
P.O. Box 979, Melton VIC 3337, Australia
www.amws.com.au/media/3RIM-guide.html

3RRR
Victoria
www.rrr.apana.org.au

3SER
Narre Warren
www.ozemail.com.au/~deaksy/3ser.html

3WK Undergroundradio
www.3wk.com
Internet-only alternative radio featuring the newest music and artists.

4ZZZ Demo Show
www.4zzzfm.org.au

5UV
University of Adelaide
www.adelaide.edu.au/5UV

6NR
Curtin University
www.curtin.edu.au/curtin/dept/6nr

The Basement
www.thebasement.com.au/frame.htm

Bondi FM
www.bondifm.com.au

Fbi Radio
Sydney
www.suburbia.com.au/~fbiradio

Gippsland FM
www.3gcrfm.org.au

HitZ FM
Victoria
www.hitzfm.org.au

JOY Melbourne
www.joy.org.au/welcome.htm

Mildura Public Radio
www.hotfm.org.au/guide

Nordic Online Radio
www.nordicdms.com/radio/site/NEW

North FM
Hornsby NSW
www.northfm.org.au

PBA FM
University of South Australia
www.pbafm.org.au

PBS
St Kilda
home.vicnet.net.au/~pbsfm

PBS Radio Unsigned Artists Show
home.vicnet.net.au/~pbsfm/indie/unsigned.html

The Planet
www.abc.net.au/rn/music/planet/planet.htm
The Planet searches out good, heartfelt, inspiring music from around the world.

Plenty Valley FM
Melbourne
pvfm.org.au/

RTR FM
Nedlands
rtrfm.ii.net

Spiral Scratch Radio Show
members.iinet.net.au/~blueboy/rtr_fm/spiral.html
A CORPORATE ROCK-FREE ZONE featuring new releases on independent labels from Australia and around the world

SRA
Melbourne
www.sra.org.au

Three D Radio
Adelaide
www.threed.suburbia.com.au

Triple J
www.abc.net.au/triplej/triplej.htm

New Zealand

95b FM
Auckland
www.95bfm.co.nz

OnAir Radio
Hawkes Bay
www.Geocities.com/CapeCanaveral/
9885/oar.html
I would enjoy any music that our staff can play.

Radio Active
www.radioactive.co.nz

Radio Woodville
www.geocities.com/CapeCanaveral/
9885/rw.html

Asia

Japan

Ramble Music
click.gaiax.com/home/ramblemusic
Singapore

Gold 90.5
Soo Sien Tay
www.rcs.com.sg/gold90fm

Turkey

ITÜ'
Üniversite Radyosu
radyo.itu.edu.tr

Üniversite FM
Süleyman Demirel Üniversitesi
radyotv.sdu.edu.tr

Africa

South Africa

Neptune KZ Net Radio
www.kznet.co.za

RMR Radio 89.7
Grahamstown
rmr.ru.ac.za

Country Radio

Includes bluegrass, rockabilly, alt-country, old-tyme country, fiddle music

United States

The Arctic Cactus Hour
www.alaska.net/~stratto
Covering the range of Americana/ Alternative Country from Bluegrass to Cowpunk and all that rocks and honky tonks inbetween. Broadcast to all of Southcentral Alaska and reaching over half of Alaska's population. Two shows a week.

Bluegrass Breakdown
www.wyso.org/wysopgs/blugrass.html

Bluegrass Junction
www.bluegrassjunction.com

Bluegrass Radio.com
www.bluegrassradio.com
Syndicated show.

Bluegrass Ramble
Bill Knowlton udmacon@aol.com
www.fmhs.cnyric.org/notes/knowlton-bio.html

Bluegrass Show
www.wbfo.buffalo.edu/programs/bgrass.html

The Bluegrass Sound
www.scern.org/programs/bluegrass_sound
A statewide syndicated production of the South Carolina Educational Network, features the best in traditional and contemporary bluegrass music each week. We do feature a good number of independent labels and artists due to the nature of our programming mission.

The Bluegrass Special Radio Show
kson.com/bluegras.htm

Bluegrass USA
www.bluegrassworld.com/bluegrassusa

Bluff City Barndance
members.aol.com/barndance1

The Cecilian Bank Bluegrass Hour
theboman.com/Cecilian.html
Bluegrass & THE BO-MAN with shows on Kentucky stations WSIP (Paintsville) and WULF (Radcliff). First Kentucky then the world!

Country Roads
www.lssu.edu/wlso/croads.html

Dirty Boogie
www.dirtyboogie.com

ETC-Country Show
www.radioetc.com/countryshow.htm

Fat Music Radio Network
www.fatmusic.com

The Fiddler's Grove BlueGrass Show
www.wantfm.com/bluegrass

Freight Train Boogie Radio
www.freighttrainboogie.com
Features Roots music with an emphasis on Alt.Country or Americana music, including some Rock, Folk and Blues and everything in between.

Front Porch Fellowship
www.solidgospel.com/frontporch.html

Hillbilly Jazz
members.aol.com/barndance1

Humble Time
www.humbletime.com

Into the Blue
www.bluegrassradio.com
An hour-long program featuring the best in bluegrass each week from Nashville, TN. The show is provided free of charge to commercial and non-commercial radio stations.

KMAG
Ft. Smith, Arkansas
www.kmag991.com

KPIG
www.kpig.com

KTTS
Springfield, MO
www.ktts.com

LakeWay BlueGrass Show
www.angelfire.com/tn/lakewaybluegrass

Made in America
www.madeinamericamusic.com

Make it or Break it Indie Show
George Austin PO Box 1044 - Sylva, NC - 28779

Mountain Folk
www.mountainfolk.com
Mountain Folk is a weekly one-hour syndicated radio, web and satellite show distributed by the Mountain Laurel Network. Hosted by "East Side Dave", the show presents acoustic bluegrass, folk and mountain music. Indie artists are encouraged to send material on cd to Mountain Folk, P.O. Box 2266, Sinking Spring, PA. 19608

Music For the Mountain
wnec.org/bluegrass.htm

Music From the Front Porch
www.geocities.com/Nashville/Stage/7568

The Papa Rox Show
www.jbotti.com/LiveMusic/PRocks.htm

Rural Free Delivery
www.sas.upenn.edu/~jlupton/rfd.html

The Santa Fe Opry
hometown.aol.com/bluespud/radio.htm

Shady Grove
www.best.com/~stevesag/shadygrove.html
An exploration through the old-time music of North America, music that originates in a time before radio and television, before paved roads and electricity. I don't play singer-songwriters on my show unless they write old-time songs; old-time is my format.

Solid Gospel
www.solidgospel.com

Swingin' West
swinginwest.4mg.com
Website dedicated to a radio show specializing in vintage and contemporary Western Swing and Western Music (not Country) and its announcer, producer and historian, Mike Gross.

Third Coast Music Network
www.accd.edu/tcmn

Topsoil
www.topsoil.net
A non-commercial free-form roots radio show on each Sunday on WXDU, Durham at Duke University. We operate on 88.7FM and stream live over the Internet.

Torch & Twang
www.msu.edu/user/depolo
We play roots-rockin', hip-shakin', soul-swayin' music. Everything from bluegrass to old-time country to folk to rockabilly to western swing has a home here.

TwangBox
www.gogaga.com/channel.php3?stationName=Country
Your source for rockabilly, bluegrass, classic country and y'alternative music. The TwangBox Radio Network presents a plethora of crooners and pickers sure to get your toes tapping like no country station available on broadcast radio.

TwangCast Radio
www.TwangCast.com
viggo.alis@mail.tele.dk

WCEN Radio
Mount Pleasant, MI
www.wcen.com

WDVR
www.wdvrfm.org

WFDU
www.fdu.edu/newspubs/wfdu

WLGN
Logan, OH
www.wlgn.com

WMLB Radio
Cumming
www.wmlb.com

Canada

Bluegrass Island
members.tripod.com/~bluegrassisland/bluegrassisland.html

Spirit of the West
www.cowboylife.com
A 60 minute weekly radio show that is also carried on the web. Rancher and Horse trainer/ broadcaster Hugh McLennan brings you music that's rich, listenable and seldom heard on commercial radio today along with conversations featuring spellbinding stories from pioneers, working cowboys and leading motiviational experts. The music is Western in nature, different than country, and features wonderfully talented Independent artists. The Spirit Of the West has won several broadcasting awards over the years.

Belgium

Country Train Radio Show
Mia Heylen mia.heylen@skynet.be
listen.to/COUNTRYTRAIN

Stetson Time Radio Show
home.planetinternet.be/~katanga

Denmark

Country Hour Radio Show
Brian Due Hansen   due@cool.dk

Country Jukebox
Birthe Skantorp   biska@vip.cybercity.dk
Sondermarken 15 A, 9280 Storvorde, Denmark

Countryknalen Radio Show
Solveig Clarkscc.country@get2net.dk

Hans-Henrik Thamdrup's Radio Show
hhcountry@adr.dk
www.homestead.com/HansHenrik

Nashville Showcase
www.freeyellow.com/members7/bjarneh
I am a country radio DJ in Denmark. Won Best of Texas Award 99, for best DJ in Denmark. I work mostly with independent artists. You can meet many of them on my linkpage.

Radio HLR
Otto Teglgaard   tecb@mail.tele.dk
P.O. Box 573, DK -7100 Vejle, Denmark

SKAGENSEXPRESSEN Radio Show
Benny Sorensen   dj-benny@mail.tele.dk
www.freeyellow.com/members8/bennysorensen

Estonia

BlueGrassRoots
Jaanus Vainu   BGR@BGR.ee
Roopa 18, Tallinn, 10136, ESTONIA
bgr.ee/RADIO
(1) Largest Web-site for bluegrass and related music links and database of recordings; (2) Independent 24h radio station for bluegrass and related music formats.

France

Country Cookin Radio Show
Viggo Jensen
www.radioalfa.net
The name of my radio show at Radio ALFA is "Country Cookin'" 4 hours weekly. I also have a two hour show at Radio Hadsten Name of show is "Country time"

Country Roads Radio Show
www.radio-rct.com

Country Roots Radio Show
Marian Lacroix   marionl@club-internet.fr
www.multimania.com/arc

Frequence Verte Radio Show
Jean Castro   castroj@club-internet.fr

Germany

I.C.M.A.G. Hoedown
www.i-c-m-a-g.org
Luxembourg

Country Club Music Show
www.ara.lu

The Netherlands

B.R.T.O.
Alex Pijnen. Saloon.BRTO@hetnet.nl
Piusplein 46,
4621en Bergen op Zoom,
Holland.
www.noremac.nl/brto
Plays:Bluegrass,Gospel,Cajun,Zydeco,Tex Mex,Rockabilly and Modern Country.

Country Behind the Dykes
www.homestead.com/john_van_den_berg

Country Crossroads
www.gironet.nl/home/pcspaan/home.html

Country Festival Radio Show
Bart van der Pol
Bart.Vanderpol.Nwh@net.HCC.nl
Zuiderkruis 43, 2221 NW Katwijk,
The Netherlands

Country Time
www.freeyellow.com/members8/jorissmits

PeelGrass
Rein Wortelboer
Rein.Wortelboer@nld.xerox.com
Akelei 10, 5803 CA Venray,
The Netherlands
www.xs4all.nl/~peelgras
If your music is in the (traditional) country, western, or bluegrass style, just send a promotional CD for review / possible airplay.

Norway

Honky Tonk Café Radio Show
Maurits Opsahl mapso@online.no
www.homestead.com/mauritso

Spain

Wired for Sound Radio Show
Ramon Anfruns
Pratramon.anfruns@mx3.redestb.es

Sweden

Hanksville Farm News
CMR 105,5, P.O.Box 53, SE-240 30
Marieholm, SWEDEN
welcome.to/hanksville
"YOU MAIL IT - WE PLAY IT !"

Switzerland

Radio Eviva
www.homestead.com/ireneschmidt

United Kingdom

Country Corner Radio Show
www.clarefm.ie/progs/countrycorner.htm

Keep it Country Radio Show
www.downtown.co.uk

Australia

Big Country Radio
matilda.aaa.com.au/bigcountryradio

Cool Country Radio
www.coolcountry.com.au

High, Wide and Homegrown
ren.netconnect.com.au/~merom/
CntryComm.htm
Merv' Romeo...an Indi Country singer/songwriter..Radio Presenter and Producer..with an interest in Midi Files and MP3's. Merv's Cyberzine, Country Communicator will promote..you, your gig and your product.

MCR Radio
Macarthur Community Radio PO Box 1420 Campbelltown NSW 2560, Australia
www.ideal.net.au/~mcr/

Rigs, Roads and Rumours
ren.netconnect.com.au/~merom/
CntryComm.htm

New Zealand

88 Country 1593AM, 88.6FM
PO Box 1603, Christchurch New Zealand
www.geocities.com/Nashville/Opry/7692
New Zealand's only full time Country music station. Modern Country. Specialty shows include "Rural Delivery" - Bluegrass, modern twang and honky-tonk.

Dance Radio

United States

WMPH
Mt. Pleasant High School, Wilmington
www.wmph.org
Has changed their format to an all dance station. Will accept indie releases.

WOMB
Miami, Florida
www.thewomb.com

Canada

In the Mix Radio Show
Andrew Duke cognition@techno.ca
Cognition/In The Mix, 1096 Queen St #123,
Halifax NS Canada B3H 2R9
techno.ca/cognition
Andrew Duke's In The Mix has been airing weekly since 1987. The show is syndicated internationally to radio/internet and features interviews, live PAs, guest DJs, world premieres, prereleases, new, and classic tracks.

Radio technologix 2000
www.technologix.org

Chile

Radioactiva
www.radioactiva.cl

France

3BOOM.net Radio
www.imaginet.fr/kanyar

Clin d`oeil FM
www2.ac-nice.fr/radio

Radio FG
Paris
www.france-techno.fr/Radio-FG

Radio RFM
www.rfm.net

RTS FM
Nimes
www.mnet.fr/rts

Germany

Fantasy FM
www.geocities.com/SunsetStrip/Stage/4192/welcome.html

Sonix Radio
new.sonix.de/new

Hungary

Rádió Eger
www.agria.hu/radio/r_eger

Italy

Fashion FM
www.fashionfm.it
Switzerland

Basic.ch
195.141.14.74
Basic.ch live and archived DJ-mixes is a daily internet-only radio and music database covering quality electronic music and more.

Radio Couleur 3
www.couleur3.ch
United Kingdom

Active FM
www.activefm.co.uk

Dance-Radio UK
www.dance-radio.co.uk

| deephousenetwork |
www.deephousenetwork.com
A deep house website which contains up to date reviews & news along with users unreleased deep house tracks & more.

Flash Radio
Alex Kinch
www.flashfm.co.uk
24 hours a day, 7 days a week Flash FM plays Todays Best Dance to the world live from London, England. Tune in now and see why we define the future.

gaialive Radio
www.gaialive.co.uk/index.shtml

Interface Pirate Radio
Stephen Clee
www.pirate-radio.co.uk/interface

Kiss FM
www.iol.ie/~kissfm

Power FM
www.powerfm.org/index.shtml

Vibe FM
www.vibefm.co.uk

Australia

2RDJ
22 Church Street, Burwood NSW 2134, Australia
www.amws.com.au/media/2RDJ-guide.html

Fresh FM
www.freshfm.com.au

Kgrind Radio
www.kgrind.com

Mix Up Radio Show
www.abc.net.au/triplej/mixup/default.htm

Noise FM
www.freeyellow.com/members/noisefm/noisefm.html

Wild FM
www.wildfm.com.au

Internet Radio

012 WebRadio
www.zero1art.com/012.html
Electronic, groovy funk, trip hop, featured artists and virtual interviews with host Craig Bereboo.

1groovE.com
www.1groove.com

aminoRadio
www.aminoradio.com/dyn/MRN
A 24 hour station devoted completely to electronic music including techno, drum Œn1 bass, house, turntablism, and much more. It is also the first net-only station in the US to offer the widely popular Coldcut Solid Steel show from London.

Beta Lounge Radio Show
www.betalounge.com

Darkside Radio (DRiP)
www.hyperreal.org/music/library/audio/drip
DRiP (Darkside Radio Internet Program) is hosted by Iron Feather & Hanna Banana since 1997. . We play mixtapes, records and CDs and gossip about the underground scene. We welcome demos, etc to be played on our shows. We will give out contact infos and also welcome listeners to e-mail us MP3 of them doing shout outs, etc. The radio show is mostly geared towards any style of dance & electronica.

dublab Radio
www.dublab.com

eastcoasthappy.com
www.eastcoasthappy.com
East Coast Happy Radio is an underground dance music 'radio station' offering streaming, continuously mixed DJ sets in all genres of Dance/Electronic music. Our goal is to provide a location for DJs to showcase their talent and for listeners to find music that is often hard to find elsewhere. We understand the nature of the Internet and follow suit by offering fresh content on a regular basis.

EBand Radio
www.ebandradio.com/e101

Groovetech Radio
www.groovetech.com

Interface Pirate Radio
www.pirate-radio.co.uk

Media Bureau Networks
www.mediabureau.com
An online digital network which produces 13 weekly live interactive shows of original programming from their studios.

Neopulse
www.neopulse.net/

Radio Valve
www.radiovalve.net

The Rave Network
www.rave-network.com

Transmissions Radio Show
www.plus8.com/Audio/Transmissions

WOMB
Miami, Florida
www.thewomb.com

XTC Radio
www.xtcradio.com
This station SHOUTcasts a unique blend of Trance, Hard and Acid Trance, Underground Progressive House and Epic Trance in CD Quality for High Bandwidth Listeners. Listening requires WinAmp 2.05+ and a 128 kbps or above (ISDN, ADSL, T-1) connection to the Internet.

Experimental Radio

Experimental, Electronica, Goth, Ambient, Industrial, Avant Garde and Noise.

North America

United States

Acoustic Dreams
www.angelfire.com/biz/acousticdigest/dreams.html
A program is for quiet hours. We do NOT play space music or synthesized selections.

AcousticCDdreams
members.theglobe.com/rodrigotijer
Classical crossover and newage music.

Antenna Internet Radio
www.antennaradio.com
Punk, Jazz, World, Avante Garde.

Arcane Asylum
www.gl.umbc.edu/~ascott7/aa

The Black Cauldron
www.kuci.org/~alana/cauldron.html

butta-phat love songs
www.rpi.edu/~greenl

Closed Caskets for the Living Impaired
www.kuci.org/~dach

Dark Horizon
darkhorizons.darker.net

dARK mARKET bROADCAST (DBM)
www.calpoly.edu/~ryau/dmb.html

Dead Air
www.apogee.net/deadair.htm

defekt - Industrial Real Audio
listen.to/defekt

Disregarded Subculture
Apryil   let_me_brood@hotmail.com
From darkwave, industrial, ethereal, gothic to experiemental, Disregarded Subculture plays for your pleasure tuesday 8pm-10pm on real audio (www.emory.edu\WMRE).

Descent Radio Show
www.dogma.org/descent

Dominion Radio
auslander.hypermart.net/main.html

Dr. Demento On the Net
www.krellan.com/demento

Dreams of a New Age
Tani Chen dreams@wmbr.mit.edu
WMBR Radio, 3 Ames St.,
Cambridge MA 02142
members.aol.com/DreamRadio/dreams.html
Dreams of a New Age airs Monday, 8pm-10pm (EST), on 88.1 FM, WMBR-Cambridge, which broadcasts to the greater Boston area, and on the web at wmbr.mit.edu. I play new age and space music on the show. People interested in submitting CD's for possible airplay can send them to me at the above address.

Electro-Shock Treatment
www-scf.usc.edu/~schary/kscr.html

EMUSIC
Robby Aceto RA336@aol.com
www.wdiyfm.org/schedule/s_emusic.html
An electronic, ambient, and space music show. Thursdays at 11pm on WDIY 88.1 FM, Allentown and Bethlehem and 93.9 FM in Easton and Phillipsburg. Email me if you wish to submit music for airplay consideration.

Factory 911
members.tripod.com/~juntaone/factory.html

Gothic Radio
www.gothicradio.com
A Gothic, Vampyric, Industrial and Ethereal Internet radio station that has a whole channel dedicated to unsigned bands.

gothic.net Radio
gothic.net/radioframes.html

The Grey Zone
www.knon.org/Showpages/satmid.htm

Gryphoemia
www.geocities.com/SunsetStrip/Underground/8959

Grooverince Radio
www.grooverince.com/
Plays hardcore too.

Hidden Sanctuary
stations.mp3s.com/stations/2/_hidden_sanctuary.html
A Gothic friendly site dedicated to serious, professional musicians with an enduring sound (not all bands are goth on the station, yet they have found a strong fan base among folks interested in this genre).

High Voltage Circumcision Show
www.tiac.net/users/deftlyd/highvolt.html
91.5 FM WJUL Lowell MA's (USA) longest running electronic experimental music radio show. Listen online or locally every Friday night Midnight to 3AM (EST).

In Perpetual Motion Radio
c/o G. R. Perye III
1620 Lake Drive #144,
Haslett, MI 48840 USA
www.gothicindustrial.com
IPM specializes in indie artists of the gothic, industrial and electronic genres & promotes the musicians and events on the weekly internet radio show as well as at live club events.

Industrial Radio
www.industrialradio.cjb.net

industrial strength radio
www.industrialstrengthradio.uni.cc

Internet Radio Boston
listen.to/irb
Ambient and New Age music.

Internet Synthpop Radio
www.ispr.cjb.net

JUXTAPOSITION
www.umsl.edu/~s1020285/rl1

KSPC
Pomona College, CA
199.231.135.31
Any electronic, ambient, noise, industrial, experimental or strange music, as well as ANY cassettes should be sent with ATTN: Josh Weide. (Cassettes are generally rejected, but I will accept them personally).

KTRM
Truman State University, MO
index.truman.edu/extras/ktrm/Ktrmopen.htm

Loud Factory Internet Radio
www.loudfactory.com

Meltdown Industrial Show
www.subnation.com/meltdown

Musical Starstreams
www.starstreams.com
Syndicated show.

Mystic Music
www.kkup.com/ericm.html
Mystic Music on KKUP community radio in the south Bay Area of CA offers spacious, contemplative, heartfelt and psychedelic sounds. Space, ambient, electronic, neo-classical. Playlists, submission guidelines included.

Percy's Crypt
www.percyscrypt.com

Radio Distortion
kyandjules.radiodistortion.com
Bringing new music to your ears!!!

Radio Free Underground
www.stitch.com

Radio Free Zu Casa
www.zucasa.com/rfzc

Radio JJ
www.jj-jones.com

Ratmouth Vs ??????? Weekly Radio Show
www4.ncsu.edu/~marouth/radio.html

Razorburn
run.to/razorburn

Real Synthetic Audio
www.synthetic.org

Ritual
www.velvet.net/~kelly/frames

Sounds of Industry
www.industrialradio.com/800x600
Industrial music radio show on WMSE 91.7 FM from Milwaukee, WI USA

sursumcorda Radio
www.sursumcorda.com

T.sonic Subspace Radio Station
Lumir Castka t.sonic@atlas.cz
mp3.com/stations/tsonic
Internet radio station plays independent MP3.com artists.

Technotica
www1.collegemusic.com/content/livecasts/technotica.asp

Tommy T's Cyberage Radio Show
www.cyberage.cx

Transmissions From Scumsburg
www.scumsburg.web.com

Vampire Radio
www.vampireradio.com
An Internet radio station which specializes in Alternative, gothic, rock. Broadcasting 24/7, Vampire Radio offers several live shows weekly.

The Voice of Satan
the600club.com/Radio

WHUS
The University of Connecticut
whusfm.saup.uconn.edu/
Playlist: noiseweb.com/whus/
Send noise,experimental and psychedelic to JAY DUNCAN, NOISETC.DIRECTOR". I'm a community member of WHUS and have been involved over 7 years now.

The Wicca Radio Network
www.nvogel.simplenet.com/wrn.html

Wired For Sound
www.sonic-boom.com/radio

Canada

Brave New Waves Radio Show
www.radio.cbc.ca/programs/bnw/bnw.html

The Embrace
www3.cybercities.com/c/cfbuembrace/embrace.htm
Hosted by the Deacon Syth, "The Embrace" chronicles the on-going history and EVILution of the gothic, industrial and darkwave.

Feedback Monitor Radio Show
www.stainedproductions.com/feedback
Featuring new releases in electronic and experimental music.

Industrial Strength Nightmares Radio Show
www.blitter.com/~isn/
Radio show specializing in industrial and gothic music.

Mediacore
www.mediacore.org/
MP3 station.

plutonian nights
plutonia.org

The Real Synthetic Audio Show
www.synthetic.org/audio.htm

Synaptic Paradox Radio Show
www.campuslife.utoronto.ca/groups/ciut/synaptic_paradox/mainbloc.html
Also does CD reviews.

The Witching Hour
www.geocities.com/SunsetStrip/Hotel/3911
The dreamy side of goth music... Lush vocals, bold instrumentation, lyrical poetry - there's something for everyone. The Witching Hour is a radio show on CKUW (95.9 FM in Winnipeg) featuring ethereal and goth music. Special attention is given to indie bands from Canada and around the world. Contact host Danishka Esterhazy by e-mail (koshka@escape.ca)

Europe

Belgium

Darker than the Bat Radio Show
www.proservcenter.be/darkerthanthebat/radio.html

De Kagen Radio Show
KAGAN, p/a Wim Troost, Geerdegemstraat 23, B-2800 Mechelen, BELGIUM
welcome.to/dekagankalender
Kagan focusses on wave-gothic-electro-industrial, including all the related styles. It has a weekly radio-show, a gig- and party-guide including reviews, a dj-team, parties and a web-site. Each promo is assured to get a review (on both KaganKalender and web-site) and will be played on radio-shows, if it suits within the music styles we focus on.

France

The Chronicles of the Imaginary Radio Show
Michael Croitoriu   croitoriu@aol.com
19 Place des Quinconces, 78960 VOISINS-LE-BRETONNEUX, France

Dark Wave Radio Show
www.multimania.com/darkwave
The metal radio show of Radio P.FM (99.9) in the North of the France (Arras). The main aim of Dark Wave is to promote and help the bands who play an extreme style of music and more precisely, the heavy, gothic, doom, death, black, grind.... bands. This collaboration between Dark Wave and the bands is realized by the help of the label whatever their importance on the metal scene (big or small) .

Dark Wave isn't a support only for the label. The radio show is equally a support for the underground bands (French or foreign) which try to promote their productions in France and the world. Dark Wave allows to them to promote their demos, EPs, CDs....

Perrine FM
www.chez.com/perrinefm
La Roche sur Foron.

Utter Dark
www.geocities.com/utterdarkradio
Germany

The Black Channel Radio Show
www.blackchannel.de

Lametta Radio
www.muenster.org/lametta
Advertising for music.

Radio Decay
come.to/radiodecay
The best radio show in the s/w of Germany.

Radio Future II
www.radiofuture2.purespace.de

Italy

Chain the Door Radio Show
dune.fionline.it/chaindlk/radio.html

[K O A N] dEE-jAy
www.geocities.com/SunsetStrip/Disco/5058
It's one of the most known Italian resources on the Net about Goth music and it's written in English, Italian and French! It's full of reviews, infos, downloadable files and great stuff such a personalized webmail! Anyone can send me his infos and I will add it into the News section (bands, artists, poets... if you have an intersting project, write me. I like any kind of music so everyone can contact me to exchange opinions... Goth, Electro, Punk, Alternative, Dub, Metal, Noise, Industrial, Jungle, Ambient, Classical... OK? I'm waiting for your emails...

Radio Blackout
www.ecn.org/blackout/radio.htm

Stargate
utenti.tripod.it/deepspace
Stargate is a program that goes on the air every friday night, from 10pm to midnight, on Radio Beckwith Evangelica (web.tiscalinet.it/rbeonline). The genres played during the program are: New Age, Electronica, Space Music, Acid Jazz, World Music, Trance, Etno, Celtic etc. Please visit our website.

The Netherlands

DFM rtv
desk.nl/~dfm

Radio 100
www.desk.nl/~radio100

Radio De Vrolijke Noot
members.spree.com/reactie/reactie.htm
We transmit Country music and Relaxation music: Ambient, New Age, Electronic Music,

Romania

Fun Radio
Christian Busuioc
crisbus_funradio@hotmail.com
OP. 74, CP.71,, BUCURESTI-6, ROMANIA
Specializing in underground music, from noise, dub, electro to alternative, punk, and metal. We are looking for all types of new promo and music. We will assure serious promotion and airplay.

Russia

Back to the Universe Radio Show
www.geocities.com/Broadway/Alley/9925

Spain

El Baile de las Sombras (The dance of shadows)
teleline.terra.es/personal/sogonz/radioBDLS/EL_BAILE.html

La Hora Muerta (The Dead Hour)
Rafa lahoramuerta@yahoo.com
www.infectiousunease.com/LaHoraMuerta
EVERY & ONLY dark ambient radioshow. Every style, unknown bands specially. Monday Night 24.00 -2.00 101.5 FM Pamplona.

A Santa Companha (The Saint Company)
www.terradixital.com/asantacompanha

Sweden

Virus Radio Show
www.mds.mdh.se/~frv96atl

United Kingdom

Fresko FM
www.geocities.com/SunsetStrip/Disco/1481

Global Goth Radio Show
www.ggrs.freeserve.co.uk

Radio Free Abattoir
samsam
www.slaghuis.net
Features a track of the week, and all previously featured tracks can be found in the mp3 archive. There's a 24-hour on-demand WindowsMedia broadcast featuring the best *new* Gothic, Darkwave, & Industrial music. Changed every 2 weeks.

XFM Dublin
Ireland
www.isis.ie/xfm

Yugoslavia

Radio B2-92
xchange.re-lab.net

Australia

Atmospheric Disturbances
listen.to/atmosdis

Behind the Mirror Radio Show
members.networx.net.au/~mercury

Blood & Black Dahlias Radio Show
www.users.on.net/placebo/blackdahlias

Darkwings Radio Show
dominion.iinet.net.au/darkw

Dawntreader
www.geocities.com/claudine_dawntreader

Difficult Listening
members.iinet.net.au/~bryce/difflist

Gothic Industrial Radio
www.dominion.iinet.net.au/darkw

Infectious Unease Radio Show
www.infectiousunease.com
We also do CD reviews.

Sacrament
sacrament@darker.net
www.darker.net/~sacrament
Gothic Music & Information programme, every Wednesday night from 10pm until Midnight, on 2RRR 88.5 FM

Skreamin' Korpse
msowww.anu.edu.au/~hola/SK

New Zealand

GUNZ Radio
www.mp3.com/stations/gunz
We hope the tracks featured here will serve as an accurate reflection of the myriad styles of Goth, Industrial, Darkwave, Black Metal and dark experimental music from New Zealand. Visit our website for a comprehensive guide to the Gothic Scene in New Zealand.

Hip Hop Radio

United States

88HIPHOP.COM
www.88hiphop.com
The oldest and premier show on the 88HIPHOP.COM channel, 88 HIP-HOP has developed a large following of loyal viewers. Each week, 88 HIP-HOP features interviews and live performances, both entertaining and educating our viewers. 88 HIP-HOP is honest and straightforward; we stress creativity rather than vulgarity. Past guests include some of the biggest names in Hip-Hop, including Afrika Bambaataa, Crazy Legs, The Roots, Phase 2, De La Soul, Nas, Wyclef of the Fugees, The Wu-Tang Clan and others.

Art12 Radio
www.art12.com

Basementalism Radio
www.redrival.com/basementalism

BeatBandit Radio
www.geocities.com/Hollywood/Club/8457

blackmusicamerica.com
www.blackmusicamerica.com
BMA is the new online epicentre emanating music, information, culture and entertainment for the Black community and those interested in that culture.

BombRadio
www.bombradio.com

bringthenoise.com
www.bringthenoise.com

Change up the Groove Radio Show
Columbus
www.wcbe.org
Local DJ and globetrotter Poppa Hopp spins an hour of acid jazz, jungle, hip-hop, trip-hop, drum 'n' bass, new-school breaks and big beat. Our own crossfader dominator features mixes including unavailable white label tracks, commentary, and now guest contributions from artists and DJs from around the world. Wicked!

The Core
www.pixelshow.com/core

Drastic Radio
PO Box 592722 Orlando, FL 32859, USA
www.insomniacmagazine.com/
Drastic Radio is a 7 year old Saturday night hip hop radio show that plays the best in indie hip hop Music. If you have an indie release on vinyl or cd, send it through for review for possible radio play

Gotcha Open Radio
www.lyricistmag.com

Hip Hop Hemisphere Radio
multimedia.breakaway.org/unityone/hiphop

HipHopBoomBox.com
www.hiphopboombox.com
A hiphop underground site with two radio shows and real audio for unsigned and independent artists, a music store, and much more hip hop info.

The Internet Ghetto Blaster
www.igb.com/

KBXX
Houston, TX
www.kbxx.com

BEST MUSIC BOOKS offers HUNDREDS of music books that can help to shape your career including *"How To Be Your Own Booking Agent and Save Thousands of Dollars"* by Jeri Goldstein and *"How To Promote Your Music Successfully on the Internet"* by David Neuve

www.bestmusicbooks.com

KJMM
Tulsa, OK
www.kjmm.com

KMJK Radio
Phoenix, AZ
www.kmjk.com

KMOJ
Minneapolis, MN
www.kmoj.com/home.html

KQBT
Austin, TX
www.beat1043.com

KXHT
Memphis, TN
www.hot107.com

MixMatrix
www.gogaga.com/channel.php3?stationName=Hip_Hop
MixMatrix throws down the best hip hop music at the cutting edge of turntablism. In addition to great mix sets, catch interviews and performances from top turntablists.

NTS Radio
nationtime.com/onpoint

Mafia1.com
www.mafia1.com

PHAT JAMZ.COM Radio
dj e-love
www.phatjamz.com

rap3000.com
www.rap3000.com

Radio Rukus
remus.rutgers.edu/~imielin/radioruckus

Rapmusic.com
www.rapmusic.com
Check out our Underground Artist Section and submit your artist info and/or get on our Radio Show for free.

Rebirth Radio
www.rebirthmag.com/rebirthradio.html

Strictly Headz Radio
Statesboro, GA
www.exploitedmusic.com/wvgs.htm

UNVRadio.com
www.unvradio.com

WBLX
Mobile, Alabama
www.93blx.com

WGGO
Washington D.C.
www.gogolive.com

WNAA
North Carolina A & T State University
drum.ncat.edu/~wnaa

WOWI
Norfolk, VA
www.wowifm.com

WYBC Radio
New Haven, CT
wybc@broadcast.com

Canada

CJLO
Concordia University
www.cjlo.qc.ca

France

Black Swing Radio
www.blackswing.com

Skyrock
www.skyrock.com

Italy

Radio Centro Suono
www.radiocentrosuono.it

Australia

The Mothership Connection
Mark Pollard editor@stealthmag.com
*Sydney;'s longest running hip hop show.
Tuesdays 2pm to 4pm. Station: 2SER
107.3FM*

Jazz/Blues/Folk Radio

Syndicated Shows

Acoustic Discoveries
www.angelfire.com/biz/acousticdigest/
discoveries.html
*For acoustic, jazz or world oriented
selections in limited syndication.*

Midnight Flyer
www.fatmusic.com/midnightflyer
Blues music.

Arizona

KUAZ
Tucson
w3.arizona.edu/~kuat/radio

California

Jazz Trax Syndicated Radio Show
San Diego
www.jazztrax.com

KCBX
San Luis Obispo
www.slonet.org/~ipkcbx

KCLU
California Lutheran College
www.kclu.org

KCSM
San Mateo
www.kcsm.org/jazz91.html

KCSN
California State University
www.kcsn.org

KEZL
Fresno
www.kezl.com

KIFM
San Diego
www.kifm.com

KKSF
San Francisco
www.kksf.com

KLON
California State University
www.klon.org

KPFK
Los Angeles
www.kpfk.org

KPOO
San Francisco
www.kpoofmsf.com/kpoohome.html

KSBR
Saddleback College
www.ksbr.net

KSDS
San Diego
www.ksds-fm.org

KUOP
University of the Pacific
www.kuop.org

Colorado

KCME
Colorado Springs
www.kcme.org

KUNC
University of Northern Colorado
www.kunc.org

KUVO
Denver
www.kuvo.org

Florida

WFIT
Florida Tech
www.fit.edu/CampusLife/clubs-org/wfit/

WKGC
Gulf Coast Community College
www.wkgc.org

WLNZ
Lansing Community College
www.lansing.cc.mi.us/sas/wlnz

WLRN
Miami
www.wlrn.org/fm

WUCF
University of Central Florida
wucf.ucf.edu

WUWF
Pensacola
www.uwf.edu/~wuwf

Georgia

WWGC
The State University of West Georgia
www.westga.edu/~wwgc

Idaho

BSU Radio Network
Boise State University
radio.boisestate.edu/
Radio Vision and Idaho's Jazz Station.

Illinois

The Midnight Special
www.midnightspecial.org

Sunday Blues Radio Show
www.sunday-blues.com

WBEZ
Chicago
www.wbez.org

Indiana

WFIU
Indiana University
www.indiana.edu/~wfiu

WPTI
Indianapolis
www.cde.psu.edu/EdComm/WPSUweb

WSND
University of Notre Dame
www.nd.edu/~wsnd

WVPE
Elkhart
www.wvpe.org
88.1 FM WVPE is public radio serving 17 counties in northern Indiana and southwest lower Michigan. We are 10,500 watt station that programs NPR news/talk, network jazz, and locally produced blues and folk/bluegrass shows.

The Blues Revue *is entering it's 17th year on WVPE. Hosted and produced by Harvey Stauffer, it airs Wednesday nights from 7pm to 12am as well as Saturday and Sunday afternoons from 1pm to 5pm. Harvey often includes interviews and performances.*

The Back Porch *is produced by Norm Mast and co-hosted by Norm Mast and Al Kniola. IT airs Sunday night from 8pm to 12am and includes traditional folk and bluegrass, with some Celtic and some contemporary folk. This show also features interviews and performances.*

Iowa

KALA
St.Ambrose University
galvin.sau.edu

KCCK
Kirkwood Community College
www.kcck.org

Kansas

KMUW
Wichita State University
www.kmuw.org

KRPS
Pittsburgh State University
www.krps.org

Kentucky

WNKU
Northern Kentucky University
www.nku.edu/~wnku

Louisiana

KRVS
University of Southern Louisiana
krvs.usl.edu

WBRH
Baton Rouge
www.intersurf.com/~aevinc/aev2wbrh.htm

WWOZ
New Orleans
www.wwoz.org
Jazz, Blues, World, Bluegrass.

Massachusetts

Blues Deluxe
www.rantersworld.net

WFCR
Amherst
www.wfcr.org
WFCR, public radio for Western New England, plays classical, jazz, folk, music of the African Diaspora, and "Tertulia," a Spanish-language program. Locally produced music programs are streamed in Real Audio.

WGBH
Boston
www.wgbh.org/wgbh/radio

Michigan

WDET
Wayne State Univesity
www.wdet.org

WGVU
Grand Rapids
www.wgvu.org/radio.html

Minnesota

KBEM
Minneapolis
www.mpls.k12.mn.us/kbem

KUMD
University of Minnesota
www.kumd.org

Rose Café
Minneapolis - St.Paul
Mark Moss
www.rosemusic.com/rosecafe.htm
An independently-produced, nationally-distributed public radio show featuring in-depth interviews.

Mississippi

WUSM
University of Southern Mississippi
www-dept.usm.edu/~wusm/index.shtml

Missouri

KCMW
Central Missouri State University
www.kcmw.cmsu.edu

KSMU
Springfield
www.ksmu.smsu.edu

WSIE
Edwardsville
www.siue.edu/WSIE

Montana

KUFM
University of Montana
www.kufm.org/

Nebraska

KIOS
Omaha
www.kios.org

New Hampshire

WEVO
Concord
www.nhpr.org

New Jersey

WBGO
Newark
www.wbgo.org

WBJB
Brookdale Community College
www.wbjb.org

New Mexico

KGLP
Gallup
www.kglp.com

New York

WAER
Syracuse
www.waer.org/

WBFO
University of Buffalo
www.wbfo.buffalo.edu

WEOS
Hobart and William Smith Colleges
www.hws.edu/~weos

WGMC
Greece
wgmc.greeceny.org

WKCR
Columbia Univeristy
www.columbia.edu/cu/wkcr

WPBX
Long Island University
www.southampton.liunet.edu/stu_serv/radio/radio.htm

WSHR
Sachem High School
www.wshr.com

WSKG/WSQX
Binghampton
www.wskg.com/radiowskg.htm

YLE Radio
New York, c/o MikaMusik, 333 E 14th Street, 9th floor; New York, NY 10003
Finish Jazz Show
Prime.BCC.CTC.EDU/KBCS
Public radio specializing in Jazz, Folk, and World Music.

North Carolina

WFSS
Fayetteville
www.uncfsu.edu/wfss

WZRU
Roanoke Rapids
www.schoollink.net/wzru

Ohio

WAPS
Akron Public School System
www.wapsfm.com

WKSU
Kent State University
www.wksu.kent.edu
Songwriters,Instrumentalists,Celtic,Bluegrass,Classics,and a trip through music somewhere around the world each hour, each night, every weekend.

WYSI
Antioch College
www.wyso.org

Oregon

KLCC
Eugene
www.klcc.org

KMHD
Mt. Hood Community College
www.kmhd.org

KMUN
Astoria
www.kmun.org/main/main.html

Pennsylvania

WPSU
Pennsylvania State University
www.wtpi.com

WRTI
Temple University
www.wrti.net

WYEP
Pittsburgh
www.wyep.org

South Dakota

KELO
Sioux Falls
www.kelofm.com

KUSD
Vermillion
www.sdpb.org/radio

Tennessee

WUTC
University of Tennessee
www.wutc.org

Texas

KNTU
University of North Texas
www.kntu.unt.edu

KTSU
Texas Southern University
www.ktsu.com

KTXK
Texarkana College
www.tc.cc.tx.us/ktxk

Utah

Breakfast Jam
www.krcl.org/~susannem

KUER
University of Utah
www.kuer.org

Vermont

WNCS
Montpelier
www.pointfm.com/wncs/wncs.htm

Virginia

WJCD
Norfolk
www.wjcd.com

WMRA
James Madison University
www.jmu.edu/wmra

Washington

KBCS
Bellevue
Prime.BCC.CTC.EDU/KBCS

KEWU
Eastern Washington University
www.class.ewu.edu/class/R%26TV/welcome.html

KPLU
Tacoma
www.kplu.org

Sundry Sound Spectrum
Craig Morrison   JOHAN7777@aol.com
14087 Olympic Dr SE,   Ollala, WA 98359
My show features jazz, ethnic music, spoken word, folk, and other uniquely diverse tunes that normally don't get so much air play. Please consider sending me some promotional CD's. I will put them in my own 'Sundry Sound Spectrum' library, and mention your record company during the broadcasts. The music would be played to eclectic audiences and everyone will be better off. Also, if you have anything EXTRA SPECIAL, please send multiple copies in order for me to do a CD-giveaway.

Washington DC

WPFW
www.capcity.com/wpfwradio/

Wisconsin

WUEC
University of Wisconsin/Eau Claire
www.wpr.org/schedule/wuec.htm

Internet

Bad Dog Blues Radio Show
www.baddogblues.com

The Blue Zone
bluezone.org

Blues Boy Music
www.bluesboymusic.com

Bluesbytes Music Network
www.bluesbytes.com

The Blues Summit Internet Radio
www.broadcast.com/radio/blues/blues

Jazz Man Music
www.jazzmanmusic.com

Australia

Acoustic Harvest
www.bit.net.au/~colin
The Acoustic Harvest site gives you presenter Biogs, Program details, lists of live artists on the program and playlist archives.

Japan

Beach FM
www.beachfm.co.jp

Metal Radio

Heavy, Thrash, Grindcore, Death, Black, Doom, Speed, Progressive and Viking metal.

North America

United States

Contamination Radio
www.screachen.com

Death Metal Radio Online
www.deathmetal.com

The Epic Metal Show
SUNY Oswego
www.oswego.edu/~wnyo
Listen to my show and find out that beer doesn't kill brain cells, I do!!

Extreme Radio
rocky.simplenet.com/radio
My site is for the extremist forms of metal only (death metal, black metal, grindcore...).

FMQB - Metal Detector Radio
www.fmqb.com/fmqb/metalf.html

Hard Times Radio
www.knon.org/Showpages/thu0800pm.htm

Heaven's Metal
www.angelfire.com/wv/heavensmetal
Christian metal.

Insolvent Radio
members.xoom.com/hukkapukka/hph.htm

Into the Pit Radio Show
www.98KUPD.com

KADU
www.kadu.org
Christian hard rock, punk etc.

KCUF
www.kcuf.org
Death metal,jazz, ambient/noise, black metal, grindcore, drone, electronica, funk, and heavy metal - this is radio you can sink your teeth into.

Khaos Metal Radio
www.nwez.net/KhaosMetal
A metal radio channel that specializes in unsigned and small label bands.

KNAC
www.knaclive.com
KNAC.com Pure Rock On The Net. Have you banged you head today?

Metal 101 Internet Radio
www.metal101.com
Classic Heavy Metal and Hard Rock Online in RealAudio.

Metal Meltdown Radio Show
www.jcu.edu/wjcu
(Friday 9:35-noon EDT) & WRUW radio.cwru.edu (Friday 2-3pm EDT)

Radio Death
www.radiodeath.com

Radio Freak
www2.cruzio.com/~frsc

Save time and money at **Indie-Music.com**, a free 1000+ page portal for musicians. Find 1000's of free contacts, list your band for free, book your tour, send in your music for review. One of the biggest and best musician sites on the internet.

Come Visit!

www.indie-music.com
E-mail: indie@indie-music.com

Rock and a Hard Place Radio Show
www.rockhardplace.com
Features independent and imported Rock, Metal, and AOR, or basically anything the Radio stations and Major Labels are ignoring. It's a two-hour pre-recorded program that will is marketed to radio stations as a specialty program. It's basically a rebellion against corporate rock and radio. The show will be highly produced with interviews, parodies, and lots of over-the-top attitude liners. There's nothing else like it because all the music chosen has had very little or no airplay in the states. The bands are all very good quality, and radio friendly so that stations will feel comfortable playing it on the airwaves.

All in all, it's a great way for bands to get some exposure. Demos will be sent to various labels, promotors, and of course, as many radio stations as possible.

Rebel Radio WJKL
Chicago, IL
Scott Davidson www.rebelradio.com

Savage Rock Radio
www.savagerockradio.com
The world's first and only Christian extreme metal radio station, Netcasting live 24/7 through BroadcastAmerica.com.

ShutEye Radio
www.nosebleed17.com

Snakenet Metal Radio
www.snakenetmetalradio.com

Vomit Radio
vomitradio.com

Canada

Skull Session Radio Show
www.geocities.com/SunsetStrip/Palms/4131/sesion.htm

Europe

Belgium

The Abyss
listen.to/the.abyss

Dakka Dakka Radio Show
www.starspawn.com/foob/dakka

Overdrive
users.skynet.be/~bs173522
The oldest Metal radioshow in Belgium.

Finland

Meteliä Maan Alta Rado Show
www.saunalahti.fi/brewer/meteliradio

France

Kerosine Radio
www.kfuel.fr.st/

Germany

Radio Beefhead
home.t-online.de/home/0406301559-0001

Stahlwerk-Hannover Radio Show
ourworld.compuserve.com/
Homepages/AxelAndre
The best of all kinds of metal (Speed, Thrash, Progressive, Death, Black, Gothic, Heavy Metal, of course we celebrate classics from the 80's).

What's Metal Radio Show
Markus "Maggi" Rehm
rehm@cip.biologie.uni-osnabrueck.de

Greece

Frozen Hell - Club Play
members.xoom.com/adenon
All of the CDs I get get are played at the best and most major metal clubs in Greece.

Norway

High Voltage Radio Show
www.geocities.com/SunsetStrip/
Towers/6468/HIGHVOLT.htm

Metal Express Radio Show
www.radiotango.no/metal

Portugal

S.O.S Heavy Metal Radio Show
www.angelfire.com/mb/sosradio

Romania

Radio Sky Constanta The Underground Show
Razvan Radu undersky@Relay.modarex.ro
www.radiosky.ro/
I have the #1 radio show in Romania. If any band or label wants to make a good promotion over here, contact me.

Radio Sonic Transilvania
raresion.cjb.net/
Rares Ion raresion@yahoo.com
POBox13-9 3400 Cluj-Napoca, Romania
You can send me promotional stuff, your latest/old releases, the latest news, and I will make well known your bands/labels in my country.

Spain

Emisión Sin Fronteras Radio Show
www.arrakis.es/~servan

La Espiral Descendente Radio Show
members.xoom.com/agur/pititako.html

Metal Age Radio Show
www.gracianet.org/pica

Australia

3 Hours of Power Radio Show
www.abc.net.au/triplej/power/default.htm

Critical Mass Radio Show
www.rtrfm.iinet.net.au/crtclmas

The Hard Report Radio Show
compsoc.cs.latrobe.edu.au:6969/hardreport2000

Metal Head Radio Show
www.shoal.net.au/~metalhead

Punk Radio

Punk, Ska, Hardcore, Emo, oi

United States

All Your Favorite Bands Suck
userwww.service.emory.edu/~kander2

Thee Attick of True Punk Radio Show
punkgarage.com

Bandoppler Radio
www.bandoppler.com
Christian punk.

The Bonus Cup Radio Show
www.fau.edu/wowl/djs/ellen
Playing punk rock and indie bands that feature female members.

Concrete Radio
clix.to/crzine

DALnet Punk Radio Show
punk.w1.net/radio.htm

Dirtnap Radio
Ken Wisconsin
www.antennaradio.com/punk/dirtnapradio

Disruptive Youth Internet Radio
www.geocities.com/SunsetStrip/Birdland/5741

Frenzy Radio
www.frenzyradio.com/
Submissions must be in MP3 format.

Froggy McKillop's Radio Show
froggy@nebula-x.com
www.kdvs.org
My show is on Wednesdays from 9:30 to noon and I play mostly rock, punk, ska, hardcore, and Sacramento area bands.

The Fuddy Duddy Radio Show
home.earthlink.net/~fuddyduddy
Syndicated show.

Gift Wrapped Crap
www.antennaradio.com/punk/giftwrappedcrap

Hukka Pukka Radio
members.xoom.com/hukkapukka/hph.htm

In the Red
www.intheredradio.com

Internet Radio Pigdog
www.pigdog.threadnet.com

Johnny Chiba's World Punk Aggressive Alternative Internet Radio Webshow
www2.collegemusic.com/content/livecasts/chiba.asp
Punk-Dub-Death Metal-Hendrix-Trip Hop-Astor Piazolla. Live Wednesday, 7-9PM EST.USA - Archived Anytime.

PANX Radio
www.panx.net/panxradio

Punk Page Radio
www.punkpage.net/home.html

punkradio.com
www.punkradio.com

The Rudenet Ska Show
www.rudenet.com

Shredding Radio
www.shreddingradio.com

The Ska Parade Radio Show
rudenet.com/skaparade

WDOA.com
wdoa.com

Zombie Radio
209.3.65.37/frames.html

Canada

Flex Your Head Radio Show
flexyourhead.vancouverhardcore.com
Hardcore/punk radio program (on CITR 101.9 fm) and website.

Kicked in the Head
www.kickedinthehead.uni.cc

Mods and Rockers
home.ica.net/~tpal/mnr

On the Edge of Sanity Radio Show
Candace Mooerscamooers@hotmail.com
Wednesday night from 8 pm - 9:30 pm (atlantic times). Can tune in on the internet with Real Audio at chsr/web/unb.ca. I play punk, hardcore and maybe an occasional dose of ska and metal.

Raw Energy Radio
rawenergy.passport.ca

Mexico

Detras del ruido
www.geocities.com/SunsetStrip/Alley/8766

Belgium

Rocklabyrinth
users.skynet.be/rocklab

Finland

Ilmestyskirja Radio Show
www.yle.fi/radiomafia/ohjelmat/hilu/hilu.htm

Meteliä Maan Alta Radio Show
www.saunalahti.fi/~brewer/meteliradio/

France

Ecrasons La Vermine
ecrase.citeweb.net

Germany

Subversiv Radio Show
Timo SchliepSubversiv_Radio@gmx.de
Punk,HC,Ska in Oldenburg, every second Thursday at 5pm. Stuff will also get a review in the Benzine Fanzine.

Italy

SkabadiP Radio Show
skabadip.submusic.org

World Music Radio

Africa No. 1
www.africa1.com

Aloha Joe Radio Show
Hawaii
www.alohajoe.com
All styles of music from the Island will get airplay.

Bayou Boogie Radio Show
www.bayoubeat.com

DubWire
www.dubwire.com
The net's champion source for Reggae music. DubWire.com is a continuous stream of dub, ska, dancehall, and roots reggae brought to you by some of the nations leading reggae producers.

Eardrum
www.gogaga.com/channel.php3?stationName=World
The Internet's most comprehensive world music station, featuring international music from every culture. Music Radio Station is the Internet's most comprehensive world music station, featuring international music from every culture.

Echoes in the Wind
Valerie Cartonio echoes@customnet.com
my.treeway.com/echoes
Native American Radio Program featuring all areas of music

Gilles Peterson's Radio Show (BBC 1)
www.bbc.co.uk/radio1/djs/peterson.shtml

KBOO
Portland, OR
www.spiritone.com/~kboo

KGOU
University of Oklahoma
www.kgou.org

Linkup Radio
www.linkupradio.com
Caribbean Music.

Prairie Ceilidh Radio Show
www.escape.ca/~skinner/pc/pc.html
Celtic Music. We are especially interested in independent releases. Please send correspondence and promotional cassettes and CD's, for on-air-play.

Radio 4EB
www.4eb.org.au

Radio Blandengue
South America
members.xoom.com/blandengue
The musical style of our programs is basically Latin American, from the music of the Island of Passover to Mexican folk music.

Radio Monde
www.radiomonde.com
Quebecois Music.

Raizes Radio Show
Prime.BCC.CTC.EDU/KBCS
Roots in Portuguese, explores the music and culture of Brazil and its neighbors, with interviews and calendar.

reggaeradiostation.com
www.reggaeradiostation.com

SFB4 MultiKulti
Germany
www.multikulti.de

Vibe FM
Ghana
www.vibefm.com.gh

WLIB
www.wlib.com

World Music Radio
www.worldmusicradio.com
An independent Internet-only live-hosted radio station featuring traditional and contemporary world and folk music.

WSHL
Stonehill College
WSHL, 320 Washington Street,
Easton MA 02357
www.stonehill.edu/WSHL
We have a great interest in World Music (Latin, Asian, Spanish music etc) and also local music from the New England area.

WTMD
Towsen University, MD
www.towson.edu/wtmd

Radio Shows that Spotlight Local Musicians

"Local" is a relative term. To some stations, "local" describes anyone within the city limits, and perhaps a bit outside of them. Others consider "local" to be any person within the listening area. There are many shows that consider "local" to be musicians from anywhere within the state or province, while others consider "local" to be an artist from any region of the host country. If you're not sure if you qualify for a particular show, get in touch with the station (or host), and in most cases they will happily respond.

United States

Alabama

WLRH *Sundial (Jazz)*
Huntsville
www.wlrh.org/index.shtml

WVUA *The Lee and Wolfe Show* (live music)
Tuscaloosa Musician - University of Alabama
www.newrock907.com/

Alaska

KBBI *Homer City Limits*
Homer
www.kbbi.org
Sometimes spotlights local acts.

KSUP
Juneau
www.ptialaska.net/~ksup
No specific show but we'll play local music.

Arizona

KDDJ/KEDG *The Local Music Spotlight*
Globe/Phoenix/Sun City
www.accessarizona.com/partners/kedj

KDKB *Desert Tracks*
Mesa
www.kdkb.com

KEDJ *Local Music Spotlight*
Phoenix
www.accessarizona.com/partners/kedj

KFLX *The Local Music Hour*
Flagstaff-Kachina Village
www.kflx.com

KFMA *New Music Test Department*
Tucson
www.kfma.com

KUPD *Local 98 Rock*
Tempe
www.98KUPD.com

KXCI *Locals Only*
Tucson
www.kxci.org

KZGL
Flagstaff
www.kzgl.com
Has several shows that spotlight local talent.

KZON *Local Zone*
Phoenix
www.kzon.com

Arkansas

WXFX *The Fox Consumer Guide to New Rock*
Prattville
www.wxfx.com

KDRE *Lick at Nite: The Local Band Show*
Little Rock
www.lick965.com/

California

KALX *KALX Live! (in studio performing), The Sunday Morning Show (Rap and Hip Hop)*
Berkeley
oms1.berkeley.edu/kalx

KCPR *The Local Beat*
California Poly State University
www.kcpr.org
Music and live performances.

KCR *Jocelyne's Show*
San Diego College
kahuna.sdsu.edu/kcr

KFOG *Local Anesthetic*
San Francisco
www.kfog.com

KIOZ *Latitude 32*
San Diego
www.kioz.com

KJEE *Localize It*
Monticeto - Santa Barbara
www.kjee.com

KKUP *The Wimmin's Music Program*
Cupertino
www.KKUP.com

KLOS *Local Licks*
Los Angeles
www.955klos.com

KLYY *Local Licks*
Arcadia
www.y107radio.com

KPFA/KFCF *Across the Great Divide (folk)*
Berkeley/Fresno
www.kpfa.org

KPIG *Local Show*
Watsonville
www.kpig.com

KRFH *Local Licks*
Humbolt College
www.humboldt.edu/~krfh

KROQ *Music From Your Own Backyard*
Los Angeles
www.kroq.com

KRXQ *Local Licks*
Sacramento
www.krxq98rock.com

KRZR *Play it by Ear*
Hanford
www.krzr.com

KSDS *Local Jazz Corner*
San Diego
www.ksds-fm.org

KSDT Saturated Phat (Hip Hop), Red Hot Radio (all styles)
University of California - San Diego
scw.ucsd.edu/ksdt

KSUN *The Jungle (Hip Hop to Punk), In the Garage (Punk), Dumpster Diving (Punk), Happy Hour (Punk), The T@x Collection (variety)*
Sonoma State University
www.sonoma.edu/ksun

KUSP *The Chaos Theory (punk/ska)*
Santa Cruz
www.kusp.org

KWOD *Sound of Sacramento*
www.kwod.com

KXLU *Demolisten*
Loyola - Marymount University
www.lmu.edu/stuaff/kxlu/kxlu.htm

KXST *Backroom Break*
Oceanside
www.sets102.com

KZAP
Chico
www.kzap.com
No specific local show, but the station urges locals to submit music for airplay consideration.

KZSU *Wednesday Night Live*
Stanford University
kzsu.stanford.edu

XHRM *The Local Fix*
San Diego
www.92five.com

XTRA *Loudspeaker*
San Diego
www.91x.com/newindex.html

Z90
San Diego
www.z90.com
Plays the music of local artists. Mostly dance and Hip Hop.

Colorado

KSRX
The University of Northern Colorado
www.univnorthco.edu/ksrx
We like to spotlight Colorado bands that have recordings available.

KTCL Locals Only
Denver
www.ktcl.com

KVCU *The Local Show*
University of Colorado
www.colorado.edu/StudentGroups/KVCU

Connecticut

WCNI *Rhythmic Variations (Techno)*
Connecticut College
oak.cc.conncoll.edu/wcni

WHUS *Bluesline, One World Radio, Sunday Night Folk Festival*
Storrs
whusfm.saup.uconn.edu

WPKN *New Music Nights, Off-Beat*
University of Bridgeport
www.wpkn.org/wpkn

WPLR *Local Bands*
Hamden
www.wplr.com

WSHU/WSUF *Profiles in Folk, Acoustic Connection*
New York and Connecticut
www.wshu.org

Delaware

WRDX *Breaking and Entering*
Claymont
www.wrdx.com

WSTW *Hometown Heros*
Wilmington
www.wstw.com

Florida

Rock 104 *Locals Only*
Gainesville
www.rock104.com

WFYV
Jacksonville
www.wfyv105.com/rock105/rock105.htm
We don't specifically have a show but if something good comes down the pipe, we will definately give it consideration for airplay!

WJBX *Orbit Nightclub*
Fort Myers
www.99xwjbx.com

WJRR *Native Noise*
Orlando
www.wjrr.com

WKRO
Daytona Beach
www.wkro.com
No specific show - but are willing to play local music.

WLRN/WXEL *Folk & Acoustic Music Show*
Miami/West Palm Beach
wlrn.org/fm

WMNF *Live Music Showcase*
Tampa Community College
www.wmtx.com

WPLA *Native Noise*
Jacksonville
www.planet93.com

WPRK *WPRK Comes Alive*
Rollins College
www.rollins.edu/wprk

WRUF *Gama Radio Rendezvous*
Gainesville
www.rock104.com

WTKX
Pensacola
www.tk101.com
We'll listen to anything that is sent to us.

WVFS *Hootenanny*
Florida State University
www.wvfs.fsu.edu

WVUM *Locals Only*
University of Miami
www.miami.edu/wvum

WWRR
www.wwrr.net
The World Wide Radio Renaissance features a playlist of Independent Florida bands exclusively. The seven hour show is produced weekly.

WZTA *Zeta Goes Local*
Miami Beach
www.949zeta.com

Georgia

WKLS *The Peach Jam*
Atlanta
www.96rock.com

WNNX *Locals Only*
Atlanta
www.99x.com

WPUP *Local Noise*
Royston
www.rock1037.com

WRAS *Georgia Music Show*
Georgia State University
www.wras.org

WREK *Live at WREK*
Georgia Tech
cyberbuzz.gatech.edu/wrek

WRFG *Live at the Attic (live acoustic)*
Atlanta
www.wrfg.org

WUOG
University of Georgia
www.uga.edu/~wuog
The local music department follows the Georgia music scene (primarily Athens/Atlanta) to program local artists, as well as producing live performances of local acts at the station. We screen local music, book artists for station remotes, and help out with other Athens' events invloving local musicians.

Hawaii

KTUH *Monday Night Live*
University of Hawaii
ktuh.hawaii.edu

Illinois

WKQX *Local 101*
www.q101.com
The best of Chicago music, signed, unsigned, new and old. Send submissions to: Local 101 PO BOX 3404, Chicago IL 60654.

WDCB *Folk Festival, Strictly Bluegrass*
College of DuPage
www.cod.edu/wdcb

WEEF *The World We Play In*
Chicago
home.earthlink.net/~worldweplay

WEFT *WEFT Sessions (live performance),* SpotLite
Champaign-Urbana
www.8am.com/weft

WESN *The Local Music Show*
Illinois Wesleyan University
www.iwu.edu/~wesn

WOUI
Illinois Institute of Technology
www.iit.edu/~woui
We have a few shows that specialize in local music!

WPGU *Innerlimits*
University of Illinois
www.wpgu.com

WRCX *Chicago Rock*
Chicago
www.rock1035.com

WUIC
Chicago
www.flamesradio.com
Will play local music.

WWCT *Poor Man's Concert (live performance)*
Peoria
www.rock106.com

WXRT *Local Anesthetic*
Chicago
www.wxrt.com

WZNX *Local Rock*
Decatur
www.wznx.com

Indiana

WCRD *Local Show (Thursdays)*
Ball State University
www.tcom.bsu.edu/wcrd/

WFHB *The Local Show*
Indiana Univeristy
www.bluemarble.net/~wfhb

WRBR *Michiana's Finest Homegrown*
Mishawaka
www.wrbr.com

WRZX *Locals Only*
Indianapolis
www.wrzx.com

WTTS *Hoosier Spotlight*
Bloomington
www.wttsfm.com

Iowa

KAZR *Local Licks*
Des Moines
www.lazer1033.com

KKEZ
Fort Dodge
www.kkez.com
No specific show, but will play the music of local artists.

Kansas

KJHK *Plow the Fields*
University of Kansas
kjhk.ukans.edu

KLZR *Local Lazer Music*
Lawrence
www.lazer.com

KSDB
Kansas State University
wildcatradio.ksu.edu
Local show every Saturday.

Kentucky

WNKU *Local Heroes*
Northern Kentucky University
www.nku.edu/~wnku

WRFL *Local Show*
University of Kentucky
www.uky.edu/~wrfl

WTFX *Unsigned Primetime*
Louiseville
www.wtfx.com/wtfx.html

Louisiana

KKND *Locals At Eleven*
New Orleans
www.kknd.com

KLSU *Saturated Neighborhood*
Louisiana State University
klsu.stumedia.lsu.edu

KNSU
Nicholls State University
knsu@mail.nich.edu
listen.to/theedge
Both a local spotlight and live show are in the works.

KRVS *Dirty Rice*
Univeristy of Southern Louisiana
krvs.usl.edu

LOUISIANARADIO.com
www.louisianaradio.com

WBRH *Crescent City Sounds (Jazz/Blues)*
Baton Rouge
www.intersurf.com/~aevinc/aev2wbrh.htm

WRKF *The General Store (acoustic-folk)*
Baton Rouge
www.wrkf.org

WTUL
Tulane University
www.tulane.edu/~wtul
Local Show every Saturday.

Maine

WCDQ *Local Chords*
Sanford
www.wcdq.com

WMPG *Fabalus Folk, In Your Ear, Local Motives, The Real Placebo (Jazz), Some Like It Hot (Reggae, Ska), Swank, Us Folk*
University of Southern Maine
www.wmpg.org

WRBC *Community Forum*
Bates College
www.bates.edu/people/orgs/wrbc

Maryland

WIYY *Noise In The Basement, Friday Night Live*
Baltimore
www.98online.com

WMUC *Local Show*
University of Maryland
wmuc.umd.edu

WWDC *Local Lix*
Silver Springs
dc101.com

Massachusetts

BCR *The Ska of Boston*
Babson College
radio.babson.edu

Mass Comm Web Radio
Massachusetts Communications College
www.masscomm.edu/masscomm_radio_online/mcradio1.htm
A globally reaching radio station entirely "broadcast" over the World Wide Web. It features most prominently the music of Boston and its unsigned lesser known bands, who are on the road to fame.

RadioBoston.com
www.radioboston.com

WAAF *Bay State Rock*
Westboro
www.waaf.com

WAMH *Live Concert*
Amherst College
www.amherst.edu/~wamh

WBCN *Boston Emissions*
Boston
www.wbcn.com

WBNW *Business for Breakfast*
Newton
www.1120wbnw.com

WBRS *The WBRS Coffeehouse, The Joint*
Brandeis University
www.wbrs.org

WERS *Boston Unscene*
Emerson College
pages.emerson.edu/organizations/wers

WFMO *Hardcore Heroes, On The Town, Folk and Good Music Show*
Tufts University
www.jumbohub.com/wmfo

WFNX *Boston Product*
Lynn
fnxradio.com/home.html

WGBH *Jazz from Studio Four*
Boston
www.wgbh.org/wgbh/radio

WJUL *Live from the Fallout Shelter*
University of Massachusetts
www.uml.edu/misc/WJUL

WKPE *The Cheap Seats*
Orleans
www.rock1047.com

WMBR *Pipeline Tuesdays*
Cambridge
wmbr.mit.edu
Pipeline features a live band each week as well as new local music. We define 'local' to liberally cover all the New England states from Connecticut to Maine and Vermont.

WMRB *Pipeline, "3" (drum and bass), Bats in the Belfry (Gothic), Jam Session*
Massachusetts Institute of Technology
wmbr.mit.edu

WMVY *The Local Music Show*
Tisbury
wmvy.vineyard.net

WMWM *The Nor' Easter*
Salem State College
wmwm.star.net

WPXC *Homegrown*
Hyannis
www.pixy103.com

WRSI *Up the Creek*
Greenfield
www.wrsi.com

WSMU *Local Anesthesia*
Univeristy of Mass/Dartmouth
www.des.umassd.edu/wsmu.html

WTBU *Sublimity*
Boston University
www.bu.edu/com/WTBU

WZBC *Mass. Avenue and Beyond*
Boston College
www.bc.edu/bc_org/svp/st_org/wzbc

Michigan

WCBN *The Local Music Show*
University of Michigan
www.wcbn.org

WCEN *Backyard Bootleg (Country)*
Mount Pleasant
www.wcen.com

WDBM *The Basement*
Michigan State University
www.wdbm.msu.edu

WDET *The Martin Bandyke Program*
Wayne State Univesity
www.wdet.org

WGRD *RadioActiv*
Grand Rapids
www.wgrd.com

WIDR *Big Fat Local Show*
Western Michigan University
www.widr.org

WJXQ *The PIT (metal)*
Lansing
www.voyager.net/q106

WMHW *The Scene*
Central Michigan University
www.bca.cmich.edu/modern_rock_91.htm

WNMC *Folkaire*
Northwestern Michigan College
www.nmc.edu/~wnmc

WRIF *Motor City RIFFS*
Detroit
www.wrif.com

WWBN *The BANANA 101.5 Soundcheck*
Flint
www.banana1015.com/banana

WWGZ *Studio X*
Lapeer
www.radioxrock103.com

Minnesota

KFAI *Local Sound Department (LSD)*
Minneapolis - St. Paul
members.aol.com/TheDanOne/lsd.htm

KTCZ *Minnesota Music*
Bill Deville
www.cities97.com

KVSC *Monday Night Live*
Saint Cloud State University
www.kvsc.org

KXXR *Loud & Local*
Minneapolis
Patrickwww.93x.com

KZNZ *Popular Creeps (live performances)*
Golden Valley
www.zone105.com

Radio K *Off the Record*
University of Minnesota
www.cee.umn.edu/radiok

WHMH *Minnesota Homegrown*
Sauk Rapids
www.rockin101.com

Mississippi

WMSV *Homegrown*
Mississippi State University
www.wmsv.msstate.edu

Missouri

KPNT *The Local Show*
St. Louis
www.kpnt.com

KWJC *The Session*
William Jewell College
www.91-9.com

KWUR *The Side Trip*
Washington University
kwur.wustl.edu

WSIE *Six O'Clock Blues*
Edwardsville
www.siue.edu/WSIE

WXTM *Monday Night Metal Live*
St.Louis
www.extremeradio1041.com
Prizes include studio time.

KDHX *The Grand Tour, St.Louis' Finest*
www.kdhx.org

Montana

KBGA *The Local Show, Live in Missoula*
University of Montana
kbga.org

KCFV
St.Louis Community College
www.stlcc.cc.mo.us/fv/kcfv
Waller has a half hour local show on
Tuesdays between 2:30 - 3:00.

KUFM *Musician's Spotlight, Mountain Stage (folk/rock)*
University of Montana
www.umt.edu/kufm

Nebraska

KEZO *Z-92's Homegrown*
Omaha
www.z92.com

KIBZ *Sunday Night Buzz*
Lincoln
www.kibz.com

KVNO *River City Folk*
University of Nebraska
www.kvno.unomaha.edu

KZUM *Alive in Lincoln, River City Folk*
Lincoln
www.kzum.org

Nevada

KOMP *The Home Grown Show*
Las Vegas
www.komp.com/komp/main.cfm

Las Vegas Local Radio
Las Vegas
www.lvlocalradio.com

New Hampshire

WHEB *Local Licks*
Portsmouth
www.wheb.com

New Jersey

WBZC *Burlington County Bluegrass,
World In Tune, Roadhouse Radio*
Burlington County College
staff.bcc.edu/radio/

WDHA *Homegrown Spotlight*
Cedar Knolls
www.wdhafm.com

WFMU
Jersey City
www.wfmu.org
Many local acts perform live in the studio.

WHTG *Local Licks Spotlight*
Eatontown
www.fm1063.com

WKOE
Ocean City
www.1063theshore.com
No show - but are willing to play local music.

WNTI *Internet Music Theatre, Sweaty Palms*
Centenary College
www.wnti.org
Promotes local talent.

WSOU *Street Patrol (local hardrock)*
Seton Hall University
wsou.shu.edu/

WTSR *Dayside/Local Noise*
The College of New Jersey
www.TCNJ.EDU/~wtsr

WZXL *Open Mike Wednesday*
Wildwood
www.wzxlradio.com/open_mic

New Mexico

KRUX
New Mexico State University
www.nmsu.edu/Campus_Life/KRUX/public_html
Two Hour Local Show on Monday nights

KTAO *Acoustic Café*
Taos
www.ktao.com

KTEG *Local Edge*
www.1079theedge.com

KZRR
Albuquerque
www.94rock.com/kzrr
Local Show is in the works - now accepting demos.

New York

WAQX *Soundcheck*
Syracuse
www.waqx.com

WBAB *Homegrown*
Long Island
www.wbab.com

WBER *The Indie Show*
Monroe College
wber.monroe.edu/
Wednesday nights from 9-11pm. Specializes in only Independent label music. It also features local stuff from the Rochester, Buffalo and Syracuse area. Bands can send stuff to WBER Attn: Joey 2596 Baird Rd Penfield, NY 14526-2333.

WBNY *Local Music*
Buffalo College
www.wnymusic.com/wbny

WCMF *Home Grown*
Rochester
www.96wcmf.com

WEDG *Over & Beyond*
Buffalo
www.wedg.com

WGFR *The Local Show*
Adirondack Community College
wgfr.org

WHPC *Saturday Rock*
Nassau Community College
www.sunynassau.edu/dptpages/whpc/whpc.htm
When it comes to the local music scene nobody covers it all like WHPC.

WHRW *Local Product*
SUNY Binghamton
www.whrw.org

WICB *Home Brew*
Ithaca College
www.ithaca.edu/radio/wicb

WITR *Rochester Sessions, Rochester Beats*
Rochester Institute of Technology
www.modernmusicandmore.com

WLIR *Tri-State Sound*
Garden City
www.wlir.com

WQBK *The Local Show*
Albany
www.wqbk.com/Home/index.cfm

WRCN *Local Buzz*
Riverhead
www.wrcn.com

WRUB *The Scene*
SUNY University at Buffalo
wings.buffalo.edu/wrub

WUSB *Long Island Music Vista*
SUNY Stoneybrook
www.wusb.org

WVBR *Radio Free Ithaca*
Ithica
www.publiccom.com/web/wvbr

North Carolina

WRQR *Homegrown Music*
Wilmington
www.wrqr.com

WTPT *Upstate at 8*
Forest City
www.93planet.com

WXDU *Live From The XDU Lounge*
Duke University
www.wxdu.duke.edu

WXNR *Local 99*
New Bern
www.wxnr.com

WXRA *Localz at 11*
Winston-Salem
www.wxra945.com

WXYC *Backyard Barbecue*
University of North Carolina
www.wxyc.com

WZMB *Locals Only*
East Carolina University
www.studentmedia.ecu.edu/wzmb/index.htm

Ohio

KBUX *Tones of Home*
Ohio State University
kbux.ohio-state.edu
We also have slots once or twice every hour where djs have to play local artists.

The Village Buzz Radio
Ashland
www.village-buzz.com/
All the cool with the n/e ohio music scene.

WBGU *Second Stage*
Bowling Green State University
www.wbgufm.org

WBUZ *Local Buzz*
Toledo
www.purerock106.com

WBWC *Local Artist Show*
Berea
www.bw.edu/~wbwc

WBZX *Local Stuff*
Columbus
www.wbzx.com/theblitz

WCSB *Blue Monday (blues), The True Unda Ground (truth hip hop) Horsepower (punk)*
Cleveland State University
wcsb.org

WIOT
Toledo
www.wiot.com
No specific show - but are willing to play local music.

WJCU *Fuzz*
John Carroll University
www.jcu.edu/wjcu/schedule.htm

WNXT *HOMEGROWN X*
Portsmouth
www.zoomnet.net/~wnxt

WOBC *The Metal Storm*
Oberlin College
www.oberlin.edu/~WOBC

WOXY *Local Lixx, Homebrew*
Oxford
www.woxy97x.com

WWCD *Front Stage*
Columbus
www.cd101.com

WXEG *Joe's Garage*
Beavercreek
www.edge1039.com

WXUT *Local Show*
University of Toledo
members.tripod.com/~PunkandSka/wxut.html

Oklahoma

KATT *KATT's Local Talent Show*
Oklahoma City
www.katt.com

KMOD *Local Licks at Six*
Tulsa
www.kmod.com

Oregon

KBOO *Folk Expresso, The Church of North West Music, The Family Hours (R&B and Hip Hop) E Ho'omau Na Nohona (local Hawiian Bands), Movin' On (folky - jazz)*
Portland
www.spiritone.com/~kboo

KBVR *Locals Live*
Oregon State University
osu.orst.edu/dept/kbvr

KEOL
La Grande
www.eosc.osshe.edu/~keol/keol.html
There are many locals only shows. Some encompass only the immediate local area; others reach out to all of Oregon, and still others go beyond into eastern Washington and Idaho.

KINK *Local Spotlight*
Portland
Cindy Hanson
www.kinkfm102.com

KLCC *Friends and Neighbors*
Eugene
www.klcc.org

KLRR *Homegrown Clear Music Showcase*
Bend
www.klrr.com

KPSU *PDX Static*
Portland State University
www.kpsu.org

Pennsylvania

WDVE *The Homegrown Show*
Pittsburgh
www.dve.com

WEZX
Scranton
www.rock107.com
No specific show - but are willing to play local music.

WHYY *Folk Music with Gene Shay*
Philadelphia
whyy.org/91FM

WLVR *Radio Revolution, Michael Stockton & Brian Newbury's Show*
Lehigh University
www.Lehigh.EDU/~inwlv

WNWR/WWZK *Pipeline Radio Show*
PA, NJ and Deleware
www.ootweb.com

WPLY *Tuesday Night Music Club*
Philadelphia
www.y100.com

WPTS *Local Live*
University of Pittsburgh
www.wpts.pitt.edu

WRSK *Passed Out by the stereo, Lunch With Ahh*
Slippery Rock University
wrsk.homepage.com/

WRVV *Open Mic Night*
Harrisburg
www.river973.com

WTPA *The Homegrown Show*
Mechanicsburg
www.935wtpa.com

WVIA *Homegrown Music*
Pittston
www.wvia.org/fm/fm.html

WXDX *The Pittsburgh X-Files*
Pittsburgh
www.wxdx.com

WXLV *The Phil Stahl Show (live music)*
Lehigh Carbon Community College
www.wxlvfm.com

WXPN *Philly Local Pick of the Day*
University of Pennsylvania
xpn.org/homepage.html

WZZO *Backyard Bands*
Bethlehem
www.wzzo.com

Rhode Island

WBRU *Home BRU'd*
Brown University
www.wbru.com

WHIY *Soundcheck*
Providence
www.whjy.com

WHJY *Soundcheck*
Providence
www.whjy.com

WRIU *The Live Show*
University of Rhode Island
www.pigsfeet.net/jockrock/wriu.html

South Carolina

WARQ *Locals @ Eleven*
Columbia
www.warq.com

WHAT *Folkways*
Clemson
www.carol.net/gcb/waht/MainNoframes.html

WROQ *An Hour From Atlanta To Charlotte*
Greenville
www.wroq.com

WUSC *Locals Only*
University of South Carolina
wusc.sc.edu/

South Dakota

KDDX *New Music Spotlight*
Spearfish
www.biffs.com

KUSD *House Blend (folky - jazz)*
Vermillion
www.sdpb.org/radio

Tennessee

WEVL *The Memphis Beat*
Memphis
wevl.org

WMTS *Locals Only*
Middle Tennessee State University
www.mtsu.edu/~wmts

WRLT *Nashville Sunday Night*
www.wrlt.com

WUTK *Tennessee Tracks*
University of Tennessee
sunsite.utk.edu/newrock

Texas

Humble Time Texas Radio Showcase
Freiheit
www.humbletime.com

KACC
Alvin
forsythe@kacc-rtv.com
We have a classic and new rock format, with attention given to local artists.

KACV *The Texas Brand*
Amarillo College
www.kacvfm.org

KAZI *Local Artist Showcase*
Austin
kazinews@aol.com

KBEC
Waxahachie
711 Ferris Avenue; Waxahachie, TX 75165
A Texas artist is played once every five songs.

KBRZ
Freeport
www.kbrz.com
Programming includes local and regional artists.

KBXX *Straight From the Streets (Hip Hop)*
Houston
www.kbxx.com

KDGE *Best of Texas*
Dallas
www.kdge.com

KEGL *The Local Show, Unmodern Rock Program*
Fort Worth
www.kegl.com

KFAN *Local Licks*
Fredricksburg
www.texasrebelradio.com

KFMX *Local Lix/Hot Lix*
Lubbock
www.kfmx.com

KGSR *The Daily Demo, Lone Star State of Mind*
Austin
www.kgsr.com

KHLR *Exposure*
Bryan
www.1039.com

KHOY *Laredo*
www.goccn.org/khoy
Featuring inspirational and easy listening music, including local artists.

KHYI *Texas Music Review*
Plano
www.khyi.com

KISS *Texas Tracks*
San Antonio
www.kissrocks.com

KJBC
1903 South Lamesa Road;
Midland TX 79701
Features local and Texas artists.

KKIK
608 Moody Lane; Temple TX 76504
We work closely with the Texas Country Music Association for Texas angles on music and showcases of local artists.

KKYX *Lonestar Hour*
San Antonio
www.kkyx.com

KKZN *The Lone Star Radio*
Dallas
www.dfwradio.com

KLAK *Garage*
El Paso
www.klaq.com

KLBJ *Local Licks*
Austin
www.lbj.com/fm

KOOP *Live Bait, Around the Town Sounds*
Austin
www.koop.org

KORA *Swingin with the Armadillo*
Bryan
www.korafm.com
Programming includes many Texas acts in regular rotation.

KPAN
Hereford
kpan@wtrt.net
We host live local music on occasion.

KPFT *Lonestar Jukebox, Spare Change*
Houston
www.kpft.org

KPLX *Live From the Front Porch*
Dallas
www.995thewolf.com

KPYK
P.O. Box 157; Terrell, TX 75160
Emphasis on Texas artists with a spotlight on artists from the local area.

KRAD *Local Licks*
1300 Antelope Street; Corpus Christi, TX 78401

KSTV *The Best In Texas Music*
Stephenville
www.kstvfm.com

KSTX *Sunday Nite Session*
San Antonio
www.tpr.org

KSYM *The Live Show*
San Antonio College
www.accd.edu/sac/rtf/ksym.htm

KTRU *The Local Show*
Houston
www.ktru.org/ktru.html

KTSR
College Station
www.ktsr.com
A 3,000-watt station featuring mainstream and classic rock. Texas acts are encouraged to send us your tapes for airing.

KTXT *Lone Star Radio*
Texas Tech University
www.ttu.edu/~ktxt

KUT/KUTX *LiveSet, Folkways. Texas Radio*
Austin/San Angelo
www.kut.org

KVLU
Lamar University
hal.lamar.edu/~kvlu
Texas artists are featured on all of our local programs.

KVRX *Texas Music, Local Live*
University of Texas/Austin
www.utexas.edu/students/kvrx/index2.html

KVST *Taste of Texas*
Conroe
www.kvst.com

KVWG
P.O. Box K; Pearsall, TX 78061
Emphasis is on local entertainment featuring local and national artists.

KYKM/KHLT *Texas Six Pack at Six*
Hallettsville
coffman@cvtv.net

KZZN
P.O. Box 510; Littlefield, TX 79339
We play a lot of local talent and feature live performances.

Micro Kind Radio *Local Live Music, What's The Story Dave?*
San Marcos
Willy One Blood and Dave
www.mediadesign.net/kindmenu.htm

ZUT
Austin, San Angelo
www.kut.org
We have many shows that play the music of local artists.

Vermont

WBTZ *Buzz Homebrew*
Burlington
www.999thebuzz.com

WEBK *Local's Spotlight*
Killington
www.webk.com

WEQX *In Your Back Yard*
Manchester
www.weqx.com

WGDR *Mostly Folky, Mostly Locally*
Goddard College
www.goddard.edu/wgdr

WKVT *Blue Cadillac*
Brattleboro
www.wkvt.com

WWPV *Live and Local Music*
St. Michael's College
personalweb.smcvt.edu/wwpv

Virginia

WGMU *Local Trax*
George Mason University
wgmu.gmu.edu

WKOC
Chesapeake
www.thecoast.exis.net
Plays local music.

WMRA *Acoustic Café*
Harrisonburg
www.jmu.edu/wmra

WNOR
Norfolk
www.fm99.com
No specific show - but are willing to play local music.

WNRN *Local Motive*
Charlottesville
wnrn.cstone.net

Washington

KCMU *Audioasis, The Live Room*
University of Washington
www.kcmu.org

KGRG *Local Motion*
Green River Community College
www.kgrg.com

KISW *Seattle Zone*
Seattle
www.kisw.com

KMTT *Underground*
Seattle
www.kmtt.com

KSER *The Bluegrass Express (live)*
Lynnwood
www.kser.org

KUGS *Women Shop, The Monsters of Folk*
Western Washington University
www.kugs.org

KWCW *Folkin Excellent*
Whitman College
www.bmi.net/pfries/KWCW.html

Washington DC

WHFS *The Local Show*
Washington
www.whfs.com

West Virginia

WQZK
Keyser
www.wqzk.com
Allows local artists to post MP3s.

WWVU *The Morgantown Sound*
West Virginia University
www.wvu.edu/~u92

Wisconsin

KRBR *Homegrown Radio*
Superior
www.krbr.com

WAPL *Rockin' Apple Homegrown*
Appleton
www.wapl.com

WIIL *Rock the Neighborhood*
Kenosha
www.95wiil.com
Plays music from the Wisconsin and Illinois area.

WJJO *Local Stage*
Madison
www.wjjo.com

WLUM *Battle of the Brewtown Bands, Radio Chaos*
Milwaukee
www.newrock.com

WLZR *Local Licks*
Milwaukee
www.lazer103.com

WMAD *Over the Edge*
Madison
www.all-info.com/wmad/homer.html

WMSE *Midnight Radio*
Milwaukee School of Engineering
www.wmse.org

WMUR *Wisconsin Jukebox*
Marquette University
www.mu.edu/stumedia/wmur

WORT *Hootenanny*
Madison
www.netphoria.com/wort

WRST *Local Lookout*
University of Wisconsin/Oshkosh
www.wpr.org/schedule/wrst.htm

WWSP *Club Wisconsin*
University of Wisconsin
www.uwsp.edu/stuorg/wwsp

Canada
Alberta

CFBR *Red, White & New*
Edmonton
www.TheBearRocks.com

CJAY *On The Verge*
Calgary
www.cjay92.com
For all Canadian artists.

British Columbia

CFOX *Sunday Blues*
Vancouver
www.cfox.com
Airplay/interviews with local blues artists.

CiTR *Spike's Musical Pins and Needles, Solid State (techno, trance, house, acid jazz), By The Way, Folk Oasis, Live From Thunderbird Radio Hell (live performance), Powerchord (metal)*
University of British Columbia
www.ams.ubc.ca/media/Citr/citr.htm

CJSF *MAPL Syrup*
Simon Fraser University
www.cjsf.bc.ca
Canadian artists.

CKKQ *B.C. Grown*
Victoria
www.radioq.com

Manitoba

CJKR *The Next Generation*
Winnipeg
www.power97.com
Plays the music of local artists, and other Indie Canadian bands as well.

New Brunswick

CJMO *Action Atlantic*
Moncton
www.c103.com

Nova Scotia

C100
newedge.net/c100/c100.asp
Plays the music of Canadian artists.

Ontario

CFBU *In Your Own Backyard, Sound Foundation*
Brock University
www.cfbu.niagara.com

CFFF *Blue in the Face (blues)*
Trent University
ivory.trentu.ca/www/tr

CFRU *Jalopy*
University of Guelph
www.uoguelph.ca/~cfru-fm

CHEZ *Share Chez*
Ottawa
www.chez106.com

CHRW *A Canadian Declaration of Independents, Just Folk/For the Folk*
The University of Western Ontario
www.usc.uwo.ca/chrw/shows/canindi.htm

CJAM *Local Indie Extravaganza*
University of Windsor
www.uwindsor.ca/cjam

Quebec

CHOM
Montreal
www.chom.com
Is in the process of setting up a site where local artists can upload their song files.

United Kingdom

Anna Livia FM *The Indie Music Show*
University College Dublin, Ireland
slarti.ucd.ie/annalivia
New Bands on the Irish music scene.

BBC Radio 1
www.bbc.co.uk
National Variations. `Steve Lamacq - the Evening Session'. Session tracks and new music. For listeners in Scotland only: `The Session in Scotland'. With Gill Mills and Vic Galloway. For listeners in Wales only: `The Session in Wales'. With Bethan Elfyn andHuw Stephens. For listeners in Northern Ireland only: `The Session in N Ireland'. With Colin Murray and Donna Legge.

Session Unsigned
www.bbc.co.uk/radio1/inside_r1/session_scotland
Unsigned Scottish bands – we want your demos!

Australia

2BOB *Sounds OZ*
Taree, NSW
www.amws.com.au/media/2BOB-info.html

2RRR *Sydney Sound*
Sydney
www.2rrr.org.au

BEST MUSIC BOOKS offers many directories that can help you to promote your music including *"The Musician's Atlas 2000", "The Recording Industry SourceBook", "The 2000 Songwriter's Market", "Music Directory Canada"* and *"The Film and Television Composer's Resource guide"*

www.bestmusicbooks.com

2UNE *Loud and Local*
University of New England, Armidale
Andrew Devenish-Meares
2une.une.edu.au
The program airs 6pm-8pm Monday nights, and focuses on local other-than-mainstream and independent artists, along with the occasional "classic track".

3CR *Local and Live*
Victoria
home.vicnet.net.au/~threecr

3MU *OZ Rock, H.A.T.*
yoyo.cc.monash.edu.au/groups/3MU

3RRR *Local and or General*
Victoria
www.rrr.apana.org.au

Heartland FM
Queensland
www.onthenet.com.au/~878fm
Features live broadcasts of local country artists.

Mildura Public Radio *OZ Music Show*
www.hotfm.org.au/guide

North FM *Battle of the Bands*
Hornsby NSW
www.northfm.org.au

OzWorld
www.ozworld.com.au

PBA FM *Max Radio*
University of South Australia
www.pbafm.org.au/max

PBS *Total Exposure*
St Kilda
home.vicnet.net.au/~pbsfm

PCR *Local Bands*
Gosford NSW
www.ozemail.com.au/~elwynw/pcr
Featuring the best unsigned acts from around the world (although, I do primarily play local stuff!).

Plenty Valley FM Australian Music Review, Jazz Oz Style
Melbourne
pvfm.org.au/
Supporting local artists in Melbourne's outer North East.

Satan's Lost Dogs Home Radio Show – Local Scene Segment
Melbourne
yoyo.cc.monash.edu.au/groups/3MU
I play local demos, and releases etc of Melbourne and interstate bands. We are not just a demo show but have demo segments.

Three D Radio *Local and Live, The Sound of Museli, Dreaming Daisies, Club Fusion, Local and Live, Smash It Up*
Adelaide
www.threed.suburbia.com.au

Triple J *Oz Music Show*
www.abc.net.au/triplej/triplej.htm

"As a musician, I found [The Indie Music Forum] to be informative, organized, and motivational!"
– Billy Martin, Multi Creations, NY99 Registrant

The Indie Music Forum is a one-day regional music business education seminar.
A great opportunity for learning and networking!

San Diego October 15, 2000
New York November 12, 2000
Ft. Lauderdale February 4, 2001
Check out our web site to see where we're headed next!

The Indie Music Forum is a music business education and networking environment for managers, artists who are handling their own management, and those just starting new record labels.

The focus of this event is about education and giving you both the basics of handling your business affairs as well as providing ideas and inspiration for new and different avenues that you can explore for your own marketing and promotion efforts.

The Indie Music Forum offers a Risk-Free Guarantee and a Binder jam-packed with articles, phone numbers and URLs for you to take home.

Contact us today!
cb@IndieMusicForum.com
www.IndieMusicForum.com
tel.215.627.1308

EXPERT CD REPLICATION

Anyone can offer you a CD in a jewel case.
But, GoldenROM offers exceptional customer service!
We can handle both your DEMO runs and your RETAIL
production runs in the thousands!

- 1 Day Turn Available
- Total CD Replication, Booklets, Tray Cards
- Multiple packaging options
- Mastering Services
- Warehousing
- Fulfillment
- E-Commerce Hosting and Transaction Processing
- Online Store Management

VISIT www.goldenrom.com for Latest Specials!

SPECIALS:

100 CD's in Jewel Case, Front Card, Tray Card printed full color -- $425.00

250 CD's in Jewel Case, Front Card, Tray Card printed full color -- $650.00

500 CD's In Jewel Case, Front Card, Tray Card printed full color -- $999.00

* Replication from your supplied CD-R Master, Artwork from Electronic files, 3-5 day turn. Silver Silver or Silver Blue CD-R.

Introducing VIVIDISC!

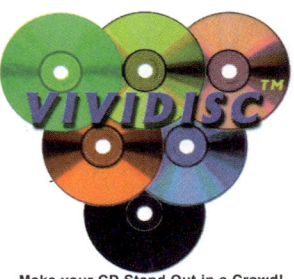

Make your CD Stand Out in a Crowd!

CALL TODAY -- 888-757-3472
Web: www.goldenrom.com
Email: sales@goldenrom.com

Section Three:
Services that Will Help You to Sell Your Music Over the Internet

The sites listed in this section are all "non-exclusive" services. Non exclusive means you are allowed to sign up with as many of the services as you like without violating any agreement. The fees and/or commissons vary from site to site. I suggest you visit as many as you can to find out which sites you get a good feeling from.

All Styles

1ie
www.1ie.com

121 Music
www.121music.com/system/shop.html

507Music
507music.com

818 Music
www.818music.com

Air Music
www.airmusic.com

Allindie.com
Tom Chernaik and Mark Roemer
www.allindie.com
All Indie was created to give independent artists and labels an advantage in today's major-label dominated music industry. We provide the services and resources independent musicians and record labels will need to compete for their share of the music marketplace. Our vision is to serve as a catalyst for artists and small record labels in the various stages of the development of their independent careers.

AmazingCDs
www.amazingcds.com

Amazon
www.amazon.com

Artist First Network
www.artistfirst.com

Artist Underground
www.aumusic.com

ArtistLaunch.com
www.artistlaunch.com

Artspheres.com
www.artspheres.com

ATOM-BOMB.COM
www.atom-bomb.com

audiohighway.com
www.audiohighway.com

audiorocket.com
audiorocket.com

audiostreet
www.audiostreet.infront.co.uk

Aural Adventures
www.AuralAdventures.com
An online music retailer dedicated to great independent music.

The AvyEgo Music Network
www.geocities.com/Broadway/5512/muscvid1.htm

bandfile.com
www.bandfile.com

Bandit
www.bandit.ICB@aweber.com
Helping unsigned acts/songwriters target their material to the right people.

Bandstore
www.bandstore.com
Bandstore has Indie Music that is Hard to Find.

BandThings
www.bandthings.com

Barnes and Nobel
music.barnesandnoble.com

Bayislandrecords.com
EL bayislandrecords@snet.net
www.bayislandrecords.com
Bay Island Records, Inc. is an independent record label dedicated to new original music in the pop/rock/alternative/ dance/blues and Island music genres.

Belham Valley Records Songwriting Contest
Gary Robilotta bvrsc@hotmail.com
theartscontest.com/index.html
An international songwriting competition featuring the largest cash awards, including a $50,000 Grand Prize, more song categories, and lower entry fees.

bfprecords.com
www.bfprecords.com
Indie site based in San Francisco Bay Area. Links, SSL encrypted online store, and resource center with contact database, trading post, and referral service.

Billboard Talent Net
www.broadbandtalent.com

bip.com
www.bipbipbip.com

Bizzario Entertainment
www.bizzario.com

borrwoORrob
www.borroworrob.com

brandnewmusic.com
brandnewmusic.com

Breakthrough Connections
www.brkthrough.com/breakthr.htm

British Unsigned Rock Band Site (BURBS)
Barry Ratcliffe www.burbs.co.uk
BURBs offers promotion, airplay, world sales, reviews and lots more!

BUGjuice
www.bugjuice.com

Callner Music
www.callnermusic.com

CD Alley
www.cdalley.com

CD Baby
Derek Sivers
www.cdbaby.com

CD Debut
www.cddebut.com
Features indie CD's and MP3's, artists get a free webpage and sell their CD or MP3 on a commission basis.

CDFront.com
www.cdfront.com
We offer multiple page sites with extensive info on the artist, including sound clips. We also provide UPC codes.

CD Music.com
www.cdmusic.com/index.cfm

CD Palace
www.cdpalace.com

CD Quest Music
www.cdquest.com
Offering over 300,000 titles from around the world allows CD Quest to reach farther into the independent world than any other site.

CD Voila!
www.cdvoila.com

CDconnection.com
www.cdconnection.com

cdlimits.com
cdlimits.com
We showcase, promote, market and sell music for Independent and Unsigned bands and artists online.

CDStreet.com
www.cdstreet.com
We enable independent music entities to add secure credit card ordering into their own website. There are no setup costs and if you do not sell anything, then there is no cost to the artist.

changemusic.com
www.changemusic.com

ChaosMusic
www.chaosmusic.com
Indie artists WANTED!!! Sell your CDs/sound files, no up-front costs.

CheckOut.com
www.checkout.com
*The CheckOut Entertainment Network is the recognized online entertainment leader. It develops, maintains and markets online entertainment destinations including CheckOutMusic.com, CheckOutMovies.com, CheckOutGames.com, The Lounge and the Wherehouse Online Stores.
In November 1999, The CheckOut Entertainment Network entered into a strategic partnership with Wherehouse Music to become the exclusive Internet arm for the nearly 550 Wherehouse retail locations nationwide.*

Children of the Virtual Revolution
moonmark chvr@chvr.net
www.chvr.net
On-line music platform (Spain).

collegemusic.com
www2.collegemusic.com

cranberry grove
www.cranberrygrove.net

Cyber Songs
www.cyber-songs.com

D-Day Records
www.angelfire.com/wi/Dday
Our goal isn't to become a huge label, it is to become a well known company that is alive because our goal is to help the bands and not just ourselves.

Degyshop
www.degyshop.com
The Musicians' Network for all Independent artists.

DELMORE RECORDING SOCIETY
Mark Linn delmores@home.com
www.delmorerecordings.com
A record label offering non - exclusive deals to artists / bands that are melodious to the ears of me!

Digital Wax Entertainment Inc.
www.digi-wax.com

Disgraceland Records
www.disgraceland.com

Duckweed Records
Mark duckweedseattle@yahoo.com
2442 NW Market St Box 354,
Seattle WA 98107 USA
members.tripod.co.uk/duckweed

E-Magine
www.emaginemusic.com
A "new type" of record company founded by former BMG Entertainment executives Christoph Rücker and Christian Jörg. Our Talent Pool offers new artists the prospect of a full retail presence once certain goals and sales milestones are reached. In this section we are permanently looking for new talent. Check it out, send us your music, and let us know what you think in general about E-Magine.

Ear Buzz
www.earbuzz.com
Sell your CDs. VISA/MC. Free sign-up. mp3s. up to $11/CD.

EMusic (formerly Cductive)
www.emusic.com/

enet 7
www.enet7.com

EvO:R
www.evor.com

extremeaudio.com
www.extremeaudio.com

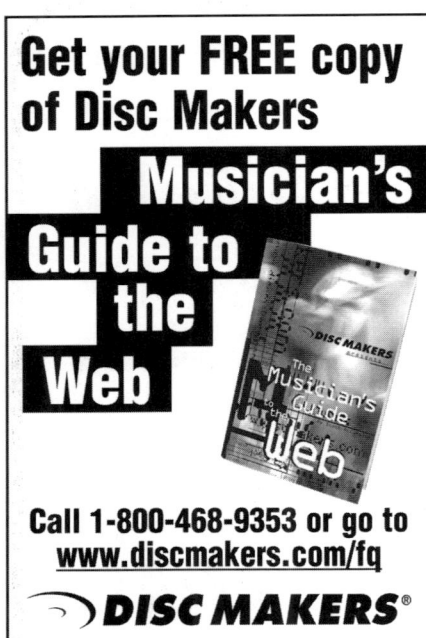

Fossil Records
Gary W. Franklin fossil@empowering.com
fossil.homepage.com
Fossil Records is a union of progressive and instrumental rock and metal artists providing manufacture, promotion, and global sales.

FrontStage.com
www.frontstage.com

GEMM
www.gemm.com

GetIndie.com
www.getindie.com

GIG Masters
www.gigmasters.com

Girl Musician Online
www.girlmusician.com

The Global Muse
www.theglobalmuse.com

Global Stage
www.globalstage.com

Grass Roots Entertainment
www.grassrootsentertainment.net

Greenpoint Music Works
www.greenpointmusic.com

Hardluckcafe.com
www.hardluckcafe.com
Hardluckcafe.com is an on-line music cafe designed to bring together independent musicians and music appreciators across the web. Hardluckcafe offers web pages, marketing, CD sales transaction processing and promotion, to unsigned musicians with original music.

Hive Music
Susan Bibeau info@hivemusic.com
www.hivemusic.com
Indie lable & production company. Not your average indie, but a partnership of artists working in a co-op fashion.

Home Made Music (Gajoob)
www.gajoob.com

Hollywood Recordings
www.hollywoodrecordings.com

HollywoodMusic.com
www.hollywoodmusic.com
A full service entertainment company with a FREE website dedicated to marketing unsigned musicians. Offering MP3, Realaudio, Live video on demand and webcasting. Come see the music!

HomeGrownBuzz.com
www.homegrownbuzz.com

Hot Bands.com
www.hotbands.com

Hungry Bands.com
www.hungrybands.com

iFill
www.ifill.com

iMusic
imusic.com

Interactive Music Promotion
www.imusicpromo.com
We are the first company dedicated to the promotion of it's artists exclusively on the web. 1999 saw some terrific changes in the way music is marketed and distributed. The web has now become an integral part in the exposure and distribution of an artists music to fans around the world. While major record labels fight for control over distribution, the savvy independent artists have seized the opportunity to put their music in the web spotlight.

Incredibly Small Concert Hall
www.smallhall.com

Independent Music Market Online
(timmol.com)
www.timmol.com

Independent Musicians Marketplace
www.secondfret.com
Music brings the world together... don't screw it up!

IndepenDisc Music Club
www.independisc.com
We listen to every submittal for review, representation, & promotion, regardless of genre. See "Artists Submissions" on our web page.

Indie Audio.com
www.indieaudio.com

INDIE Central
www.indiecentral.com/store

Indie Connection
www.indieconnection.com
Our most complete and well know aspect is that we put Original muis into Independent films! Please check out our site!

Indie Pro
www.indiepro.com

IndieCDShop.com
www.IndieCDShop.com
The record shop on the corner. A select but diverse roster of quality Independent Recording Artists. Buy great music. Sell your music. It's All About the Music!

Indiegrrl
www.indiegrrl.com
Indiegrrl was set up by Holly Figueroa in May of 1998 as a forum for information, networking and conversation about independent music from a female perspective. The list welcomes women and men interested in women's role in the independent music industry. Indiegrrl has evolved into several entities, including Indiegrrl Records (a not for profit label, releasing 4 compilations per year) Indiegrrl Inc. (a non profit organization supporting women in the industry) ITA, and Indiegrrl Events.

Independent Music Site formerly **Indie-Zone**
www.indiemusicsite.com

IndiSonic
www.indisonic.com/newweb

Indymusic.com
indymusic.com

Insound
www.insound.com/index.cfm

Interactive Music Promotion
Scott Meldrum imusicpromo@flashcom.net
www.imusicpromo.com
I-Music Promotion is the first company dedicated to the promotion of its artists exclusively on the web. Our clients are among the most highly visible acts on the internet.

Internet Music Association
www.theima.com

IUMA
www.iuma.com

JoeRecords
www.joerecords.com
An online record site that specializes in compilations, hard-to-find, ethnic and unusual music.

Juno Beach
www.junobeach.com

Kanoodle.com
kanoodle.com

The Knowledge
www.theknowledge.com
We feature news, reviews, soundclips, exclusive interviews, merchandise, a music careers guide, competitions and gigs - It's where alternative music's @!

K-Space
www.kspace.com

Kweevak's Tracks
Richard J. Lynch
www.kweevak.com
Specializing in new music promotion and advertising.

Large Orange
www.triclops.com
We actively promote Independent artists on the Internet when they subscribe to our service.

Lazy Dog Records
Kostas lazy@magnet.gr
www.lazydog.gr/
Indie record label in Greece. Photos, lyrics, real audio,mp3, interviews, news about many local bands and international artists like Astronauts, Mecano, Patrik Fitzgerald, the Mob, the Zounds etc

Licence Music - Unsigned Artist Program
customerservice@licensemusic.com
330 Townsend Suite 212, San Francisco, CA 94107, USA
www.LicenseMusic.com
Expose your music to Film, TV and commercial producers worldwide. No sign up fees and no rights transfers!

"Seeking and Selling Ethnic, Weird, Unusual, World and Hard to Find Music"

Listentothis
www.listentothis.com

localmusicstore (CMAG)
www.localmusicstore.com/backstage/new.html

localsongs.com
www.localsongs.com/sell.html
We sell Independent releases and don't take any commission!

localstation
www.localstation.com

Mytown Records
Claymcmurray   mytownrecords@aol.com
mytownrecords.com
Independent record label that offers non exclusive CD releases to local artist.

Magex
www.magex.com
A new digital commerce service which provides a safe and easy way to buy and sell digital content on the Internet - like music, software, videos, games and business information. Magex provides copyright protection and a secure payment facility with the backing of an international clearing house and supported by leading DRM technology.

Main Street CD
www.mainstreetcd.com
MainStreet CD is an Independent Record Company that works with unknown, independent artists to assist them in world distribution, and artist development.

Make it Big Records
www.makeitbigrecords.co.uk

Mazur Public Relations
Michael Mazur michael@mazurpr.com
P.O. Box 360, East Windsor, NJ 08520 USA
Tel: 609.426.1277   Fax: 609.426.1217
www.mazurpr.com

Manifest Music
www.freeyellow.com:8080/members/manifest

Milk Records
Dan Augustyn dan@milkrecords.com
milkrecords.com
Milk Records provides independent recording artists the opportunity to sell their albums over the Internet.

Millennium Music Media
www.millennium5.com

Moonletters Records
hometown.aol.com//shaunaskye/moonletters.html

MorphCity.com
www.morphcity.com

Morusa Records
www.morusarecords.com

museek.net
museek.net/home.html

Music Choice
www.musicchoice.com

Music Evolution
www.MusicEvolution.com

Music Exchange
www.musicexchange.net

Music Media International (CAZ)
www.cazmedia.com

Music Pyramid
st1.yahoo.com/musicpyramid

The Music Site
www.the-music-site.com

MusicBuilder.com
www.MusicBuilder.com

musiceditor.com
www.musiceditor.com
The new, online A&R industry resource to help unsigned bands get signed. New Music Reviews - MP3 picks - win free CDs!

musicoffice.com
musicoffice.com

www.PlanetCD.com

Providing more bang for your promotional buck since 1997!

MusicQuotesAndInfo
musicquotesandinfo.com
A website designed to bring together, via email, those interested in buying or selling music and music-related goods and/or services.

Musik International
Musikintl@aol.com
154 Berasso Road,
Boulder CO, 80302, USA
Est. 1977, provides publicity, radio and retail promotion for all styles, except rap, hip-hop and country. Distribution, marketing, graphic design and more. Clients include: Rykodisc, Begger's Banquet, ARK21, Hearts of Space, Real Music, Electra, Mikey Hart, Natacha Atlas, Lunar Drive, dozens more. Ask about our One Hour Crash Course conducted by phone.

muXic.com
www.muxic.com

Muzik Plaza
www.musikplaza.de

NetBeat
www.netbeat.com
A musical portal, where people can find information about artists and labels (bios, photos, gigs, gossip), buy a cd or a vinyl and download exclusive mp3 from indie labels. There is also live webcast and video interviews. And radio is coming soon.

NetJammer
www.netjammer.com

NetMartMusic
www.netmartmusic.de
Germany based agency mainly for unsigned bands looking for record companies, publishers, distributors, booking agencies and so on.

Netthis Television
Rob Steiner music@netthis.com
www.netthistv.com
Live concert performances on internet television.

NETUNES.com
www.netunes.com
Wholesale, Interactive Record Store. All CDs only $8.99 shipping included.

NewTech Music
www.newtechmusic.com

Not Lame
www.notlame.com
3 power pop labels and music distributor of power pop-oriented music.

On the Row
www.ontherow.com

Online Express Music
www.onlineexpressmusic.com

Online Rock
Roland Goity roland@onlinerock.com
www.onlinerock.com
A Web-based music community for bands and musicians to promote, distribute and sell their music online.

The Orchard
www.theorchard.com
A leading supplier of independent music on the Internet, that offers worldwide non-exclusive distribution.

Outer Seventh Records
outerseventh.com

peoplesound.com
www.peoplesound.com
You will be seen and heard by a 1 million users at THE leading "quality" new music site.

Planet CD
planetcd.com
Planet CD has been serving the needs of the independent musician since 1997, featuring the BEST in independent music. We provide SECURE online ordering of your music, audio samples, and 2 professionally designed web pages dedicated to your music! We provide your customers with unsurpassed customer service, a free newsletter, free bumper stickers and monthly prize drawings to keep them coming back for more. Come visit us!

PlatinumCD.com
www.platinumcd.com

PlayHear.com
playhear.com
PlayHear.com(tm) is the platform and gathering place for the music community: the fans, artists, and publishers. As the Hub for a network of sites, publishers, and independent bands, PlayHear.com is the premier destination on the Web for music news, resources and products. You choose your mix of mainstream and grassroots media.

Pop Swap
www.popswap.com/#

Radio Jukebox
www.radio-jukebox.com

Raging Smolder Music Store
www.avmcyber.com/rsms
An Internet webzine comprised of music reviews featuring high quality recordings by independent bands and musicians. Each recording on the RS Music Store site is recommended 100% by Raging Smolder. If we don't like a recording, it won't be there!

Red Button
www.redbutton.com

Riffage
riffage.com

Riviera Publishing
Spike & Chrissy Sykes
sjs@rivierapublishing.co.uk
148 Park Rd, Barnsley,
South Yorkshire, UK
www.rivierapublishing.co.uk
The first on-line music publishers in the UK promoting new original songs, bands, artists and licensed product to the music industry using real audio streaming. We promote and accept product worldwide.

Rock Record Collectors Association (RRCA)
www.eol.ca/~thrash
An international rock music association dedicated to the promotion, distribution and preservation of rock music. Has large on-line resources.

Scout Indie
www.scoutserv.com

sellyoursongs.com
www.sellyoursongs.com/
A new and revolutionary way for songwriters, known and unknown, to direct market their music to potential consumers.

Siltown Records
www.siltown.com
An independent music/entertainment site with extensive content.

songs.com (NOMA)
songs.com

Soundclick
www.soundclick.com

SOUNDSBIG.COM
www.soundsbig.com
The SOUNDSBIG Broadcast Network is the easiest and most comprehensive music experience on the Internet - a place to hear, see, learn and buy music from both mainstream and undiscovered artists. With over 100 channels of music, video and live events spanning 17 genres, and a program dedicated to helping unsigned/independent artists, SOUNDSBIG.com is your one-stop music destination.

Spawner Records
Kyle Richardson spawner1@yahoo.com
www.spawnerrecords.com
100% indipendent non profit label run by bands for bands from Vancouver B.C. Canada!

SpinRecords.com
www.spinrecords.com
SpinRecords.com gives the best independent musicians across all genres a comprehensive Internet presence to place them directly in front of their fans.

Starplace
manager@starplace.com
www.fortunecity.com/tinpan/wuthering/806/Starplace/Page_1x.html

Stinkweeds Online
www.stinkweeds.com

sursumcorda.com
www.sursumcorda.com

TalentBox.com
www.talentbox.com
Online promotion services for bands, singers, dancers, actors and models.

TheTop5.com
www.thetop5.com
We sell over 200,000 CDs, DVDs and Videos at some of the lowest prices anywhere. We feature extra-low sale prices on The Top 5 bestselling items in hundreds of music and video categories.

ThirdRoad
www.thirdroad.com

Throttlebox.com
www.throttlebox.com
Promotion for independent musicians and record labels, featuring customized artist web pages and unique multimedia music files for public download. ThrottleBox.com receives over 3.5 million hits every month, and features music from the newest indie artists to the biggest industry superstars.

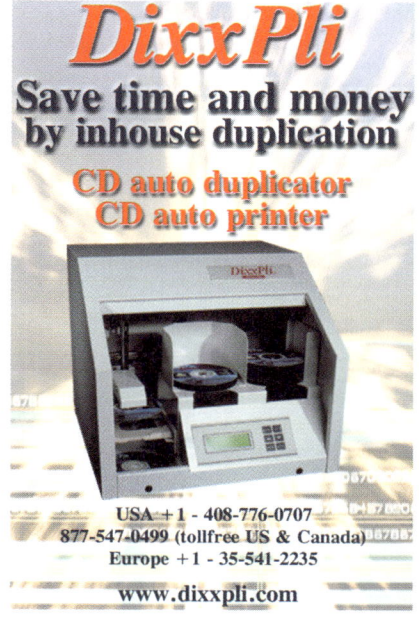

To The Bone
www.tothebone.com

Tropia
www.Tropia.com

Tune Vault
tunevault.com

Twee Kitten
www.tweekitten.com

unazone
www.unazone.com

Unsigned Artists Organization - UAO
uao.org

Unsigned On-Line
www.unsigned.au.com

unsigned-music.com (formerly indieforce)
www.unsigned-music.com

800-363-8273　　　**800-928-3310**

35 STAFFORD RD. UNIT 4
NEPEAN, ONTARIO K2H 8V8

WWW.CANATRON-WAVE.COM
E-MAIL rondrake@sprint.ca

25 years of audio-video experience on everything we do. **Fast** and efficient without sacrificing quality. **Call** us for a comparison quote.

Complete range of on-site services: mastering, graphics, production and packaging; fulfillment and shipping.

Member: International Recording Media Association and cassette shell standards committee.

You have questions
We have answers

Vitaminic
www.vitaminic.com
You can register with Vitaminic online and upload music, images, biographies, etc. or you can send your material to us and we'll do it for you. You'll get your own homepage and gain exposure throughout Europe and the US, building new fan bases at the same time. Best of all, it's free!!

Warm Cola
info@warmcola.com
PO Box 8301 Northland Vic Australia 3072
www.warmcola.com

Wired Planet
www.wiredplanet.com

World of Indie
Kale Kaposhilin   kale@netstep.net   1-800-260-7550 x-201
www.worldofindie.com
Definitive online promotion of independent music with multi-media content. Potential advancement onto labels with distribution, production, and management.

World Records
www.Worldrecords.com

Worldwide Radio
www.worldwide-radio.com

Xact Records (formerly MusicSports.com)
xactrecords.com/
A site that promotes unsigned bands and sells their merchandise. We review all types of bands, have band contests, giveways and much more.

Y2K Music
www.y2k-music.co.uk

Zen Music
www.zenmusic.co.uk

Specialty

Country

Affinity Music
www.affinitymusic.com

Bandstand
www.saradon.co.uk
UK - Country Music.

Country Music In Britain
www.countrymusic.saltire.org/

KIC – Soundtrack
www.kic-soundtrack.com
A promotion recording label, which produces every month promotion CD's with independent artists for Radio Station all over the world.

Lonnie's Music Store
www.freeyellow.com/members3/lonniec

Miles of Music
www.milesofmusic.com

Just Bluegrass Music
www.jbmsound.com

RealCountry.net
www.realcountry.net

Saradon
www.saradon.co.uk

Shop Records
www.shoprecords.com
Independent Americana and Traditional Singer Songwriters Including Lacy J. Dalton, Larry Hosford, Beans Sousa, Freddy Powers and more.

BEST MUSIC BOOKS has books on MP3's including *"The MP3 and Internet Audio Handbook"* by Bruce Fries, *"The Official Guide to MP3"* by Michael Robertson & Ron Simpson and *"MP3 Power!"* by Justin Frankel & Greely Sawyer
www.bestmusicbooks.com

Tall Grass Records
www.tall-grass.com

Texas Worldwide CDs
www.texasworldwidecds.com

Tsab, ink
www.2steppin.com/tsab.htm
Specializing in the promotion of country music on the Internet. Creators of 2Steppin.com.

Dance

303net.com
www.303net.com

DanceMusicShop.com
www.dancemusicshop.com

e-frenchsound
www.e-frenchsound.com

PCDJ.com - Visiosonic
www.pcdj.com

Psychedelic Mind Expander 2000
www.cs.umu.se/~tdv94ati/dj/djmag.html

Experimental

b: group records
info@bgrouprecords.com
P.O. Box 181,
New Hudson, MI, 48165-0181, USA
www.bgrouprecords.com
Detroit's home of instrumental music and ambient-space. b: group/ records is also the home of Matt Borghi and most all of his audio endeavors.

Baba Luba
www.babaluba.com
Ambient, Electronic, Industrial, Dance & Experimental Music-CD, Vinyl, Cassette.

Bands Online
bands-online.com
Experimental/Goth ter. Specializing In Complete Online Musical Promotional Packages

Carpe Mortem Records
400 Bagley Avenue, Suite 707,
Detroit, MI 48226
www.records.carpemortem.com
A Detroit based record label specializing in Gothic, Industrial and Darkwave music.

Digital Intersect
www.digital-intersect.com
Electronic music.

Interbeat Records
Tim webmaster@interbeatrecords.com
www.interbeatrecords.com/
Industrial, Gothic, Techno and more store and record label

StarVoice
www.starvoice.com
Music, Chats and More: Over 10,000 chatrooms boasting up to a million hits per day, offering SoftCD Singles downloads from Independent Record Labels.

Hip Hop

basically-hiphop
www.basically-hiphop.com
Basically-HipHop.Com Was Created For The Sole Purpose Of Playing Under Ground, MainStream, And HipHop On The Net In Real Audio. We Feature Up And Coming Acts Managed By Us And We Only Play Music That Is Considered HipHop.

Beatbreaks
www.beatbreaks.com

CiPHER DIVINE
cipherdivine.virtualave.net/main.html
Definitive resource for underground hip hop music on the web.

Deep Rooted Productions
Carlis Phillips drp_llc@hotmail.com
www.deeprooted.com
Production & Recording for Hip-Hop/R&B. Home of Nappy Roots, Klientel, and more..

Digital187.com
www.digital187.com

Down-South.com
www.down-south.com

GrooveControlOnline.com
www.groovecontrolonline.com

Hip Hop Closet.com
www.hiphopcloset.com

HipHopBoomBox.com
www.hiphopboombox.com
A hiphop underground site with two radio shows and real audio for unsigned and independent artists, a music store, and much more hip hop info.

Insomniac Record Pool
www.insomniacmagazine.com
Insomniac Record Pool is a hip hop record pool that helps indie labels by our servicing members (radio, club, internet and party djs) with quality indie hip hop. If you are a label and want to get your group played by our dj's just give us a call: 877 213 7747 x 7625 or email insom@mindspring.com

Rap.de
www.rap.de

Support Online Hip Hop (SOHH)
P.O. Box 6300,
Bronx, New York 10451-1704
www.SOHH.com

UndergroundHipHop.com
www.undergroundhiphop.com
The Official Home of Underground Hip Hop. Listen to tons of Real Audio, Singles, Albums, Radio Shows, Old School, Instrumentals, Videos, etc. Meet others in our chat room and message boards. Updated daily.

Urban Anthem Records
www.urbananthem.com/indie.htm
Premier online store specializing in independent, underground, and old school hip hop.

WholeTeam Entertainment
www.wholeteam.com
An entertainment resource for independent artists in search of online distribution, management, production, photography, and web design.

Jazz/Folk/Blues

The Blue Zone
bluezone.org
Blues bands only.

Christer's and Vanja's P.A.W.S.
home5.swipnet.se/~w-53855

efolk Music
www.efolkmusic.com
Home of the 49 cent mp3, features a discriminating collection of legal folk, bluegrass, and Celtic mp3s and cds by independent and signed artists.

House of Blues
www.hob.com

InterJazz
www.interjazz.com

Jazz Country
www.jazzcountry.com

Jazzpromo.com
www.jazzpromo.com

Metal

BANDINDEX
www.bandindex.com

Digital Death
Simon Miller
www.digital-death.org
Online Metal Ordering and underground artist promotional services.

Hard Radio
www.hardradio.com

Headbanger's Delight
www.headbangersdelight.com
Our Indie Store is here to help promote independant heavy metal bands or any metal band without major distribution.

Loud! Online
www.geocities.com/SunsetStrip/Stage/4599
Australian Metal.

Shoutweb.com
www.shoutweb.com

Punk

Interpunk
www.interpunk.com

truepunk.com
www.truepunk.com

World Music

The Ethno Trip
members.xoom.com/sahua
This site is in Russian!

Reggae Warehouse
Omar Hakim rwinfo@web.com
www.reggaewarehouse.com
We specialize in the promotion of reggae ska jungle & worldbeat music. We also love selling indepentent reggae products.

Other

2LOUD4U
www.2loud4u.de
Hard Alternative.

AnonymousBands.com
www.anonymousBands.com
Independent Christian Bands.

Debut Music
www.younameit.com.au/dmo/index.shtml
Australian bands only.

GetChristianMusic.com
getchristianmusic.com
GetChristianMusic.com is an online retailer with the goal of getting your music to industry people, the consumer and other songwriters/artists. Get sales and help your career at the same time.

Goldenrod Music
www.goldenrod.com
Handles many "extreme" genres.

Greg's Music World
www.musicworld.com.au
Australian bands.

Harmony Ridge Music
www.rahul.net/hrmusic
Dedicated to Female Singer Songwriters.

Indie Pool
www.indiepool.com
Distributing over 1000 Canadian indies to over 500 Canadian retailers.

Indie-cds.com
www.indie-cds.com
RealAudio and MP3 sample tracks, CDs for sale, and four webradio channels 24 hrs a day. Secure server, world/roots/folk music specialist. Australian bands only.

Ladyslipper.org
www.ladyslipper.org
Female artists only.

NY New Music
nynewmusic.com
New York Musicians.

Unsigned-Indie.com
www.unsigned-indie.com
Christian.

Section Four:
Sites that Will Allow You to Upload Music Files.

As is the case with Section Three, the sites in this section vary a great deal cost wise. Many will allow you to upload your files for free, while others charge a fee or commision.

All Styles

507Music
507music.com

52ndStreamMedia
www.52media.com

A and R Online
www.aandronline.com

afternight
www.afternight.com/music/rates.htm

AmateurMP3.com
www.AmateurMP3.com
THE ultimate free resource for Amateur singer and songwriters.

AMP3.com
www.amp3.net

The Anti-Elitist Audio Zine
subrealsongs.com/antielitist

Area Music.com
www.areamusic.com

Atlantic Satellite Marketing Ltd.
www.atlantic-satellite.com/unsigned.htm

The Audio Hub
www.sounds-online.com
The Audio Hub is an audio portal for music lovers and music makers, you will find mp3s to download, hardware and software info, free music hosting, radio, webcasting, chat, and tons of useful links.You can find us by simply typing aud.io into your browser.

audio-bot
www.audio-bot.com

Audiogalaxy
www.Audiogalaxy.com

Audiopia
www.audiopia.com

audiorocket
audiorocket.com

AudioSurge.com
www.AudioSurge.com

AudioVideoweb.com
www.musiciansweb.net/
A high quality low cost hosting service for Real Audio, Real Video.We create RealAudio, RealVideo, MP3,and Quicktime files for your web site. Live Netcasting. Server Space.

bandfile.com
www.bandfile.com

Bandradio
www.bandradio.com/botw
You can also send a CD in to try for BOTW.

Better Dayz
www.betterdayz.com

The Indie Link Exchange
A new free and easy way to promote your website!
www.indielinkexchange.com

The Big Red Cat MP3 Page
www.bigredcat.com
A home for independent music.

bowienet
www.davidbowie.com

Breakthrough Connections
www.brkthrough.com/breakthr.htm

Broadband Talent Net (formerly Billboard Magazine Talent Net)
www.broadbandtalent.com

Broadcast.com Jukebox
www.broadcast.com/music/cd_jukebox
Yahoo!'s Broadcast CD Jukebox will host, stream and sell your album FREE to you and your listeners.

Busca MP3
www.buscamp3.com.br
In Spanish.

buttermonkey.com
www.buttermonkey.com

Callner Music
www.callnermusic.com

CD Debut
www.cddebut.com
Features indie CD's and MP3's, artists get a free webpage and sell their CD or MP3 on a commission basis.

The CD Music Page
www.cdmusicpage.com/index.shtml

cdart
www.cdart.com/cgi-bin/cdweb/new.cgi

CDIY
www.sean.co.uk/var

ChangeMusic.com
www.changemusic.com/default-fr.html

CDNOW – Cosmic Music
cosmic.cdnow.com

ChaosMusic
www.chaosmusic.com
Indie artists WANTED!!! Sell your CDs/sound files, no up-front costs.

Clovis Records
www.clovisrecords.com

Crazy Mary's Electronic Underground
members.xoom.com/_XOOM/crazymary23/EUindex.htm

cybertropix
www.cybertropix.com

Cybtribe
www.cybtribe.com/

Degolpe.com
www.dgolpe.com

DemoTape2000
www.DemoTape2000.com

Digital Danny
www.DigitalDanny.com
Offers an MP3 area where artists can have their MP3 music listed, reviewed and available for download.

dmusic
www.dmusic.com

eatsleepmusic.com
www.eatsleepmusic.com
Easy MP3 uploads and excellent band promotion pages.

Elf World
www.effworld.com
Upload your music onto the EDJ - a jukebox going into bars. Free promotion. Free Stats. Money for your song's play.

EMusic.com
www.emusic.com

extremeaudio.com
www.extremeaudio.com

EZCD
www.ezcd.com

farmclub.com
www.farmclub.com/

Firstlook.com
www.firstlook.com

FranceMP3.com
www.francemp3.com
The leading MP3 files distributor in France with over 150.000 visits per month, 500 artists and 1500 songs currently on line.

The Free Music Archive
free-music.com

Freetrax
www.freetrax.com
World's first democratic record company lets users decide the content. You can download mp3-files, listen to music (streaming), or publish your own songs.

garageband.com
www.garageband.com

getsigned.com
www.getsigned.com

Gigmania
www.gigmania.com

GimmeFiles
www.gimmefiles.com

Goodnoise
www.goodnoise.com

GrandCentralMusic
www.grandcentralmusic.com

Grip Monthly
www.virginiamusicflash.com

Hangover Square
www.hsq.co.uk
Free* music archive for all musical genres (MP3/RealAudio only).

Home of the Unsigned Musician's Page (TheHUMp)
www.thehump.com

iHearYou.com
www.iHearYou.com

in2tv
www.in4.com

Independent Musicians Marketplace
www.secondfret.com
Real Audio and MP3: All kinds of indie music.

The Independent Musicians MP3 Archive
www.thedigitalalchemy.net/imma

Indie Journal
www.strangecloud.com/indiejournal
Reviews, interviews, Internet radio, mp3 site guide, poetry, art and more.

indielive.com
www.indielive.com

IndieUnite
www.indieunite.com
Created to promote independent music on the Internet. Realaudio/MP3 clips.

The IndX
www.fortunecity.co.uk/explore/area/madchester.html

Indulged
www.indulged.com/mp3s.html

Indy Hits
www.indyhits.com
Promotes the best in independent bands and artists to record labels, press, radio etc...

Insound
www.insound.com/index.cfm

IUMA
fozzie.iuma.com/Artist_Uplink

Joe'sGrill
www.joesgrille.com
Also does CD design and replication.

Jukebox
https://www.islandnet.com/~songbird/addsong.htm#CONTACTINFO

The Jukebox
www.thejukebox.org
A free searchable database for new indy music and music videos.

Just Music
justmusic.simplenet.com

Kanoodle.com
kanoodle.com

Laser Trax
www.lasertrax.com
Store, recording studio, live music venue, Record label, distibutor, and website. Host band webpages with info, photos & downloadable music.

Liquid Audio
www.liquidaudio.com

Listen.com
www.listen.com

ListenSmart
listensmart.com

Listentothis
www.listentothis.com

Local Music
www.localmusic.com

Local Music Store
www.localmusicstore.com

localbroadcast.net/KNDR Radio
www.localbroadcast.net

Lycos Listening Room
listeningroom.lycos.com

Minstrel Avenue (part of TMPB)
www.Minstrels.com

Mjuice
www.mjuice.com

mono.net
www.mono.net
The ultimate resource for Australian music information, encompassing both the recognised and the undiscovered. Featuring hundreds of artists along side their respective noise.

MOZ Music
www.mozmusic.com
Popular music site with free promotion for indie & independent artists.

MP123
www1.mp123.com

MP3 Artist Archive
www.mp3artistarchive.com
MP3 Artist Archive lists independent musicians, links to their music and CD's for free. Bulletin board, chat room and Shoutcasts.

MP3 Box
www.mp3.box.sk

MP3 charts.com
www.mp3charts.com

MP3 Chicks
www.mp3chicks.com

MP3 Hangout
come.to/mp3hangout

MP3 Park
www.mp3park.com

The MP3 Place
www.mp3place.net

The MP3 Shack
mp3.shack.dk

MP3.ca
www.mp3.ca

MP3.com
www.mp3.com

MP3.com.au
www.mp3.com.au

MP3DOM.com
MP3DOM.com

MP3Fever
www.mp3fever.net
Submit samples of your music and get a link back to your official band page.

MP3now
www.mp3now.com

MP3vault
www.mp3vault.com

MPSOL
www.mpsol.com
"Tune In, Log On, and Hear Your Music Here"!

mudhut.co.uk
www.mudhut.co.uk
Mudhut is the independent music channel catering for all musical needs. Artists sell music at mudhut via download or custom cd, publish and license it at mudb2b, hear it on mudradio or read the hottest reviews in the mudmag.

Music corner
www.musicorner.com

Music Global Network
musicglobalnetwork.com

The Music Note
www.musicnote.com
The site for Indie Music enthusiasts. Free Classifieds, Email, Message Forum, great links, music and lots more.

Music4Free.com
www.music4free.com

MusicBroadcast.com
www.musicbroadcast.com

musician.com
www.musician.com
Members can become artist of the month.

Musician's Network
www.MusiciansNetwork.com

Musician's Network
www.bytes4u.mb.ca/mn

Musician's World
www.your-game.com/music

musicmaker.com
www.musicmaker.com

Musicstuff
www.musicstuff.de

MyPlay
www.myplay.com

NeTube.com
netube.com
Home of the famous Mp3 Jukebox and Lube Quarterly.

The New Artist Review
www.newartistreview.com

The New Music Showcase
www.newmusicshowcase.com
The ultimate Internet promotion medium available to Independent artists.

NewTech Music
www.newtechmusic.com

netDrives.com
www.netdrives.com/home_layers.htm

Oddbox
www.oddbox.com

On the Row
www.ontherow.com

OnLine Rock
www.onlinerock.com

The Open Mic
www.theopenmic.net

Orbit music
www.orbitmusic.com

Original Music Net
www.originalmusic.net

peoplesound.com
www.peoplesound.com

Planet Jam
www.planetjam.com/

pn4u.com
Laurent Y. TESTUD
1555 Mesa Verde Drive East
Apt #41B Mesa Verde Villas, COSTA MESA CA, 92626 (USA)
pn4u.com
Pn4u.com is unique and different. It is the place for art, music and emotions. This site is absolutely free of ads, distracting banners and silly flying logos. At Pn4u.com, your talent has a name and you are not one more entry in a database. Signing up is simple, contact webmaster@pn4u.com

PopSceneRadio
www.popscene.com

popwire.com
www.popwire.com
A site where unsigned bands can expose there music for free!

PureMP3
www.puremp3.org

Recycled Music
www.recycledmusic.com/home.htm

reelscreen.com
www.reelscreen.com
New music, new films, creative thinking and the hottest new talent on the planet.

Resort Records
www.resortrecords.com

ROCKCOVERS.com
www.rockcovers.com

RollingStone
www.rollingstone.com

Search MP3
www.searchmpthree.com

Siltown Records
www.siltown.com
An independent music/entertainment site with extensive content.

SomeMusic.com
www.somemusic.com

Songfiles.com
www.songfiles.com

The SongPost
www.roadsideattraction.net/webmaster.html

songs.com (NOMA)
songs.com

Sonic Abyss
www.sonicabyss.com

Stains
stains.highspeedweb.net
This is a zine style site that has everything from music to graff to comics. We'll put just about anything on our page.

StarVoice
www.starvoice.com

Streamsearch
www.streamsearch.com

StreamSeek
www.streamseek.com

Sunnymead
www.sunnymead.org

The Synthesis
www.thesynthesis.com/framem.html

takeoutmusic.com
www.takeoutmusic.com

theindependentartist.com
www.theindependentartist.com
"Uniting Your Alternatives." Website, print magazine, tv show, live events, productions, Artist affiliate programs, indie-Artist catalogue, community.

TUCOWS Music
music.tucows.com
An MP3 site that finally checks the QUALITY of music that is uploaded.

Tune Vault
tunevault.com

Tune-Land
www.tune-land.com
Holds the Internet Battle of the Bands.

UBL
www.ubl.com

UKSounds
www.uksounds.com

Unicycle Records
www.unicyclerecords.com/
unicyclerecords.com - "Morning After Singles" - artist selected, live tracks for internet distribution. A free service with revenue sharing. Get Up For The Download!

Unsigned Artists.com
www.unsignedartists.com

The Unsigned
www.UNSIGNEDRADIO.COM

USGIGTV.NET
www.usgigtv.net

Unsigned Bands MP3 Files
www.stax98.freeserve.co.uk/unsigned.htm

Unsignedacts.com
www.unsignedacts.com

Virtual Radio
www.vradio.com

Virtual Tunes Music
www.virtualtunes.com/music/index.shtml

Voquette
www.voquette.com

Wabbit Wadio
www.tagyerit.com/xchange.htm
Wabbit Wadio is also the home of Bandwidth: Discussion of web design as it relates to bands, labels, and other music related sites. Everything from adding audio and video; format types, linking strategies, site promotion, search engine placement. To subscribe: www.onelist.com/subscribe. cgi/bandwidth

Web 'n' Zic
webmestre@webnzic.com
www.webnzic.com/enter.htm

Weekly Indie MP3
www.weeklyindiemp3.freeservers.com

Well Cut Recordings
www.wellcut.com

Wired Planet
www.wiredplanet.com

WMP3.net
www.wmp3.net
Get your music streamed over the Internet for free!

WorldWideBands
www.worldwidebands.com

www.recycledmusic.com
www.recycledmusic.com

www.unsigned.com
www.unsigned.com

Y Zap
www.yzap.com
Your Indie Music Connection.

Your Music
www.YourMusic.cc

YourMusicSource.com
www.yourmusicsource.com

ZeBox
www.zebox.com
Over 2000 artists, 3500 songs in every genre, music videos, city lists, gig lists, genre jukebox, and showcase.

ZincAudition
www.zinc-audition.com
...a simple web interface between musicians & masses.

Zorilla Music
www.zorilla.com
Zorilla - A Site For Sore Ears. Zorilla is the best place on the web to find the best in international independent music. It's free, it's legal and it's dangerously habit-forming.

Specialty Sites

Country Music

Country Music Showcase
freezone.exmachina.net/
Country_Newcomers

Cowpie Corral
www.roughstock.com/cowpie
COWPIE (COuntry and Western Pickers of the InternEt) catalogs thousands of chord and tablature files to all genres of country music. Uploading is free and a great way to get your music in front of other guitar pickers.

Cybergrass
www.banjo.com

Original Song Site
www.evansville.net/~aires

ZestspearMusic
members.xoom.com/blueraven
Leans towards country music/country rock. Dance Music

303net.com
www.303net.com/

DanceCity Network
www.geocities.com/~loudmusic
Voted the #1 DJ site. A community of DJs & producers geared towards the dancefloor via the mp3 vehicle.

Med Techno Zone
www.imaginet.fr/kanyar

Psychedelic Mind Expander 2000
www.cs.umu.se/~tdv94ati/dj/djmag.html

Tribe
www.mp3-tribe.com/tribe.shtml
Techno/Dance.

Experimental Music

44k
hustle@44k.com
www.44k.com
Electronic music.

Ambience for the Masses
www.sleepbot.com/ambience

Bloodsoaked Promotions
bloodsoaked.simplenet.com
Only extreme music is accepted - free.

CLAN Analogue
clananalogue.org
Australian Experimental Music.

Darkland
www.ifrance.com/darkland
Goth.

Demo Bank
www.carbonsolutions.se/demo/startsida.asp

Epitonic
www.epitonic.com
Mostly experimental.

The Gauntlet
www.thegauntlet.com
Any type of music but mainstream.

Goth Like
huizen.dds.nl/~gothlike/

The Gothic Jukebox
gothic.virtualave.net
A place where you can hear your favorite gothic songs in RealAudio.

gothik.nu
gothik.nu

Industrial Music Digest
www.vl.kharkov.ua/%7Eben

Jtronic
www.jtronic.com
Electronic Music.

The Midi Farm
www.midifarm.com
Contains the latest industry news and information to equip the modern artist.

no type
www.notype.com

Noiseweb
www.noiseweb.com
Experimental Music.

sugarRUSH
www.sugarrush.com
Electronic music.

Hip Hop

beatsnatcher
www.beatsnatcher.com

Blunted Migration
www.bluntedmigration.com

Dee Jekyll's Hip Hop Site
www.multimania.com/deejekyll?

Hip Hop Boulevard
members.xoom.com/hiphop_quest/
If your a underground/net mc, please send your audio files to me along with a small bio about your self and were your repin' & i will do a whole page on you along with your pictures and what ever you want on there, FREE, of course send your files in real audio, please encode them in 28.8.

Hip Hop Infinity
hiphop.simplenet.com/Underground
An underground music site specializing in unsigned artists from established indie emcees to bedroom/ basement musical hobbyists. All hip hop related music, regardless of production quality (or lack thereof), will be sold through the site's online store.

Ill Crew Universe - Global Hip Hop Nation
www.illcrew.com

The Italian Turntablism Newsletter
members.xoom.it/turntablism

Mix-Tape
www.mix-tape.com

rapsoundz 2000   (formerly Realsoundz)
www.rapsoundz2k.com

Rapworld
www.rapworld.com
Get a free E-Mail or a Free Redirection URL @ The Biggest Rap, HipHop, R&B Music Archive On The Net. This site has everything a good site needs, audio, pictures, videos , join the bannerexchange.

The Source
www.thesource.com

Urban Earth
www.urbanearth.com

Wodie.com
www.wodie.com
The only unbias hiphop magazine.

Jazz/Folk/Blues

efolk Music
www.efolkmusic.com

Jazz Scene
jazzscene.no

Metal

A Cry From the Dark Dimensions
www.geocities.com/SunsetStrip/Studio/2584

A Village of Underground Metal and People
www.geocities.com/SunsetStrip/Palladium/6235

Al's Metal MP3 Page
www.angelfire.com/pq/metalmp3

Arizona Metal
www.coffinz.com

AUSMETAL
www.ausmetal.net
Australian metal bands only.

Carnage zine
come.to/xnendex

The Enchanted Castle
come.to/enchantedcastle
Dark Metal.

Les Filles du Metal
metal.citeweb.net/
Female bands only.

The Gates
get.to/thegates

thegatesofhell.org
www.thegatesofhell.org
Australia - Metal reviews, MP3's, band hosting and web site creation.

True Metal
www.truemetal.org

True Norwegian
www.juniks.org/~loke
Norway metal.

Punk

Boston PUNK!
bostonpunk.thegeek.net
Boston area only.

Classless Society
members.tripod.com/~ClasslessSociety
A political crust punk site with tons of sounds, links, and pics.

Dork Magazine
www.bigdork.com

Downsided
www.freespeech.org/downsided

East Side Revolution
www.members.home.net/ese

FUCKIN EH!
www.geocities.com/canadianpunkeh

F.U.B.A.R. Zine
www.geocities.com/SunsetStrip/Pit/3216/index2.htm

Headbanger's Heaven
headbanger.virtualave.net

loudnet
www.loudnet.com

Mad MP3s
www.angelfire.com/pa2/madmp3s/main.html

BEST MUSIC BOOKS offers HUNDREDS of music books that can help to shape your career including *"How To Be Your Own Booking Agent and Save Thousands of Dollars"* by Jeri Goldstein and *"Guerilla Marketing"* by Bob Baker.

www.bestmusicbooks.com

Neil's Page O Punk
members.tripod.com/~retard82/index1.html

New Music Network
www.newmusic.net

Pennsylvania Hardcore
members.tripod.com/~pahxc
PA style hardcore and philly graffiti.

Poppunk.com
www.poppunk.com
The one stop resource and online zine for punk music. Sponsored by Epitaph, Tomato Head, Fastmusic, and Springman Records.

The Punk and Ska Page
www.lino.com/~landry/MLL

Punk: Exploited and Pist
www.deepnet.com/~punk

Sound Check
www.soundcheck.simplenet.com

Subversion Network
acornweb.com/subversion
If any independent bands want their mp3s up, I will definitely help them out.

UK Punk
members.tripod.com/ukpunk
UK artists only.

Who's Got the Punk?
wgtp.tripod.com

World Wide Punk
www.worldwidepunk.com

Other

Any Swing Goes
www.anyswinggoes.com
Swing Music.

Bandas
www.bandas.com.ar
Argentina Bands.

Beat Magazine
www.beat.com.au
Australian bands.

Boston Soundcheck
www.bostonsoundcheck.com
Boston area only.

BostonBands.com
www.BostonBands.com
Boston area only.

Club Culture
club-culture.com
Mostly French Canadian.

C.R.U.M.B.S.
www.serve.com/music
Albany NY.

Crunch
www.crunch.co.uk
UK only.

Cerberus
www.cerberus.co.uk
UK Only.

Cosmic Hermit
stop.at/chp
Many services for bands in and around Ohio.

Cyber Sound
www.cyber-sound.co.uk
London, England bands.

Dreamatic
www.dreamatic.com
Only accepts 4 and 8 track recordings.

Foundation For Local Music
www.flmusic.com
Ithica, NY area.

jesusfreak.com
home.jesusfreak.com
We are dedicated to helping out the independent Christian band. What you find here is not typically the stuff you'll hear on Christian radio.

"As a musician, I found [The Indie Music Forum] to be informative, organized, and motivational!"
– Billy Martin, Multi Creations, NY99 Registrant

THE indie MUSIC FORUM

The Indie Music Forum is a one-day regional music business education seminar.
A great opportunity for learning and networking!

San Diego October 15, 2000
New York November 12, 2000
Ft. Lauderdale February 4, 2001
Check out our web site to see where we're headed next!

The Indie Music Forum is a music business education and networking environment for managers, artists who are handling their own management, and those just starting new record labels.

The focus of this event is about education and giving you both the basics of handling your business affairs as well as providing ideas and inspiration for new and different avenues that you can explore for your own marketing and promotion efforts.

The Indie Music Forum offers a Risk-Free Guarantee and a Binder jam-packed with articles, phone numbers and URLs for you to take home.

Contact us today!
cb@IndieMusicForum.com
www.IndieMusicForum.com
tel.215.627.1308

Louisville Rocks!
members.aye.net/~tucker
Louisville, Kentucky area.

MP32000
216.55.32.235
Asian pop music.

MP3s @Boston.com (Boston Globe)
music.boston.com
New England area bands.

Nightshift
nightshift.oxfordmusic.net/
Oxford, England.

Oz Music Project
www.ozmusicproject.net
Australia only.

PDX Bands
Matt Mair Lowery matt@pdxbands.com
www.pdxbands.com
*What Portland, Oregon sounds like.
Streaming Audio from Local Artists.
Updated frequently.*

Radio Freedom
www.radiofreedom.com
Canadian Indie artists.

The Review
www.review-mag.com/
Michigan - Accepts cd and cassette submissions for consideration for review.

Rocksie
www.rocksie.de
European Music Network for Women.

South Australian Music Site (SAMS)
www.senet.com.au/~paulhas

Webtunes
www.webtunes.com
NYC bands.

www.musicofcornwall.com
www.musicofcornwall.com
Cornwall England only.

Save time and money at

Indie-Music.com,

a free 1000+ page portal for musicians. Find 1000's of free contacts, list your band for free, book your tour, send in your music for review. One of the biggest and best musician sites on the internet.

Come Visit!

www.indie-music.com

E-mail: indie@indie-music.com

Section Five:
Sites that Will Allow You to Post Information About Your Band For FREE

If you find that any of these sites are now charging for this service, please let me know and I'll remove them from the list.

All Styles

All Media Guide (AMG)
www.allmusic.com/AMG.html

All Musician Network
www.geocities.com/Nashville/3150

Artist Forum
www.ArtistForum.com

Artists In Residence
artists-in-residence.com

Bandradio
www.bandradio.com/botw

BandTools
www.bandtools.com

BasementBands.com
www.basementbands.com
Our Basement Bands List is comprised of people from around the World that just love to sit around the Basement and JAM. If you would like to be listed here drop us a line. If you don't have a WebSite but you would like to have page on the web we will set aside a page just for you on this site that will give you a place to tell the World about yourselves. So check out the Basement Bands List for more details.

Beats E-Zine
www.beatsezine.com

Below the Surface
freespace.virgin.net/chinch.mu
The foremost underground music 'zine. Nuff said. With slight seriousness.

bestmusiczines.com
www.bestmusiczines.com
A free site that showcases the best music zines, magazines, artists and Independent music resources on the Internet. EVERY style of music is covered. Submit your site today! Each listing contains a photo, logo or cover scan along with contact information and a lengthy description of your site. All that is asked in exchange for your listing is a return link.

BusyMusician.com
Richard Dutchman
dutchman@busymusician.com
Phone: (202) 478-0319 (Washington, D.C.)
www.busymusician.com
Business tips, job listings, how-to books and products, and a marketplace connecting musicians with people who need their services.

Changemusic.com
www.changemusic.com

collegemusic.com
www2.collegemusic.com

Computerized Music Association
lightning.prohosting.com/~orpipop
The place for talented musicians to get published over the Internet, CDs and Local radio stations, Free of charge.

Direct Access Link
www.fusic.com

Endless Entertainment
endlessentertainment.com

Fishtank Soundworks
www.fishtank1.com

Flick Music
www.flickmusic.com

Freemusic.org
www.freemusic.org
This is a great place to promote your music for free! Expand your fan base now. All genres are welcome.

FromDownTown.com
www.fromdowntown.com

Gig Connection
deepblueblack.com/gig_connection

Gigmania
www.gigmania.com

GigMasters
www.gigmasters.com

Grand Central Music
www.grandcentralmusic.com

HitQuarters
www.hitquarters.com
The most detailed data base of names, companies, addresses, numbers, recommendations, links, charts, contacts, classifieds etc. ever made within the music business, free of charge.

Hot Bands.com
www.hotbands.com

in2tv
www.in2tv.com

Independent Artist Services (IAS)
www.idiom.com/~upend/ias

The Indie Link Exchange
www.indielinkexchange.com
The Indie Link Exchange contains a list of music people who wish to exchange links with other music related sites. Everyone involved with Independent music is welcome!

Indie Rock Alaska
www.velvetclub.com
Music, Record Label, News, Shows in Alaska.

Indiecenter
www.indiecentre.com
IndieGroup
www.indiegroup.com

Indie-Zone (Independent Music Site)
www.indiemusicsite.com

IndiSonic
www.indisonic.com/newweb

Internet Music Association
www.theima.com
Gateway to the Next Millennium for Unsigned Bands.

InternetDJ.com
www.internetdj.com/archive
InternetDJ.com hosts and plays MP3s and Real Audio from Independent musicians, bands, and DJs from around the world. Including instant web page creation, free email, streaming net-casts, classifieds, and live chat!

IUMA Artist Uplink
fozzie.iuma.com/Artist_Uplink

KNAC Live!
www.knaclive.com

LocalScene
www.indiebands.com

LyricsReview.com
www.LyricsReview.com
Send your lyrics in for review!

Magic Bus Music
www.mbus.com

Mi2N
www.mi2n.com/submit_top.html
A powerful database driven industry newswire service for music professional, firms and pr agencies.

Midwest Music Review (was Midwest Monster)
clubs.yahoo.com/clubs/midwestmonster
Online Midwest state-by-state rock guide for bands/fans.

mojam
www.mojam.com

Music and Audio Connection
www.musicandaudio.com

Music Genome Project
www.beatsezine.com/submitlink.shtml
The Music Genome Project will identify and map the components which make up what we call the Online Music Industry.

musictourbus.com
www.musictourbus.com
A website designed as a service to assist bands in networking with other bands across the country so that they can more successfully book tours and perform with bands whose styles are similar to their own.

Musicunsigned
www.musicunsigned.com

musicoffice.com
musicoffice.com

muzone.co.uk
muzone.co.uk

Neo Synthpop
www.path.unimelb.edu.au/~new_wave/Neosynth.html

North American Band Name Registry
www.bandname.com

NuSounds.net
www.nusounds.net

Phreak Zine
surf.to/PhreakZine.com
We have a place for bio/press kits, deals, tour date posting and other stuff.

planet radio (empire net)
www.PlanetRadio.net

Published.com
www.published.com

Sites that Jam
www.surfjam.com
Sites that Jam is a directory for artists who have made it possible to listen to their music from their web site. If this is you, please add your site by visiting the Sites that Jam directory.

Soundclick
www.soundclick.com

Stomping Ground
www.stompinground.com
Promote your music for FREE!

SUBS – Scottish Unsigned Bands
www.geocities.com/SunsetStrip/Pit/1015
Whilst the stuff on this site is primarily intended for Scottish bands, please feel free to post anything you like, no matter where you're from.

tourdates.com
www.tourdates.com

TuneTrade
www.tunetrade.com

UASL (Unsigned Artist Site List)
tbq.hypermart.net/UASL.html

Ultimate Band List
www.ubl.com

UnsignedWeb.net
www.unsignedweb.net
We provide valuable services to unsigned musicians allowing them a cost effective way to establish a web presence. We provide a free web site hosting service with an option to upgrade later on, free online profiles, an unsigned music resource search engine and much more.

Virtuoso (New Artist Showcase)
www.virtuosoedusys.com/lobby.html

World Records
www.Worldrecords.com
Search engine for music, free homepage system for bands/labels.

Y Zap
www.yzap.com

Specialty Sites

Country

The Future of Country
members.tripod.com/~cowboyhat

In the Spotlight
www.geocities.com/Nashville/Opry/2578

Women in Bluegrass
www.visuallink.net/murphy/wib.htm

Experimental

Brain
brainwashed.com/brain/

Carpe Mortem
www.carpemortem.com
Constinople Sound
members.tripod.com/~constinople

Frozen Guild
www.multimania.com/blacks
European GotH

The Gas Stations
www.the-gas-station.com

Music Database
KZSU.stanford.edu/eklein

Shadowplay Band Descriptions
www.gothic.net/~dhouse/band-descriptions.html

Sub-Fennica
www.kolumbus.fi/scorpius/

Hip Hop

Hip Hop Boulevard
members.xoom.com/hiphop_quest/
An underground music site specializing in unsigned artists from established indie emcees to bedroom/ basement musical hobbyists. All hip hop related music, regardless of production quality (or lack thereof), will be sold through the site's online store

Onlinehiphop.com
www.onlinehiphop.com

Metal

Belgian Metal Underground (BMU)
members.tripod.lycos.nl/FPP
Registered bands are given a chance to perform on stage.

The Metal Guide
www.geocities.com/SunsetStrip/Pavilion/ 6075
Australian bands.

Nameless
www.zewoc.com/nameless

Rikard's Heavy Metal Page
www.geocities.com/SunsetStrip/Club/4573

The Shxt
crash.to/TheShxt
A music website 2.0; Free band promotion for hard, heavy rock bands; Sell your band tee shirts online.

www.deathrock.com
www.deathrock.com/
Send your material for review and to be included in our index of related bands. I am also putting together an unnofficial site for bands that do not have any informative web presence or very little.

Punk

Make a Scene
thepunkpage.com/makeascene
A site intended for punk indie bands, with goodies like bands, distros, labels, zines, and more.

Oregon Ska Pages
www.pdxnet.net/bands
Oregon/Washington/Idaho area.

Punknet 77
www.hiljaiset.sci.fi/punknet/punkidx.htm

punksite.com
www.punksite.com

Skaville.com
www.Skaville.com

thepunkpage.com
www.thepunkpage.com/zines.html
Your best source for punk rock on the web, period.

Other

Available in Shops
diskant.future.easyspace.com/shops
British Pop Bands.

Baltimore Bands.com
www.baltimorebands.com
Maryland area.

Big Heavy World
www.bigheavyworld.com
Burlington, Vermont.

Broken Pipe
www.omen.net.au/~elhornet
Perth, Australia region.

Dayton Local Music Page
www.dayton.net/~rwarrick
Dayton, OH region.

The End
members.tripod.com/~The_End_
pgreen@newcomm.net
Canadian bands.

Girl Unity
girldesign.com/natalia/
Bands with at least one female member.

GoGirlsMusic.com
www.gogirlsmusic.com/gogirls

Jam Music
www.canoe.ca/IndieBands/home.html
Canadian artists.

kickinthehead.com
www.kickinthehead.com
Canadian bands only.

Orange County Bands
www.ocbands.com
Orange County, CA.

Red Sun Zine
www.listen.to/redsun
Texas.

Scooter
www.emucafe.com.au/scooter
Female musicians.

SLAB (Southern Local Area Bands)
www.slabmusic.com
We offer services, awards, annual festivals, and opportunities for FREE to 700+ members who are all local bands from the Southeast United States.

Southern California Pure Rock Local Bands
www.moshking.com

Starplace
www.fortunecity.com/tinpan/wuthering/
806/Starplace/Page_1x.html

Prince Charming, Wallingford, CT

BAY ISLAND RECORDS, INC. ARTIST / EL

www.bayislandrecords.com

Fill out this card – send it to Big Meteor Publishing and you will receive a FREE Indie Contact Bible update by e-mail. The update will contain all the addresses that have changed since the 2nd Edition was printed. The update will also contain several hundred NEW contacts.

Your name: ....

Your phone number: ....

Your e-mail address: ....

(please print clearly)

Comments:..
....
....
....

Big Meteor Publishing
P.O. Box 6043
Ottawa J
Ottawa, ON
Canada
K2A 1T1

Postage Required

Advertising Rates for
The Indie Contact Bible

The Indie Contact Bible is now being distributed *worldwide* by Omnibus Press. Everyone involved believes that sales will be tremendous in The US, Canadian and European markets!

If you would like to advertise in the Indie Contact Bible, the rates are as follows (note that ads will remain in the resource for one FULL year, regardless of how many editions or updates are printed).

RATES (all prices $US)

FULL PAGE COLOR (front or back inside cover) $2000
FULL PAGE COLOR (regular placement) $1500
FULL PAGE BLACK & WHITE $750

HALF PAGE COLOR $800
HALF PAGE BLACK & WHITE $400

QUARTER PAGE COLOR $450
QUARTER PAGE BLACK & WHITE $250

EIGHTH PAGE COLOR $250
EIGHTH PAGE BLACK & WHITE $150

For further information phone (613) 596-4996 and ask for David, or e-mail me at: bigmeteor@home.com

Do Independent Musicians deserve national distribution?

...At Oasis® CD & Cassette Duplication, we feel they do.

Now, if you manufacture a CD project at Oasis® Duplication, your title automatically qualifies for national distribution at all of the big Internet/Web music superstores, including CDnow, Amazon.com, barnes and noble.com, CDUniverse.com, Buy.com, and the rest.

Your CD is also automatically eligible for distribution to national retail chain stores, including Camelot and many others, where it will be available for special order.

Let's be clear. This is old-fashioned, mainstream, get-it-to-retail national distribution. The kind the labels get. The kind indies could never get before. The real kind. The good kind. And you get it automatically if Oasis manufactures your CD.

Five Reasons Oasis Should Manufacture Your Next CD:
1) Our national distribution program.
2) OasisSampler Program—free, professional radio promotion.
3) Oasis Jewel-Free™ Box—patented, innovative CD packaging.
4) Oasis Rough-Look™ Packaging—funky brown cardboard, very-recycled packaging.
5) The best reputation for quality in the industry—for 12 years running.

We manufacture CDs and cassettes in quantities that begin at 300 units. Popular packages range from 1,000 CDs + 500 cassettes for $2185 to 10,000 CDs + 5,000 cassettes for $12,885. Shipping and overruns are additional.